*Fictions of Affliction*

# **Corporealities:** Discourses of Disability

David T. Mitchell and Sharon L. Snyder, editors

Books available in the series:

*"Defects": Engendering the Modern Body*
  edited by Helen Deutsch and Felicity Nussbaum

*Revels in Madness: Insanity in Medicine and Literature*
  by Allen Thiher

*Points of Contact: Disability, Art, and Culture*
  edited by Susan Crutchfield and Marcy Epstein

*A History of Disability*
  by Henri-Jacques Stiker

*Disabled Veterans in History*
  edited by David A. Gerber

*Narrative Prosthesis: Disability and the Dependencies of Discourse*
  by David T. Mitchell and Sharon L. Snyder

*Backlash Against the ADA: Reinterpreting Disability Rights*
  edited by Linda Hamilton Krieger

*The Staff of Oedipus: Transforming Disability in Ancient Greece*
  by Martha L. Rose

*Fictions of Affliction: Physical Disability in Victorian Culture*
  by Martha Stoddard Holmes

*Foucault and the Government of Disability*
  edited by Shelley Tremain

*Bodies in Commotion: Disability and Performance*
  edited by Carrie Sandahl and Philip Auslander

*Moving Beyond Prozac,* DSM, *and the New Psychiatry:*
  *The Birth of Postpsychiatry*
  by Bradley Lewis

*Disability in Twentieth-Century German Culture*
  by Carol Poore

*Concerto for the Left Hand: Disability and the Defamiliar Body*
  by Michael Davidson

*Disability Theory*
  by Tobin Siebers

# Fictions
## *of* Affliction

## Physical Disability
## *in* Victorian Culture

*Martha Stoddard Holmes*

THE UNIVERSITY OF MICHIGAN PRESS
*Ann Arbor*

First paperback edition 2009
Copyright © by the University of Michigan 2004
All rights reserved
Published in the United States of America by
The University of Michigan Press
Manufactured in the United States of America
♾ Printed on acid-free paper

2012   2011   2010   2009    5   4   3   2

*A CIP catalog record for this book is available from the British Library.*

Library of Congress Cataloging-in-Publication Data

Stoddard Holmes, Martha.
    Fictions of affliction : physical disability in Victorian culture /
Martha Stoddard Holmes.
        p.   cm. — (Corporealities)
    Includes bibliographical references and index.
    ISBN 0-472-09841-1 (alk. paper)
        1. English literature—19th century—History and criticism.   2. People
with disabilities in literature.   3. People with disabilities—Great
Britain—History—19th century.   4. Great Britain—Civilization—19th
century.   I. Title.   II. Series.
PR468.P35   S76   2003
820.9'3520816—dc21                                              2003012932

ISBN-13: 978-0-472-06841-8 (pbk. : alk. paper)
ISBN-10: 0-472-06841-5 (pbk. : alk. paper)

Cover illustration: "Miss Wren Fixes Her Idea." From a woodcut by
Marcus Stone reprinted in Charles Dickens, *Our Mutual Friend.*
Courtesy Dartmouth College Library, Rauner Special Collections.

This world's no blot for us,
Nor blank; it means intensely, and means good . . .
—Robert Browning, "Fra Lippo Lippi"


In memory of
*Mary Beatrice Dingle Stoddard,*
1900–1983

# Preface

This book began with my own questions about bodies, emotions, and representation, and how we learn to feel about bodily variation in others and ourselves. What kind of bodies are represented as feeling bodies—stocked with pain, sympathy, disgust, desire, and laughter, not just blood, organs, tissues, nerves, and muscles? Why, and in what contexts, do we read our own or others' physical bodies as slates on which feelings are writ large, or as markers in an emotional landscape? What cultural texts inform those readings, what intelligence guides them, and what power do they wield (and for whom)? When we fume or cry over a story or film, what kinds of bodies raise our hackles or tears? What does it mean to evoke pity or fear, desire or disgust, through the look of our bodies and the cultural meanings other persons garner from them? Looking historically, what are the longer-term effects of the coding of all of our bodies—through the recurrent stories that shape our social relations—as bodies instructed to feel in limited ways? And finally, how have people scrambled these codes to feel or to mean otherwise?

I had no good answers to these questions. In my classes on cultural studies and the body, my students seemed to lack answers as well. While they were perfectly easy discussing "freaks," when we read and talked about disability, they expressed discomfort: a mix of detachment, guilt, irritation, and anxiety. The women, happy to discuss the cultural con-struction of women (while the men looked detached, guilty, irritated, and anxious), were uncomfortable talking about disability. The Lati-nos/as in the room, happy to engage the wild words of Gloria Anzaldúa (while the Anglos, especially the men, looked detached, guilty, irritated, and anxious), were perturbed as well; in fact, we were all troubled by talk about disability. "I never thought about disability and sexuality as having anything to do with each other before," they wrote. "I would not want to date a disabled person. I'm not sure I can say why." Yes, they were spir-ited and angry at overt messages devaluing disabled people, and ugly words like *retard* or *defective*. They loved joining in the heartwarming mood dictated by the road trip in the film *The Waterdance,* when four dis-abled men of different ethnicities steal the keys to the van and sneak out of rehab to a strip club (there was little support for the comment that these guys got their bonding on the backs, as it were, of women).

They were unsure, however, how to navigate a middle range of feel-ings, or how to take our discussions on the road. A student complained that after one class, she had seen a disabled person and, attending to our discussions of the stare that makes disabled people both ultravisible and invisible, had smiled and said hello, but had been rebuffed. Now she had no idea how to be and was much more uncomfortable than she had ever been about disability, thanks to this class. Palpable tension filled the room when we talked about education and inclusion; silliness domi-nated a role-play of receiving prenatal test results. These moments dropped us into issues about disability that neither goodwill nor right-eous anger could address.

Trying to work out the relationships between disabled bodies and nondisabled ones made my students feel vulnerable because it was liter-ally unimagined territory. They imagined they would date and marry a nondisabled person who would stay that way; they imagined they would always be nondisabled. The likelihood that any long marriage or part-nership would end up with both people variously disabled was not in that world of imaginings. Even the people who shared the facts of their own disabling conditions seemed to need, in this social space of the class-room, to disavow full participation in the identity "disabled person." Their valuable comments were couched in a variation of "I'm not a fem-inist, but . . ." They did not, in Simi Linton's terms, "claim" disability. Coming to teach these classes straight from an NEH Summer Institute on disability studies, in which many people in our group had visible disabilities and/or assistive devices, I was shocked at how suddenly difficult it was to talk about this central experience of being human.

I knew that all those uncomfortable spots in my classroom were just where we might begin the real work of understanding ability and disability; just when we were all hoping I would call for a break or return to the text, we were on the edge of something exciting and valuable. But how could we get there? Critical analyses never seemed to reach this place, much less tell us how to work through all the shades of feeling about disability without resorting to individual psychology or class discrimination. Fiction came much closer, but even with a wealth of new nuanced, situated, historicized scholarship that let us engage disability as we engaged gender, "race," ethnicity, or class, we had the same conversations about compassion and inspiration, followed by defensiveness and boredom. If discomfort was the sign of real learning, or at least its potential, why could we not make more of our discomfort about disability?

The class's failure of imagination with regard to disability was not simply a sign of lack of experience or of some essential immaturity. These were thoughtful, interesting, smart people, who responded earnestly to the series of difficult questions and troubling texts I gave them to wrestle with over the semester. Rather, I believe that our imaginative impasse was a product of those dominant cultural narratives—fictional and otherwise—that teach us what embodiment means, when it is desirable and when it is fearful. When these narratives speak at all about disability, they teach us that it is alien, terrifying, tragic; that it transforms your life in overwhelmingly negative ways; and that it is normal to feel horrified, relieved, and inspired, all from a safe distance, when we encounter disability: "I'm so glad I'm not disabled. I'm so impressed with the achievements of those who are." My objection here is not with any of these feelings, per se, but with the fact that there are so few others suggested by the textual and visual narratives that train us how to picture, talk about, and enact the relationships to our own and others' bodies shaped by the able-disabled binary.

This book offers part of the story of how we got here.

## *Affect in the Academy*

It is not always easy to study "feeling bodies" in the context of the academy, which doesn't always know how to feel about bodies, or feelings, or the scholars who study actual bodies rather than "the body" as an intellectualized, textualized entity. Disability by cultural definition makes visible that which will not be disappeared: the body and its sensations and needs, not all of which involve *jouissance,* at least not in the relatively limited terms imagined by nondisabled culture. Disability also makes visible that which must disappear, despite our best efforts: the body that is impermanent and will die. Disability reminds us of that which is most personal (and thus shameful) in the intellectual life, that which is not aesthetic or abstract. This same body is also what is least personal, most generically human—that which we in academia hope to surpass with distinctive and irreplaceable creations that usually celebrate our minds. This tension between the personal and the generic—the solid and the ephemeral—contributes to resistance to thinking of disability as a scholarly subject that requires or confers authority; because it is a basic human experience, we can speak about it without doing our homework ("We are all disabled"). Because it is a particular experience of individuals, what knowledgeable individuals say about it is often discounted as lacking scholarly authority ("That's just her experience"). Even finding the words to engage the body, should we dare, is a problem. Sharon L. Snyder and David T. Mitchell point out that writing about the disabled body is not only difficult to do without producing a new frame of pathologization, voyeurism, leveling humanism, and so on, but more fundamentally challenging because there is no "sensual and sensory language to theorize the body itself." Snyder and Mitchell turn to "body poetics" and the work of disabled writers and artists to show how culture can render the "elasticity" of the body; the challenge remains how to do this in academic writing (381–82).

Feelings are dangerous associations for scholars as well, to such an extent that

> literary historians sometimes distance themselves from sentiment
> in the very act of talking about it. By studying the "ideological
> work" that sentiment is performing in [a] text or cultural milieu,
> the scholar allies himself or herself with ideology as the analytical
> term. (Ellison 6)

We often find ourselves using linguistic tongs to handle bodies and feelings, using phrases like "grammar of affect" or "economies of emotion," to bring out some of my own. We are happier, perhaps, to anchor the study of emotion to science, analyzing ever more complex and yet limited exteriorizations of affect such as images of "the palette of emotion" yielded by PET scans of the brain.[1] We need more situated, theoretically nuanced analyses of bodies and feelings that honor their social, intersubjective, and historical status and engage our actual lives in our feeling bodies.

Throughout this book, I use "we" not only as a convenience, but also to indicate the fact that we are all affected by cultural representations of disability, even those rare few who do not become somehow disabled in the course of a lifetime. At the same time, I can't offer the same "we" that a disabled scholar could bring to this book, or unpack disability representations from the perspective of anyone whose negotiations with those representations are habitual and mandatory. The book's early versions were written during a decade of invisible, context-specific bodily impairment, an experience that is nowhere in the book, though it loomed large in the energy I brought to writing it and (even more) received from meeting the wonderful friends and scholars now central to my academic and social life. When it appeared in 2004, I had just emerged from a life-changing experience of disablement, having experienced a cancer diagnosis and its treatment. At this moment, living with minor side effects from surgery and chemo, I am more displaced from a disability experience, but in future moments, I can count on being closer to it again. From a shifting spot on the margins of disability, this book does its best to articulate a perspective of alliance and advocacy for those who identify or are identified as living at its heart.[2]

## Acknowledgments

Research for various parts and stages of this book was supported by a George W. Reynolds Dissertation Fellowship from the University of Colorado, a Walter L. Arnstein Dissertation Award from the Midwest Victorian Studies Association, and a National Endowment for the Humanities Fellowship for College Teachers and Independent Scholars. I thank William Ferris, NEH chair at the time of the award, for his personal support of this project and of disability studies as a field of scholarship.

An expanded, earlier version of parts of chapter 1 appeared as "Performing Affliction: Physical Disabilities in Victorian Melodrama," *Contemporary Theatre Review* 11 (2001): 5–24 (see Taylor and Francis journal

Web site, http://www.tandf.com). An earlier version of parts of chapter 2 appeared as "The Twin Structure: Disabled Women in Victorian Courtship Plots," in *Disability Studies: Enabling the Humanities,* edited by Sharon L. Snyder, Brenda J. Brueggemann, and Rosemarie Garland-Thomson (New York: MLA, 2002), 222–33; it is partially reprinted by permission of the Modern Language Association of America. A version of chapter 3 appeared as "'Bolder with Her Lover in the Dark': Wilkie Collins and Disabled Women's Sexuality," in *Reality's Dark Light: The Sensational Wilkie Collins,* edited by Maria K. Bachman and Don Richard Cox (Knoxville: University of Tennessee Press, 2003). Parts of chapter 5 appeared as "Working (with) the Rhetoric of Affliction: Autobiographical Narratives of Victorians with Physical Disabilities," in *Embodied Rhetorics: Disability in Language and Culture,* edited by James Wilson and Cynthia Lewiecki-Wilson (Carbondale: Southern Illinois University Press, 2001), 27–44 (© 2001 by the Board of Trustees, Southern Illinois University). I am grateful for permission to reprint these excerpts.

Teachers, colleagues, students, and staff helped this project at various stages. At the University of Colorado, James Kincaid, Margie Ferguson, John Allen Stevenson, and Bruce F. Kawin were inspired teachers and mentors. Above all, Kelly K. Hurley always "got" this project, always imagined it in terms of its best potential, and always knew the right questions to ask to help me move in that direction. "Dissertating women" Rebecca Dickson, Siân Mile, and Kayann Short contributed tea, cookies, smart comments, and sustaining friendship. Plymouth State College colleagues Patricia Cantor, Richard Chisholm, Alys Culhane, Bonnie Epstein, Meg Peterson, and Annie Valdmanis gave sage advice on early drafts. At California State University San Marcos, Yuan Yuan and Susie Lan Cassel offered constant encouragement and never asked when it would be done. The students in my Body Studies classes at Plymouth State and Cal State San Marcos reminded me why I needed to keep doing this work. The students in my graduate seminar Bodies and Feelings in Victorian Fiction gamely read a series of impossibly long novels, expanded my ideas with their own, and made Thursday evenings a time of feasting and flowers. Karen Sutter Doheney eased the burdensome aspects of teaching and brought her intellectual energy, editing finesse, and energizing collegiality to my last semester of struggling with this book. Amy Bolaski offered helpful manuscript comments on very short notice. Zachary A. Pugh gave his boundless energy to the index. Administrative coordinators Anita Nix and Jill Martin set the mark for patience, effectiveness, and kindness.

Various libraries helped me track down sources and gave me quiet and tidy havens to work in when I, like many adjunct instructors and independent scholars, had no office space. Norlin Library's Interlibrary Loan Department and the Center for British Studies at the University of Colorado gave me access to most of my primary sources; the helpful and knowledgeable staff of the Special Collections libraries of Princeton University, Dartmouth College, and the New York Academy of Medicine supplemented these beginnings, as did the wonderful Lori Whittemore of Cal State San Marcos. The Stowe Free Library in Stowe, Vermont, gave me many warm and happy hours of writing as the snow fell (and fell) outside.

Many others, too numerous to name, through their words, activism, and collegiality kept me attuned to the reasons why I wanted to do and teach this work. Thanks in particular to Simi Linton, Tammy Gravenhorst Berberi, Brenda Jo Brueggemann, James Wilson, Cynthia Lewiecki-Wilson, Georgina Kleege, Catherine Kudlick, Lillian Nayder, Felice Aull, Andy Potok, Johnson Cheu, Penny Richards, Jennifer Sutton, Julia Miele Rodas, Robert McRuer, Cindy LaCom, Sue Schweik, and Kim Hall. Dr. Lawrence J. Schneiderman listened to me ramble over many cups of coffee, and bought the coffee to boot. The ds-hum, Victoria, and literature and medicine discussion lists provided constant companionship, intellectual provocation, and speedy generosity with ideas and citations. Conference audiences at Modern Language Association, Interdisciplinary Nineteenth-Century Studies, Nineteenth-Century Studies Association, Society for the Study of Narrative, American Society for Bioethics and Humanities, and the Dickens Project conference offered useful and encouraging comments on various versions of these ideas. Phyllis Franklin and Karin Bagnall of the MLA facilitated an environment that welcomed disability studies. Hilary Schor and many others at "Dickens Camp" made me and my work feel welcome. I thank Robyn Warhol for authorizing my interest in bodies and feelings with her own inspired and carefully historicized work in this realm.

At the University of Michigan Press, LeAnn Fields gave this book lots of encouragement and lots of patience. Marcia LaBrenz and Allison Liefer were endlessly helpful and kind. I met the Corporealities series editors, Sharon L. Snyder and David T. Mitchell, at the first-ever conference on disability studies in the humanities—the one at which we named what we were doing and found our cohort. It is a great pleasure to be able to thank them for their work, their friendship, and their support of this book.

Heather Richardson Hayton, my academic "twin," was not only constant in her intellectual and personal support but also knew all the best ways to be helpful, from wicked humor to soul-sustaining food. Catherine Belling's intelligence and cheer got me through the revisions. Suzanne Lane dispensed deft editing suggestions and other life advice with constant wisdom and generosity. Sue O'Neill proofread and praised at a crucial time. Diane Freedman's contributions to my life long precede this book, and will never go out of print or be remaindered. She helped me begin the project by the side of the swimming pool over ten years ago and has encouraged it—and me—ever since.

Rosemarie Garland-Thomson has mentored, sustained, nurtured, and challenged me for the past ten years. Her own scholarship continues to "transfigure disability within the cultural imagination" and dazzle every venue in which she presents it ("the Beauty and the Freak" 181). To be in Rosemarie's company is to experience her energetic interest in stimulating others to do and present their own work, and her passion for connecting scholars who don't know each other, but should. Rosemarie originated many of the fora for our most crucial and exciting conversations about the body, some taking place even as you read these words. I can't thank her enough for these gifts, and for her kindness, wit, and friendship.

My wonderful family remained loving and kind as I missed all of their birthdays, took boring books to the beach, and muttered unintelligible things while distracted by my work. My mother, Ruth Dougherty Stoddard, encouraged my love of literature and gave me my first model of a passionate reader. My wonderful siblings Sally Collier, Susan Durant, and Sam Stoddard, along with their delightful families, cheered me on and made me travel to places too sandy, rustic, or entertaining to work on the manuscript. The support of my late grandmother, Pat Stoddard, made it possible for me to work and write independently for a whole year.

My late father, George Chaffee Stoddard, Jr., understood this project immediately, and even suggested books to include. My late mother-in-law and reading partner, Helen Wisowaty Holmes Hallenbeck, kept my husband and son happy and well fed on countless occasions so that I was free to write, and always was proud that I was doing this work. I wish both of them could read the book they helped me to write.

My biggest thanks, of course, go to my immediate family. My wonderful husband Jake kept me—and the household—going when my spirits and energy ran out. My son Josh's birth in the middle of this project was the peak of my own body's melodrama. He is my life's miracle and continuing delight. I rely on them to invite me daily back to the world.

# Contents

Introduction   1

1   Melodramatic Bodies   16

2   Marital Melodramas
    *Disabled Women and Victorian Marriage Plots*   34

3   "My Old Delightful Sensation"
    *Wilkie Collins and the Disabling of Melodrama*   74

4   An Object for Compassion, An Enemy to the State
    *Imagining Disabled Boys and Men*   94

5   Melodramas of the Self
    *Auto/biographies of Victorians with Physical Disabilities*   133

    Conclusion   191

    Appendix
    *Physically Disabled Characters in Nineteenth-Century
        British Literature*   197

    Notes   201

    Works Cited   211

    Index   223

# Introduction

> "God bless us every one!" said Tiny Tim, the last of all.
>
> He sat very close to his father's side upon his little stool. Bob held his withered little hand in his, as if he loved the child, and wished to keep him by his side, and dreaded that he might be taken from him.
>
> "Spirit," said Scrooge, with an interest he had never felt before, "tell me if Tiny Tim will live."
>
> "I see a vacant seat," replied the Ghost, "in the poor chimney-corner, and a crutch without an owner, carefully preserved. If these shadows remain unaltered by the Future, the child will die." (Dickens, *A Christmas Carol* 47)

Every December, countless people across the United States watch this scene from hard seats in high school auditoriums or from comfortable living-room couches in front of flickering TV screens. For many, the annual resurrection of *A Christmas Carol* is an occasion for enjoying the worry that Tim will die, the relief of hearing that he "did NOT die" (76), and the anticipation of taking the same affective excursion again next year. Just as it is Tim who pries open Scrooge's hard heart, it is Tim, with his "active little crutch," who prods us to respond emotionally to Dickens's story (45).

Whether he moves us to tears or derision, whether we see him as touching or maudlin, the emotionality of our responses to Tiny Tim may seem normal and natural. If we identify ourselves as able-bodied people, the narrow range of emotions the character evokes may also feel more natural, or at least more comfortable, than our responses to the actual people with disabilities who share our world, who may spark a complex mix of surprise, sadness, curiosity, longing, irritation, uncertainty, shame, boredom, identification, excitement, worry, fascination, love, collegiality, or any number of other feelings beyond the simple tonics of pity, laughter, terror, or anger.

Tim's own feelings, as drawn by Dickens, are also conveniently limited. The conviviality of his feeble hurrah, his famous "God bless us, every one," are much more memorable than his quiet distaste for the toast Bob offers to Scrooge, the "founder of the feast." For the most part, Tim is full of fellow-feeling, and glad to be looked at in church on Christmas Day "because he was a cripple, and it might be pleasant to them to remember . . . who made lame beggars walk, and blind men see" (45). While we might linger over this statement, the story itself does not. It moves us on to the plum pudding without inviting a more complex negotiation of how we or the characters feel about disability.

The emotional landscape of Tim's disability—what the characters feel, and what we feel in response—tends to obscure other questions we might have about it. While Dickens draws in detail the streets and interiors of Victorian London and even the abjection of many of its inhabitants, we don't know enough about Tim to ascertain whether his disability is the result of poor nutrition, a factory injury, or some other material cause. We know—and only need to know, as engaged readers of this story—that Scrooge's Malthusian, emotionally closed stance toward poverty is the cause, and that as soon as Scrooge regains the ability to melt and weep in response to his own and others' lives, Tim will not die an early death.

The specific things we know as we read *A Christmas Carol* are part of a general knowledge of bodies and feelings collaboratively produced by countless such narratives. From experiencing the movie *Scent of a Woman;* a telethon for Jerry's Kids; a soap opera plot involving wheelchairs, white canes, or fatal illness; or any news story on cancer, paralysis, blindness, deafness, or amputation, we know that when we enter a story about disability, we enter a world of pitying or heart-warmed tears, inner triumph, mirror-smashing rages, suicide attempts, angst and abjection, saintly compassion, bitterness, troubled relationships, and courageous overcoming.

The connection between emotion and impairment has become a kind of cultural shorthand: to indicate or produce emotional excess, add disability. The makers of *Sleepless in Seattle* (1993), for example, borrow this commonplace from *An Affair to Remember,* the 1957 film to which *Sleepless* makes habitual and reflexive reference. Neither film is about disability in a central way; both are about missed connections and finding true love against all odds. *Sleepless* both pokes fun at melodrama in a specifically gendered way (women who weep at commercials, for example) and traffics wholeheartedly in the same goods, featuring, for example, a motherless boy whose widowed father hasn't gotten over the loss of his perfect marriage. In order to ratchet up its emotional tension even beyond this, however, *Sleepless* draws on *Affair* as its shadow self. As the hero and heroine approach each other, *Sleepless* references the fact that *Affair*'s heroine almost misses out on love because she is hit by a taxi and disabled on the way to a rendezvous. As a *Sleepless* character whispers at the crescendo of an increasingly weepy plot summary, "He doesn't know . . . she is . . . *crippled!*" Both productions know that if you want to double the anguish of missed love, you cripple the heroine. If you get to a happy ending from *those* depths, you can get there from anywhere. Disability is melodramatic machinery, a simple tool for cranking open feelings, and everyone involved—disabled and nondisabled, viewers and actors—is somehow placed and defined by what floods out.

The stories that pervade our lives make disability resound so intensely in emotional terms that all other possible registers (scientific, environmental, artistic, sexual, economic, geographic, epistemological, statistical, sartorial, political, and so on) are often informed and overshadowed by affect. All these registers clearly work together: emotional messages about disability are both motivated by and shored up by economics, for example. In public discourse, however, an emotional context or subtext tends to be obligatory when disability is the subject, while a host of other possible contexts for its meaning are optional or secondary. Thus, while emotion is undoubtedly part of the individual and social experience of disability, it disproportionately defines those experiences in ways that inform not only the popular imagination, but also, as a consequence, public policy.[1] More significantly, we have neither attended to the connection between disability and emotion nor asked what purposes are served or other forms of social organization masked by describing bodies on the basis of feelings.

In this book, I want to question, analyze, and disrupt the "natural" connection between disability and feeling, recast it as naturalized rather than natural, and suggest some of the cultural work that produced it. The focus is Victorian Britain, a time in which "afflicted" and "defective" bodies permeated not only the plots of popular literature and drama but also published debates about heredity, health, education, work, and welfare. These texts' recurrent ways of representing bodies and feelings helped produce not only a social identity for disabled people that was significantly defined in emotional terms, but also the distinctive identity of "disabled," and its co-product, "able," in a century in which disability and ability were not the established (if ambiguous) rhetorical categories that they are in Anglo-American culture today.

Victorian discourses of disability, and the texts that convey them, are overwhelmingly "melodramatic." This term invokes not only the recurrent use of disabled characters in stage melodramas, but more broadly the habitual association, in literary and other texts, between physical disability and emotional excess. Just as the nineteenth-century melodramatic stage diffused the entire culture as a significant mode of expression and understanding, a specific historical connection between the melodramatic stage and disability evolved into a generalized, melodramatic mode of imagining disability.[2] The results of this long-term connection were to formalize and institutionalize disability's connection to a particular set of emotional codes and to permanently associate the experience of disability with an expectation of melodrama.

Examined in the context of Victorian culture's particular concerns about reproduction, production, and disability, the melodramatization of disability represents not so much the perfect marriage of an emotionally extremist genre with an emotionally extreme state as it does a resonant, multiply determined connection. Melodrama's emphasis on external identities served the need to elide theater licensing restrictions on the spoken word with bodies that spoke volumes, but it also thematized Victorians' concerns with identifying what kinds of bodies should marry and what kinds of bodies could work. The meanings that accrue to the "emotional excess" at the core of melodrama—the intensely real, and the false or unearned—dovetail with a parallel lexicon of meanings associated with representations of disabled people across a wide range of literary and nonliterary texts exploring disability and disease, heredity, education, labor, and indigence. Finally, the formulaic endings of melodrama, in which the emotional overflow of the middles is neatly put to rest, offered a mode in which to imaginatively resolve tensions that in reality were much too complex to settle with a closing curtain or final chapter. While disability had much to offer to melodrama, the emphasis here is on what melodrama had to offer a culture concerned about disability.

A significant element of this exploration is attention to those texts in which melodrama fails as a way to narrate disability: the neat resolution doesn't work, or melodramatic conventions are modified, abandoned, or scrambled. Thus, I trace not only recurrent patterns but also their variations, as both fiction writers and autobiographers negotiate with the obligation to be melodramatic about impairment.

The Victorians went far beyond Tiny Tim in exploring the meaning of disability and ability and the ways in which disabled and able people might relate. Exploring these representations, then, is not simply an exhumation of the past that has defined our limited ways of thinking and feeling in the present, but also an invitation to reopen our own narrative explorations of disability—to move beyond Tiny Tim ourselves.

My use of the term *melodrama* requires some articulation, with particular reference to the concept of emotional excess and its connotations of intensity and falsity, and this is one of the tasks of chapter 1. After a summary of the historical connection between stage melodrama and disability, I suggest the spread of a melodramatic mode of representing disability across various nonliterary genres. Various relationships of corroboration and complementarity characterize the relationships between literary and nonliterary representations of disability.

Chapter 2 develops a specific example of the cultural utility of melodramatic plots of disability, focusing on the recurrent dramatic and literary figure of the disabled woman of marriageable age. These plots teach us how to feel about disability and how disabled women feel, with the specific purpose of locating disabled women in relation to marriage and reproduction. D'Ennery and Cormon's popular 1874 stage melodrama *Les deux orphelines* is a key text for the century's negotiations with ideas about disability, ability, and marriage. This immensely popular melodrama, which gives "twin" sisters physically, emotionally, and socially divergent fates on the basis of blindness and sight, retained its popularity well into the twentieth century.

Before this resilient cultural message about disability and marriage entered the twentieth century, however, melodramatic fiction offered a host of variations on the same plot, each of which uses emotional excess as a principle for organizing women's bodies into the marriageable and the unmarriageable. Two novels from early in the century, by Dickens and by Bulwer-Lytton, move disabled women from centers of pathos that support others' emotional development (and further others' marriage plots) to figures with desires of their own. Dangerous in any context, women's desire in conjunction with disability produces a particular instability in the plot that is never completely settled by the narratives' melodramatic endings.

In 1850 and 1860, novels by Craik and by Yonge shift the site of emotional excess from disabled women to nondisabled women, making disabled women "passionless" and thus "marriageable." Both works also produce a more generalized and so less melodramatic construction of disability by representing most of the main characters as disabled in one way or another. Dickens's last novel, *Our Mutual Friend* (1864–65), is a third exploration of disability, marriage, and emotional excess that suggests that disabled women can be marriageable rather than simply the midwives of others' unions. Dolls' dressmaker Jenny Wren's melodramatic excess is fragmented and intermittent, complicated by her verbalized identity and the novel's dispersal of melodramatic energy throughout many characters and multiple plots. Jenny's relationship to the marriage plot, to pathos and eros, and to the courting couple of Lizzie and Eugene is more complex than can be resolved in her final parceling off in a suggested romance with Sloppy, another "good" disabled character.

These plots about disabled women and marriage are increasingly nuanced in their negotiations with the emotional excess of melodrama. While all the fiction represents women with disabilities as women who long to enter the marriage plots they facilitate, the early works merely reiterate the impossibility of this desire, while later ones carefully map out the terms on which disabled women can achieve it.

The increasing richness with which Victorian writers imagined women with disabilities in marriage plots, however, masks two significant issues. First, no matter how close they get to the traditional Victorian heroine's plot of courtship, love, and marriage, disabled women characters almost never become biological parents. Second, out of several decades of texts exploring disability and marriage, the one work that is popular into the twentieth century is *Les deux orphelines,* in which the blind woman is not only unmarried at the end, but also happy in her single state.

Why was it so dangerous to imagine disabled women as desiring women or biological mothers? Characters like Bertha, Nydia, Olive, Ermine, and Jenny were not simply metaphors for the social impairment of "woman in general," or warnings for nondisabled women to be happy in their lot, but also sites for investigating and managing particular concerns about the bodies and feelings of actual disabled women. These fictional explorations, I argue, were shaped and fueled by Victorian medical science's concern about the transmission of physical illness and impairment, which made it irresistibly interesting to imagine a disabled woman as a sexual being, but far too alarming to allow her to reproduce. By their conclusions, these plots either eliminate the desiring, emotionally excessive disabled woman, or rehabilitate her into a properly feeling woman; they provide, with varying degrees of success, a melodramatic fictional solution to what was perceived as a biological and social problem. Goldie Morgenthaler (35) writes insightfully of Dickens's fascination with heredity, but beneath the melodrama of his and other writers' works is also fear of heredity, and a current of eugenics.

The fiction of Wilkie Collins, unique in its use of melodramatic resolutions to excite and encourage the exact fears that other writers tried to calm, suggests just how important melodrama was as a mode of keeping eugenics under wraps. Chapter 3 explores Collins's representation of disabled heroines in the marriage plots of *Hide and Seek* and *Poor Miss Finch,* which pushed explorations of disabled women's sexual feelings— as well as notions of what melodrama could hold—too far for many critics. While other late-century writers expanded the possibilities for imagining physically disabled women beyond the emotional excess of melodrama, Collins crafted *Poor Miss Finch,* the century's most radical novel about blindness and sexuality, as a heady mix of melodrama and antimelodrama, medicalization and "history." Even more than Dickens, who alloys the melodrama of Jenny Wren and makes it hard to feel one way about her, Collins scrambles the codes of melodrama and disability. Lucilla Finch is an agent of melodrama, an emotionally excessive, desiring disabled heroine who evokes pathos only when she becomes sighted. Collins not only returns her to blindness and desire, but actually rewards her with marriage and biological children, bringing about a classic melodramatic ending to a plot about blindness and sight, but on very unusual terms.

Chapter 4 touches on melodramatic representations of disabled boys and men in Dickens as a gateway to parallel representations by educators, social workers and charitable reformers, and journalists and their debates about disability, dependency, charity, and work. The paired figures of the innocently afflicted disabled boy and the begging adult male impostor, which appear both in fiction and nonfiction, thematize the debates that built the social category of "disabled" (as opposed to "afflicted and neglected"). As Deborah Stone argues in *The Disabled State*,

> [T]he unitary category of "disability" in contemporary social policy . . . began as a series of separate conditions more unified in the notion of vagrancy than in any concept of common cause. The concept of need embodied in these categories was the mirror image of the concept of work. (55)

The notion of need was frequently translated from material terms (impairment and function; home and work; transportation and money) into emotional ones, as part of an affective economy that enmeshed both able and disabled bodies in a web of complex feelings and meanings. Like fiction, nonfiction about disability works through the slippage between "innocent" and "guilty" indigence by positing two character types that embody the dual meanings of emotional excess. The victimized afflicted child is a figure of pure intensity and authentic pathos; the villainous begging impostor, in contrast, evokes the emotional clarity of rage, but also the ambivalence of suspicion, or the conviction that pathos or "emotional excess" is fakery, a coin that disabled people use to trick the nondisabled into inappropriate giving. This melodramatic opposition between affliction and imposture served to "place" disabled males in the social world and to organize nondisabled people's complex feelings about work, unemployment, dependency, and systems of social support.

The fact that the strained opposition between the afflicted child and the begging impostor often failed suggests how disability disrupts and disorganizes many binarist discourses, among them the melodramatic discourse of social reform, which was based on the assumption that innocent and guilty need could be seen and differentiated. As pressing as this tension was, however, it was underpinned by the greater anxiety produced by the disabled worker, the one figure that was hardest to imagine.

The texts explored in chapters 2 through 4 were written primarily by nondisabled people and in service of their interests, desires, and fears with regard to disability. The people who were born into these cultural constructions, however, were not simply passive recipients or victims. Chapter 5 interrogates narratives by people with physical impairments themselves, written within a culture that tended to construct them as emotionally excessive women, pathetic children, or begging malingerers. Autobiographical statements by disabled Victorians reflect not only the constraints of contemporary assumptions about disability and feeling, but also the possibility of engaging those figurations of disability in personally empowering ways, whether through direct resistance or more subtle discursive and behavioral strategies.

The chapter discusses the autobiographical statements of Henry Mayhew's disabled interviewees in *London Labour and the London Poor* as well as life writing by and about four middle-class Victorians with disabilities: influential writer and intellectual Harriet Martineau, religious writer John Kitto, statesman Henry Fawcett, and blind activist and philanthropist Elizabeth Gilbert. These precursors to modern life writing on disability and illness suggest the surprising range of strategies Victorians with disabilities used to create, perform, promote, and protect (though not necessarily in that order) a self within the limitations of melodramatic cultural scripts for disabled identity, including physical and rhetorical "public" gestures and behaviors in "private" life. Most of the narratives I examine are framed by a nondisabled biographer or reporter, which helps to illustrate the tensions that beset a disabled person's social body and the pervasiveness of performance in the construction of disabled identity. It was impossible for disabled Victorians to live without reference to melodrama, but many were adept and intelligent brokers of the very cultural constructions of "affliction" that restricted their lives. These texts suggest that while nineteenth-century writing posited an interiorized psychology of disability, disabled subjectivity was of necessity a mix of interior and exterior, private and public, secret and dramatic.

## Critical Contexts

Disability as a literary trope is obviously not a new idea, but the questions we have asked about disabled characters have been fairly limited until recent years. Similarly, literary scholarship has often glossed the connection between disability and emotion without really questioning it. While chapter 1 will discuss this tendency with reference to melodrama studies,

I want here to note two outstanding essays on Victorian fiction that open the door for a discussion of disability but do not seem to realize the significance of that threshold or attempt to guide us through it.

In "Who Is This in Pain?" Helena Michie explores how the bodies of Dickens's heroines, which usually "occupy the place of the unrepresented, the unspeakable" in his novels, enter the text through "illness, scarring and deformity" (199), and how Esther Summerson of *Bleak House* and Jenny Wren, the crippled dolls' dressmaker of *Our Mutual Friend*, "turn their ailments into . . . narrative power" (200). Jenny, Michie argues, turns not only her own pain but also the pain of the courting couple Lizzie Hexam and Eugene Wrayburn into "pathways to self-knowledge" and the marriage that results; Jenny narrates and thus makes possible the story of Lizzie's desire for Eugene. "Dickens can allow Jenny fantasies of an erotic future," Michie argues, "precisely because she is crippled, precisely because she does not function traditionally as a heroine. . . . By making Jenny a child and a cripple, Dickens outlines a safe space for the articulation of female sexuality" (212).

These statements are wonderfully insightful. They move a much-discussed novel and character into new realms, and bolster and corroborate my own discussion of this work in chapter 2. Note, however, where Michie stops: "Jenny, of course, can neither be heroine nor narrator of the text in which she appears." What combination of her being "a child and a cripple" and "a 'minor' character" produces the "of course"? Which of these social identities is most important in making Jenny a character who can "use her 'poor shoulders' to open up the text for Bellas, Lizzies, and Esthers in their journeys toward . . . the self"? (211).

Audrey Jaffe's remarkable analysis of "scenes of sympathy" in nineteenth-century texts has been another significant intellectual wedge, opening up new perspectives on what it means to see and imagine another person's experience of misfortune, and how such scenes with this particular specular dynamic are imagined and weighted with cultural meaning in Victorian fiction. These are central issues for all constructions of "difference" that are based (as disability habitually is) on an assumption that suffering and need are central to difference and that suffering can be assessed by visual inspection. Jaffe brilliantly articulates the way that "the scene of sympathy in effect effaces both its participants, substituting for them images, or fantasies, of social and cultural identity" (4).

One of the most exciting aspects of Jaffe's critical perspective is her attention to "objects, persons, and scenes that are already spectacular in

Victorian culture: already invested with cultural value and desire" (32). Her discussion of *A Christmas Carol* attends briefly to Tiny Tim's participation in such a scene and his self-imagining as a "sympathetic spectacle" in church, and makes a wonderful connection between the plenitude of the Christmas turkey ("twice the size of Tiny Tim") and Tim as the real founder of that feast with the commodity of his specularity (44). Jaffe's analysis of *A Christmas Carol,* however, like Dickens's narrative itself, is more interested in Scrooge and how scenes of sympathy constitute the nonsuffering, middle-class perceiving subject, whose identifications with the role of suffering spectacle are temporary. Like Adam Smith's reflections on Philoctetes in *The Theory of Moral Sentiments,* Jaffe's analysis sees suffering from outside. Even as she problematizes that view in very significant ways, she does not explore the perspective of those who inhabit the cultural spectacle of disability.

Both these works demonstrate that it is quite possible to make provocative and important contributions to literary scholarship by building on the cultural function of disability while leaving that cultural function more or less undisturbed, following the lead of the Victorian narrative and its assumptions about disability a shade too closely even while asking provocative questions about other issues.

Michie and Jaffe represent unusually nuanced analyses of disability for literary studies, which has treated it as something of a free zone, a last repository of essentialism. In a time of obligatory contextualization in which a responsible piece of scholarship by definition does not essentialize women, people of color, ethnic minorities, the working class, postcolonial subjects, or people who identify as queer, bisexual, or transgender, disability can be a realm where a trope is just a trope and characters have no cultural history. If *A Christmas Carol* is a place where the general public can forget both what the Victorians learned about disability and what we have learned after them, it is also such a place for literary critics. As social constructionism, the aging and disabling of the baby boom generation, and the increased visibility of disability as a claimed, activist, and minority-group identity challenge us to rethink bodies, feelings, and social relationships, disability forms a space of nostalgic and uncritical looking alongside those other spaces (gender, "race," sexualities, ethnicities, class) that have lost their safety from critical and politicized analysis.

There are clear benefits to disability's unexamined status. For one thing, as an uninterrogated anchor, the trope of disability enables the exploration of many other tropes (*pace* Mitchell and Snyder, disability has long been a *critical* prosthesis). More generally, it's easier not to explore disability because it, like all body studies, raises difficult questions about the bodies in which we live, work, and relate, especially with reference to power relations, values, justice, and communication. These questions permeate the academy and affect our teaching, hiring practices, and collegial relations; it is hard to know either how to ask critical questions about issues so close to our lives, or exactly how to pursue them outside a punitive "positive images" discourse.[3]

The coalescence of disability studies as an emphasis within humanities scholarship has begun to map out this new territory. Many scholars have not only taken up historian Douglas Baynton's statement that "disability is everywhere in history, once you begin looking for it," but also asked increasingly complex questions about what the visibility (and invisibility) of disability has produced in the way of cultural meanings and social relations ("Disability and the Justification of Inequality" 52). As Rosemarie Garland-Thomson articulates it,

> This new critical perspective conceptualizes disability as a representational system rather than a medical problem, a discursive construction rather than a personal misfortune or a bodily flaw, and a subject appropriate for wide-ranging cultural analysis within the humanities instead of an applied field within medicine, rehabilitation, or social work. From this perspective, the body that we think of as disabled becomes a cultural artifact produced by material, discursive, and aesthetic practices that interpret bodily variation. . . . Such an approach focuses its analysis . . . on how disability is imagined, specifically on the figures and narratives that comprise the cultural context in which we know ourselves and one another. ("The Beauty and the Freak" 181)

The discussion here is in conversation with several recent works in disability studies, notably Garland-Thomson's *Extraordinary Bodies* and Mitchell and Snyder's *Narrative Prosthesis,* as well as essays in volumes edited by Snyder, Brueggemann, and Garland-Thomson *(Disability Studies),* Mitchell and Snyder *(The Body and Physical Difference),* Davis *(The Disability Studies Reader),* Deutsch and Nussbaum *(Defects),* and Longmore and Umansky *(The New Disability History),* all strong examples of work that strives "to transfigure disability within the cultural imagination" (Garland-Thomson, "The Beauty and the Freak" 181). Readers may consider this book on British texts alongside the works of Garland-Thomson, Mary Klages, and Mitchell and Snyder, which emphasize American literature, and thus speculate about a developing Anglo-American discourse of disability. My focus on emotion as the currency that disabled bodies are made to represent suggests links to the works of other writers on bodies and feelings in British and American literature and culture, such as Julie Ellison, Jaffe, Adela Pinch, Shirley Samuels, Karen Sánchez-Eppler, Julia Stern, and Robyn Warhol.

On a broader scale, then, this study participates in a growing universe of books that study "the body" not as an essence but as a representational effect that helps to constitute the material bodies (and feelings) in which we live.

In writing about disability in the nineteenth century, I had to make decisions about terminology and scope. First, the Victorian terms *afflicted* or *defective* are not used here to describe disabled people, except when I refer to an explicitly Victorian perspective. Elsewhere, I use *impaired* or *disabled* as relatively neutral ways of describing bodies represented as having difficulty with "fundamental" physical functions and actions, while acknowledging that both terms and the concepts that underpin them are culture- and context-based. I tend to use *disability* and *impairment* interchangeably, partly for linguistic variation and partly because I'm not convinced that impairment is a more objective term. After deliberating on the nuances of *disabled people* and *people with disabilities,* I chose the former for general usage, influenced in large part by Simi Linton and the concept of claiming disability.[4]

In writing about "physical disabilities" I draw several provisional lines. I include deafness and blindness in the category of disability, as the Victorians would have, acknowledging that in our own time, proponents of Deaf culture and others may find that inclusion both inaccurate and specious. On the other hand, I draw a very un-Victorian line between the body and the mind.[5] Most of my primary sources assume their meshing; the need to distinguish body and mind and locate impairment in one or the other seems to emerge with the rise of the welfare state and the need to scrutinize bodies (moving inside with the ophthalmoscope, speculum, and other advances in medical hardware) in order to distinguish those who would receive financial support. The body-mind distinction is much more firmly based in current culture, which responds very differently to "mental" disabilities than to "physical" ones and is often flummoxed by conditions that blur those categories. Further, in the interest of pursuing the common cultural status of all people with disabilities in Victorian culture, I have attended less assiduously to the ways in which particular conditions are constructed as different from each other. Blindness, to take the most obvious example, receives more emphasis than other conditions, reflecting the abundance of representations of blindness in Victorian texts. While the cultural status of blindness is clearly distinct from that of deafness or of mobility impairments, I tend to merge those differences in the cause of making broader statements about people who were not only singled out as blind, deaf, or "crippled," but also batched together as "the afflicted and neglected classes."

Choice of the terms *physical* and *disability* as delimiters reflects the current cultural-historical moment and its theorized separation between body and mind, as well as certain practicalities. I wanted to engage issues unaddressed by important studies of Victorian illnesses of the body/mind by Diane Price Herndl, Maria Frawley, Athena Vrettos, Sally Shuttleworth, Jane Wood, Elaine Showalter, and others, whose impressive scholarship has provided models for what a productive cultural study of the Victorian body looks like. My work draws on these scholars, but moves in somewhat different directions.

I also do not explore nineteenth-century "freaks," partly because of the wealth of fine scholarship in that area.[6] Most of the texts examined here represent bodies that do not have a clear location at the "abnormal" pole of most imaginary continua of bodily variation; their disabilities are common experiences to anyone who lives long enough (and many of us sooner than later). While they were not always represented as such, the disabilities represented in these texts were close to the experience of the average Victorian; the bodies were imaginable as one's own body at a later date. It was very common to know someone with mobility impairment or chronic illness, or to have a relative who was deaf or blind. In contrast, few Victorians of any class had a family member or close associate whose body approximated Joseph Merrick's or Julia Pastrana's. Thus, the representational distance the texts insert between ability and disability responds to a different kind of anxiety and desire than that produced by "freaks." Despite their coexistence on a continuum that includes all forms of embodied difference, including gender and "race," the proxemics (visual, linguistic, physical, and emotional) that governed the situation of the "afflicted" person and that of the "monster" were substantially different.[7]

The starting point for this study was fictional characters who were not isolated as "freaks" but rather placed parallel to "normal" lives, close enough to mark a notable falling-away from normative outcomes (marriage, for example) and thus to build a compelling and melodramatic "if only" gap that the works themselves never explain in full. In Eliot's *Mill on the Floss,* for example, Maggie Tulliver's marrying Philip Wakem is imaginable enough to make the fact that she does not marry him a rich issue, as is the question of why, in Dickens's *Cricket on the Hearth,* Bertha Plummer's dreams of marriage are even farther from her grasp than the pretty cottage and kind employer her father invents for her. In *The Old Curiosity Shop,* by contrast, Nell's avoidance of Quilp—and more compelling, Mrs. Quilp's alliance with him—gives him an aura of pathology, not pathos, a difference that merits development in another critical space.

In the realm of nonfiction, similarly, a shifty gap separates a crippled man's business operations from anything Henry Mayhew can call "work." His anxiety about that gap suggests that (as Freud argued about the *heimlich* and the *unheimlich*) the near-normal is a more troubling cultural issue than the freak, and the one that we most resist unpacking. In both fiction and nonfiction, representations of disability may be invoked to construct or shore up the unstable category of ability, but they seem just as liable to critique and erode ability and normalcy. This complex, subtle dynamic is what fascinates me.

This book explores rather than defines or concludes, and it will raise questions, provoke disagreement, and inspire corrections. May these results be gifts to a larger and more nuanced conversation about bodies and feelings in Victorian culture and our own.

# 1

Melodramatic
Bodies

A first step toward discussion of specific texts is to particularize the meaning of "melodrama" and the concept of emotional excess that is central both to it and to contemporary discourses of disability. Critics have already anatomized melodrama's shifting shapes, its relations to other popular dramatic and literary forms, and its potential for conservatism or subversion. There is general agreement about certain recurrent characteristics: melodrama features victims and villains in suspenseful conflicts that, through a series of coincidences and revelations, are neatly resolved by the end of the play, often with reference to Providence. Conflicts and resolutions take place in a surface world; we need not look for meanings hidden below the immediately visible or audible. On the Victorian stage, these surfaces became increasingly visible and audible. Actors used extravagant acting styles and technical staging effects to reach large audiences within an expanded theater space, making melodrama even easier to read as a genre opposed to the interior, the psychological, and the individual. Melodramatic characters have little "character" per se; their Manichaean moral states can be seen in their bodies and heard in the tenor of their words. The emotions they express and inspire are physical and unalloyed: the villain performs pure malignity (and we hiss him); the victim, pure pathos that brings our tears. If melodrama begins on the stage, by the play's end it reshapes the audience in its own image, enmeshing both sides of the stage in a universe of unthinking, expressively feeling bodies.[1]

This is melodrama's primary emotional work. With this affective purpose as a guide, the boundary drawn around the terms *melodrama* and *melodramatic* can be capacious and imprecise, blurring historical distinctions among popular genres.[2] The texts I discuss as melodramatic have also been called sensational, or sentimental, with the three terms often overlapping or competing. For example, while Charlotte Yonge's *The Clever Woman of the Family* has decidedly melodramatic and sensational threads—a public trial, for example—it is probably most properly termed a sentimental and domestic novel. While Wilkie Collins actually subtitles *Poor Miss Finch* "a domestic story," both its improbable coincidences and its comic subplots feel more like melodrama, and critics term its plot "sensational."[3] For all that distinguishes these two novels, however, both use affect to represent disability and ability.

While most if not all literary works represent emotion and engage our emotional participation, melodrama enacts emotion as a visual, performative, and social entity, an aspect of the social body. Further, it both defines the world as a place of emotional excess and attempts to transform that excess, through plotting, into a particular kind of social order.

The visual nature of melodrama, which has predisposed it to a rich afterlife in film, lends itself to an ordering of its emotional world based on visual identification.[4] Differences of the body—biological sex, performed gender, skin color, bodily signs interpreted as ethnic or class identity, and those visible variations from perceived norms of function and configuration we term "impairment," "defect," or "disability"—are evoked as the core of character. Melodrama codes them with reference to the flow of vision and places them within a dynamic of looking and knowing (or failing to know). Through its dual emphasis on the visible and the emotional, melodrama shows us who we and others are, and how to feel when we see each other. When Bertha Plummer of Dickens's *The Cricket on the Hearth* cries out, "O Heaven how blind I am! How helpless and alone!" her visible identity ("Blind Girl," as the text announces) and her emotional state are so transparent to each other that they dictate our response of pity (222). Millicent, the heroine of John Wilkins's play *The*

*Blind Wife* (1850), aggrandizes and sacralizes her love for her gambling husband and her physical identity as correlated truths:

> The Breath! The Blood! The Spiritual Essence of the Divinity that lurks within the soul! The self! The incarnated Being of the Heart's Creation! That lives thro' all perils, all dangers, to the end, and dies not save with the gentle life of which it formed the best, and holiest, noblest part . . . such a love is the love of the Blind Girl, beaming like a bright star thro' her eternal Night. (N.p.)

Milly's verbal hyperbole, in turn, is matched and substantiated by the sheer physical drama of her role: she throws herself down a cliff, is kidnapped by begging impostors and beaten, and is accidentally shot by her own husband.

When these plots end, all this physicality and emotional excess is out, resolved, and done, like a wonderful tonic with no aftertaste. When Bertha cries, "Nothing is gone. . . . Everything is here. . . . And I am *not* blind . . . any longer!" (224), we can forget her anguish and close the book, at least in theory. We have wept for the victim, hissed the villain, and finally cheered the triumph of goodness. We do not wonder what Tiny Tim will do for a job when he grows up, or what would have happened if the wonderful women of *Terms of Endearment* or *One True Thing* survived their cancers (would either one's philandering English professor husband reform?). Melodrama works with emotion in a measured, highly structured, and definitive way. It delineates feelings within limited choices and organizes—or tries to—the unruly world they invoke, then leaves us with the comfortable clarity of expressed pity, fear, and anger.

Sometimes, however, we do wonder after we close the book; thus, a model for melodrama needs to include failure, those moments when emotional closure is incomplete, as often happens when this feeling genre enters the more complex narrative space of the novel.[5]

The concept at the heart of melodrama's function, as well as its critical reception, is "emotional excess." Like all aspects of the affective dynamic of melodrama, excess is located somewhere between the narrative and its audience. It is user-defined, articulating an assessment of the emotional effects of melodrama. The terms *melodrama* and *melodramatic* ultimately tell us as much about audiences and critics as they do about works. Eric Bentley comments on both in his defense of the genre:

The tears shed by the audience at a Victorian melodrama . . . might be called the poor man's catharsis, and as such have a better claim to be the main objective of popular melodrama than its notorious moral pretensions. . . . Once we have seen that our modern antagonism to self-pity and sentiment goes far beyond the rational objections that may be found to them, we realize that even the rational objections are in some measure mere rationalization. Attacks on false emotion often mask a fear of emotion as such. Ours is, after all, a thin-lipped, thin-blooded culture. (198)

Bentley argues eloquently not only for the utility of crying at a melodrama, but also for its appropriateness, melodrama's *lack* of excess as experienced by the appreciative audience for whom too much is exactly right. His often-quoted passage, then, posits two stances toward melodrama: that of the weeping Victorian audience member, for whom the term *excess* may be irrelevant, value-free, or laudatory; and that of the modern critical viewer, who calls it melodrama to express both disdain for the falsity of its emotion and an underlying fear of all feeling.

If we appreciate melodrama, its emotional excess is simply intensity, a feeling so concentrated that, expressed (as emotional excess must be), it immerses characters and audience in its flood. This is the stance of critics like Bentley, who endorse that intensity and explore its cultural functions. If we perceive emotional excess this way, we worry when Edmond, James Kenney's Blind Boy, stands on a precipice over the raging Vistula River; we weep when Squeers beats the hapless, tubercular Smike in *Nicholas Nickleby,* or when Maggie Tulliver's mother finally speaks up on her behalf and offers to leave home with her shamed daughter. The music that provides the *melos* in melodramas of stage and screen simply heightens or enhances the intensity of "too much." The pleasure of this "excess" is partly based on an uncomfortable sense that if it went on too long, it would not be pleasure but pain, especially in plots in which emotional intensity is located in characters whose misery can't be eased.

The sense of emotional excess, in these cases, is tied to the audience's acceptance of melodrama as a token of the real. While theoretically opposed to a "realist" or mimetic mode in its intensification of the performative aspects of lived experience and its erasure or even denial of interiority, melodrama concentrates and ritualizes that aspect of real life which is uncontrollable, subject to enormous changes at the last minute, and physically and emotionally intense. Melodrama is a synecdoche for experience, though not necessarily interior experience. As Juliet John asserts in her excellent analysis of Dickens's ambivalence toward interiority, in melodrama "surfaces are synonymous with depths," and in a successful melodrama, the audience is willing to accept those surfaces as being good for the depths they signify (111).

John's reading suggests that melodrama's shorthand of intense exteriors does not refer to a mode of experience in which there is an interior life where "depths" and a discrete, privately owned self exist and generate true value. Rather, melodrama refers to a mode of experience in which value ("depths") resides in the embodied moment itself. Pre-Freudian audiences, especially, would not even be working with our model of interior/exterior, depths/surfaces, as Robyn Warhol's study of nineteenth-century acting manuals' model of feelings and embodiment ("As You Stand") testifies. The melodramatic mode, more than any other, preempts Judith Butler's concept that gender and other aspects of social identity reside in repetitive social acts rather than expressing an interior, individually owned essence.

Victorian theater audiences were certainly aware of melodrama's distance from the daily. The recurrent frozen tableaux and effusive acting styles reminded them that they were at a performance; these marks of staginess, burlesqued even early in the century by plays like Thomas Dibdin's *Melodrame Mad!* (1819), were probably central to the experience of theatergoing. That very gap between the ritual and the daily, especially in terms of emotional concentration, did not preclude melodrama's connection to the real but rather proposed an alternate model of mimesis, with a pre-Freudian version of Virginia Woolf's model of life as a series of "moments of being" in which "being" is exteriorized and interpersonal.

A second use of "emotional excess," much more familiar as a critical commonplace about melodrama, commemorates an unsatisfactory experience of unreality, a distasteful or shoddy lack of correspondence between the emotion circulating around a situation and the situation's realities. The gap that separates melodrama's emotional excess from lived experience marks a representational and aesthetic failure that takes place both on the stage or page and in the body of the viewer or reader. The music, in this case, prompts us to feel because the narrative itself has failed to evoke feeling; music functions like a laugh track or cue card, other symbols of inauthenticity.

Unlike an appreciative framing of emotional excess, this version is often end-determined; it is not until the end that we can fully assess whether the middle earned our tears. Melodrama's very tendency to resolve those middles habitually undercuts the value of what has spilled out, if it can be so easily cleaned up.

While Bentley locates the experience of emotional falsity and emotional denial in twentieth-century audiences, Victorian critics expressed it as well, like the annoyed and anonymous *Blackwood's* reviewer in 1859 who defines "melodramatic" as

> the expression of a strong sentiment without a sufficient cause: it is feeling without a base of reality. If people go off into the melting mood, and waste away in tears when they learn that a little boy bought rum for his father on a Sunday, what is to become of them before the greater calamities of life? (526)

Emotional excess here is produced by the gap between what is expressed and its cause, but may also—and here I offer a variant on Bentley—be constructed by the gap between what an audience member wanted to feel and what happened. Perhaps, as Bentley suggests, we do not like being made to cry unless it is on our terms.[6] Perhaps we wanted to cry and didn't. In either case, we encountered the line that the critic above articulates, between "earned" and "unearned" emotions. Despite the difficulty of locating *where* emotions are dispensed, whether among the characters or in the body of the audience, emotional excess in this case is attached to an idea of a merit- or work-based flow of feelings.

The tension between the earned and the unearned relates to that between the real and the unreal. About some events, it is completely appropriate to cry buckets; this is not emotional "excess" but reality; in the metrics of emotion that govern such critical assessments, aesthetically full works deploy—and we experience—a correct measure of emotion relative to events described. We engage this complex of ideas linguistically when we tell our loved ones, "For God's sake stop being melodramatic; it's just a cold," or, in contrast, "Christopher Reeve fell from a horse and is paralyzed—what a terrible tragedy." If the term *melodramatic* may memorialize a critic's sense of gap between the feelings deployed (by characters, the audience, the critic) and what stimulates them, it also inscribes a gap between works of melodrama and those other, tragic, works that do deliver the goods, whose aesthetic plenitude is confirmed by the fact that they not only make us cry, but also seem to have earned the tears. The blinding of Oedipus or Gloucester is generally termed tragic, whereas the blinding of Rochester in *Jane Eyre* is melodramatic. We cried at Sophocles and Shakespeare, and felt good about crying. It was an earned sorrow. Brontë either didn't get to us, or got to us against our better judgment. Critics who write from this perspective are cranky or even angry; they have been cheated of something.

The two meanings, as Bentley suggests, are not completely discrete. A charge against melodrama as bilking us of tears can mean a sense of an inappropriate (false) degree of emotion for the cause, or discomfort with emotional intensity, or both at once. (The potential slippages between all the meanings of emotional excess—real and unreal, earned and unearned, and so on—will be a point of discussion in chapter 4.)

The above examples suggest how frequently we refer to melodrama when we talk about disability. If the disabling of a public or private figure invariably invokes the concept of tragedy, most narratives of disability—even or especially autobiographical ones, curiously enough—must also negotiate with an expectation of melodrama. The best thing we can say to introduce a movie about disability is that it transcends this expectation. A quick Web search for sites that combine the terms *melodrama* and *disability* yields kudos for a movie-of-the-week on disability that is "not melodramatic," a doctor-website discussion of patients who melodramatize their disabilities, and advice to law school applicants not to overemphasize any access needs.[7] While Garland-Thomson observes that visible disability, unlike pain, works as a manifestation of suffering (whether suffering exists or not), even visible disabilities seem liable to provoke a sense of uncertainty and suspicion as often as they do a sense of too much reality ("Seeing the Disabled" 373 n. 16). In twenty-first-century culture, then, melodrama and disability are associated with each other, and aligned in being susceptible to being read as too real, too fake, or both at once.[8]

## Melodrama and Disability: History and Criticism

We can posit a provisional beginning for that long-term conjunction of melodrama and disability, moving from its specific theater history to its generalized usage ("the melodramatization of disability") elsewhere in Victorian culture. Disability's connection with the emotional excess of melodrama dates at least to the early 1800s. When Louis James calls one of Wilkie Collins's characters "that cliché from melodrama, the deaf-mute" (196), he is not just making a dig at Collins's fiction. "Picturesque affliction" as figured by deaf, mute, blind, or crippled characters is a significant feature of the best-loved works of this popular genre. Thomas Holcroft's *A Tale of Mystery* (1802), the first English play billed as a melo-drama, originated for British audiences the genre's recurrent mute char-acter, "a sympathetic figure with a terrible and mysterious past . . . meant to evoke great pity" (Booth 70–71). Deaf-mute characters appear in a host of very successful melodramas, including Holcroft's *Deaf and Dumb* (1801) and B. F. Rayner's *The Dumb Man of Manchester* (1837). Blind characters are central to James Kenney's *The Blind Boy* (1807), George Dibdin Pitt's *Belinda the Blind; or, the Stepmother's Vengeance* (1845); John Wilkins's *The Blind Wife* (1850), and the numerous English adaptations of D'Ennery and Cormon's *Les deux orphelines* (1874).

Melodramatic representations of speechlessness and other disabili-ties are historically rooted in eighteenth- and nineteenth-century cen-sorship of theatrical performances. Royal patents in England and France permitted a limited number of theaters to perform those "legitimate" plays that used spoken dialogue; thus

> consolidation of an "illegitimate" theater depended on the entre-preneurial development of former folk and popular entertain-ment traditions for their capacity to evade official restrictions: dumb show, pantomime, harlequinade, ballets, spectacles . . . the exhibition of animals and freaks, and, above all, musical accom-paniment and song. (Gledhill, "The Melodramatic Field" 14–15)

Because "the monopoly of the patent theatres was . . . a monopoly of the word," bodies distinctive enough to "speak" without words were invalu-able to early melodrama: "Subjects were evidently conceived for their plastic figurability, the dramatic interplay of posture and gesture" (Brooks, *The Melodramatic Imagination* 63).

There has been no sustained analysis of disabled characters in melo-drama that connects them to actual disabled people, that segment of society whose presumed "helpless and unfriended" state was the focus of increased public interest and anxiety during melodrama's rise.[9] We can, however, piece together a repertoire of interpretive frameworks based on what critics say. As some critics read it, melodrama's adoption and promotion of disabled characters was an aesthetic move substantially inflected by class politics. Laura Mulvey emphasizes that working-class entertainments were the source of melodrama's nonverbal modes of expression and that working-class audiences also participated in melodrama's development of an aesthetic relevant to melodrama's "speaking bodies." Disabled characters' dramatization of a "crisis of expression, in which language is either inappropriate or inadequate to the emotional burden of the subject matter at stake," had particular resonance for non-literate audiences with limited access to written expression or political representation (72). Robertson Davies, similarly, writes that "mutes" and "idiots" not only alluded to "the uncanny, the instinctive, the world of feeling" but also

> appealed powerfully to audiences containing many people who, without being either mute or idiotic, nevertheless had difficulty in holding their own in the voluble world in which they lived. (227)

Thus, disabled characters were resonant figures not because of disability per se, but because disability worked as a metaphor for the situation of the working classes.

Even later, when the restrictions on spoken dialogue were lifted in 1843 and audiences were composed of more middle-class people, disability continued to be popular not just because of an overdetermined emphasis on visuality that shaped melodrama's mise-en-scène (Gledhill, "The Melodramatic Field" 22), but also because there was always a new group of "helpless and unfriended" people to whom melodrama and its disabled characters were relevant. Disabled characters might solidify melodrama's ability to be "a cultural touchstone for large sections of society that felt both in awe of and unclear about the benefits of the new society being built around them" (Vicinus, "Helpless" 128). Christina Crosby, who like Vicinus does not attend to disability per se, argues that melodrama's binarism shores up middle-class domesticity, "recognizing otherness only to confirm the domestic, familial, homely identity of that class" (78). Within this framework, disability plausibly functions as that essential otherness which produces the same, an argument suggesting Mitchell and Snyder's concept of prosthesis as well as Robert McRuer's concept of compulsory able-bodiedness.

Peter Brooks's *The Melodramatic Imagination*, "a book about excess," remains a significant prod to contemporary literary scholars to reassess the importance of melodrama to cultural history and critical study (ix). Brooks pays specific attention to disability in melodramatic plots, suggesting that these recurrent characters represent

> a repeated use of extreme physical conditions to represent extreme moral and emotional conditions: as well as mutes, there are blind men, paralytics, invalids of various sorts whose very physical presence evokes the extremism and hyperbole of ethical conflict and manichaeistic struggle. (57)

Brooks suggests that the genre's reliance on extremes (represented, in part, by disability) is an attempt to supplement the nineteenth-century erosion of the sacred with an ethical framework for viewing the world (15). He reads the use of "the halt, the blind, and the mute" as furthering a more transcendent mode of representation, as part of a "repertory of signs which render the world expressive of moral sentiments." This repertory also includes animal actors, tableaux, "the secret impulse by which parents and children . . . are irresistibly drawn to one another despite mistaken and lost identities," the conventions of melodramatic acting, and music itself (45–49). He thus assigns disabled characters a particular quality of mise-en-scène: thematically and spiritually resonant, critical to the workings of this particular genre, but not requiring any historical analysis outside theater history. He leaves these disability effects ungrounded in the changing cultural contexts in which disability was meaningful, and does not ask what made it possible for the disabled figure to deliver the extreme emotional or sensational experience that is the hallmark of melodrama, or what were the long-term cultural implications of embedding disability in melodrama. Michael Booth, working more historically, discusses melodramatic mute characters' origins in dumb show and observes that the mute character is often a "centre of pathos and distress" (70–71), but does not ask why this emotional shorthand works.

Those who do historicize melodrama have not historicized disability in melodrama, and yet representations of disability provide an unusually good example of the ways in which a melodramatic mode pervaded Victorian culture (one of the key points, for example, of Hadley's study). The melodramatization of disability is anything but a "literary" phenomenon. Nineteenth-century educators, social workers, journalists, and even physicians routinely articulated blindness, deafness, and "crippling" in terms of their emotional content rather than through concrete images of disabled bodies or the particulars of disabled people's material and economic lives. Writers in contexts as diverse as the medical journal *Lancet* and the *Morning Chronicle* newspaper habitually "diagnosed" people with disabilities in terms of the state of their emotions, even in texts that we would expect to prioritize particulars of the body, such as the nature, effects, and possible causes of impairment. Emotional content marked the charity-based settlement work of individuals like "Sister Grace" Kimmins—whose turn-of-the-century Guild of the Brave Poor Things had as its motto "Happy in My Lot"—but also that of groups like the Charity Organisation Society (COS), which avowed it would substitute "scientific" decisions for emotional responses to the disabled and other "suffering" people (Vicinus, *Independent Women* 235).

The professional discourses (education, social work, medicine) that often address disability offer particular confirmation of the frequency with which Victorian writers turned to the melodramatic in order to articulate "affliction," making melodrama and disability shorthand for each other. Melodramatic writings about disability form a cross-disciplinary throng that encompasses high and low culture and professional and popular contexts. The mix is something like the advertisement sections of serial numbers of Victorian novels, in which the virtues of patent medicines, hair dyes, charitable associations, and literary works are extolled side by side on the page.

As nonliterary texts engage disability in relation to the key concerns of reproduction and production, they grapple with the questions "Should disabled people marry?" and "Can disabled people work?"—not just in the discipline-specific terms we might expect (statistics, diagnoses, facts) but also in emotional terms, using poetic discourse and literary works to speak about bodies as emotional conduits.

From a twenty-first-century perspective, the emotionalism attached to disability in medical discourse is especially surprising. Physician William Lawrence's "Lectures on the Anatomy, Physiology, and Diseases of the Eye" references Milton's blindness, quotes *Paradise Lost* as a sort of literary-clinical case file, then moves on to inflammations, without ever missing a beat:

> The object of these lectures is to make you acquainted with the nature and treatment of diseases of the eye. . . . blindness is one of the greatest calamities that can befal human nature short of

# THE LANCET.

## LECTURES

### ON THE

ANATOMY, PHYSIOLOGY, AND DISEASES
OF THE EYE.

### By MR. LAWRENCE.

*London Ophthalmic Infirmary, Moorfields.*

## LECTURE I.

GENTLEMEN,

THE object of these lectures is to make you acquainted with the nature and treatment of diseases of the eye, including, under that expression, not only the globe itself, but the several auxiliary parts, called its appendages. The anatomy and physiology of the organs will be only considered shortly, and in reference to the practical part of the course.

It is hardly necessary to enlarge on the importance of the subject, or to prove to you formally how indispensable it is that you should become acquainted with it. Every one feels that sight is the most valuable of our senses; that it not only is, in itself, the most important inlet of knowledge—the most indispensable medium of our communication with surrounding persons and objects, but also that it is essential to the full enjoyment of our other senses—to the free exercise of almost all our other faculties and endowments; so that these latter lose more than half their value when sight is gone. Hence blindness is one of the greatest calamities that can befal human nature short of death; and many think that the termination of existence would be preferable to its continuance in the solitary, dependent, and imperfect state to which human life is reduced by the privation of this precious sense.

Loss of sight is the greatest misfortune even to the rich, who can alleviate it by purchasing the aid and services of others. How much more severely must it be felt by the poor, by the middle and lower classes of society, *i.c.* by 49-50ths of mankind; who, being rendered incapable of labour, and having their minds uncultivated, find their existence reduced to a dreary blank—dark, solitary and cheerless—burthensome to themselves and to those around them. Even our great poet, who might have been supposed to find every alleviation and resource that such an affliction admits of, in his highly-gifted mind, and the exhaustless stores of knowledge with which it was furnished, repeatedly reverts to his blindness, and always in a tone of anguish and despondency characteristic of recent misfortune:—

> " Thus with the year
> Seasons return; but not to me returns
> Day, or the sweet approach of eve or morn,
> Or sight of vernal bloom, or summer's rose,
> Or flocks, or herds, or human face divine;
> But cloud instead, and ever-during dark
> Surround me, from the cheerful ways of men
> Cut off, and for the book of knowledge fair
> Presented with a universal blank
> Of Nature's works, to me expunged and rased,
> And wisdom at one entrance quite shut out."

It often depends on the surgeon whether the patient shall retain or lose, recover or remain bereft of vision.

Common external inflammation of the eye, if neglected or improperly treated, by rendering the transparent anterior portion of the organ more or less opaque, proportionally injures vision; inflammation of the iris, when unchecked, causes contraction of the pupil and deposition of lymph in the aperture, which prevents the passage of light into the eye. Affection of the nervous structure, if not arrested in its beginning, terminates inevitably in diminution or loss of sight; and these distressing results are too often advanced by some plans of treatment, which have been pretty generally followed, and might plead the sanction of names that have enjoyed public confidence.

[Oct. 22, 1825.]

William Lawrence's "Lectures on the Anatomy, Physiology, and Diseases of the Eye," Lecture I (*Lancet*, 1825). Photo courtesy of Dartmouth Medical School Photography and Illustration.

death; and many think that the termination of existence would be preferable to its continuance in the solitary, dependent, and imperfect state to which human life is reduced by the privation of this precious sense. . . . their existence reduced to a dreary blank—dark, solitary and cheerless—burthensome to themselves and to those around them. Even our great poet . . . repeatedly reverts to his blindness, and always in a tone of anguish and despondency characteristic of recent misfortune:—

> " . . . from the cheerful ways of men
> Cut off, and for the book of knowledge fair
> Presented with a universal blank
> Of Nature's works, to me expunged and rased,
> And wisdom at one entrance quite shut out."

It often depends on the surgeon whether the patient shall retain or lose, recover or remain bereft of vision.
Common external inflammation of the eye . . . (Lecture I 145)

If we assume that doctors and poets use different kinds of language and engage different orders of facts to tell and authorize their truths, Lawrence's comments present a delightful case of rhetorical displacement. Surgeon E. F. Lonsdale's detailed description of a treatment for orthopedic disability in the *Lancet* in 1851, similarly, describes its physical benefits briefly and its social and emotional results at more length: "the deformity can be removed, the patient rendered a useful member of society, and his mind relieved from the never-ceasing anxiety, the consciousness of his affliction must have caused" (6). In our own time, you can usually tell a page from a journal of pathology apart from a page of verse. In the nineteenth century, they were much less distinct.

While the *Lancet* writers must eventually return to human anatomy, professionals in less prescriptive disciplines often completely submerge bodily, economic, and other material details with discussions of the feelings that physical impairment is supposed to produce. In the process, people with disabilities are often made to exist more in various affective states than in the infirm body that, in nineteenth-century discourse, is the putative catalyst of such "affliction."

There are many benefits to this emotional construction of ability and disability. In the context of social institutions and the rhetoric that defines them, constructing physical disability as primarily a *feeling* state

can minimize the importance of the material circumstances that sur-
round all disabilities, and maximize the importance of personal agency
while minimizing the need for social change. Disability can more easily
be theorized as a personal problem. Further, eliding or mystifying material details of disability (as both Victorian fiction and nonfiction do on a
regular basis) can make the person with a disability into a figure onto
which the philosophic, romantic, or other intellectual and imaginative
interests of the reader may be inscribed without regard for any conflicting information.

An emotional discourse of disability, without specific ways to structure it, produces some interesting problems. While disabled people are
always the origins of emotion in Victorian nonliterary writing, they do
not precisely contain it, but exist in a complicated interpersonal dynamic
with the emotions generated by impairment. While blind or deaf people
are frequently drawn as isolated from "normal" people through their
sensory impairments and the emotional pain blindness or deafness generates, many texts also posit an emotional exchange system in which cur-
rents of feeling, stimulated by the presence of a corporeally "different"
body, connect people who are not disabled and people who are; disability is thus as relational a category as emotion itself.

As writers articulate the emotional economy of disability—the
dynamics of the feelings that circulate around and through it, engaging
both disabled and nondisabled people—it follows no clear or consistent
logic. The identity of the "feeling person" is anything but stable. In this
respect, nineteenth-century theories about the way the emotions produced by disability move from person to person are strikingly similar to
nineteenth-century scientific theories about the transmission of impairment discussed in chapter 2.

Overpowering suspicion, for example, is said to characterize blind
men's feelings toward their sighted wives, the mutual feelings of the
blind and sighted, and deaf people's feelings toward the world at large.
Suffering and sympathy are everyone's property. Following the same
uncertain logic that characterizes the theories of impairment and its
transmission, emotional affliction has an alarming ability to circulate
from infirm bodies to "whole" ones. While deaf children are habitually
described as "stricken" beings, one educational institution asserts that
"the uninstructed Deaf and Dumb must be causes of unceasing sorrow to
their afflicted parents and friends, and in most cases useless and burdensome, often dangerous and injurious, members of Society" (*Histori-*

*cal Sketch* iv). Another school report assures that gentlefolk "need not be apprehensive of seeing anything which can hurt their feelings" when they visit (*Account* 8).

Melodramatic literature provided not only a model, but also an anchor, for these fluid emotions. The affective landscape of disability in medical, educational, and other nonliterary texts is a visual and performative realm of melodramatic extremes; the intensity with which disabled people's suffering, gratitude, fear, and affection are drawn is mirrored by the equally intense pity or outrage expressed by the nondisabled people who view, interview, and write about them. When they can, the texts work with a plotline, visualizing disability before and after education or before and after treatment, narrating emotional transformations and their social consequences by following the recognizable path of a melodramatic play or story.

What I have theorized is an interdisciplinary, collaborative relationship. Literary and nonliterary works, similar in their melodramatic rhetorics of affliction, worked in complementary ways with the concept of disability as a social identity and social problem. Not only did all kinds of texts frame disability within the conventions of melodrama—emotional excess, visual display, and tidy resolutions to emotional conflicts—they also worked on the same kinds of problems associated with disability. In fact, the tension and resolution in a fictional plot often only make sense as solutions to conflicts articulated elsewhere. Disabled women's recurrent banishment from marriage plots, as I argue in chapter 2, is completely legible only in the context of medical texts' construction of them as dangerous mothers. Melodramatic novels offer their own solutions to the perceived social problem of disabled people's reproduction. In the realm of disability and production, the collaboration is somewhat more complicated. Innocent children who cannot work and crafty disabled beggars who will not work appear in fiction by Dickens and the editorials in the *Charity Organisation Reporter.* Both texts weep for disabled victims and hiss disabled villains. This melodramatic character set only makes full sense, however, considered in terms of its excluded middle of the adult male worker. The contexts of poor-law reforms, the unemployment of "able-bodied" men, and educators and activists' insistence that disabled children can learn trades and become workers produced the bogeyman of the thieving blind beggar and the cherished image of the suffering child; these melodramatic figures were both screens for the truly threatening one of the disabled worker.

Melodrama maps these issues out in part by thematizing disabled bodies as bodies not only "seized by meaning" but also invested with affect (Brooks, "Melodrama, Body, Revolution" 18). Emotional excess makes and marks the distinction between able and disabled bodies, building a boundary that helps assess such questions as who is fit to work or receive poor relief, or who is fit to marry and reproduce. Melodrama provides a plotline and resolution to structure a world suffused with feeling. It reinscribes certain bodies as emotionally intense, others as less so, and names their narrative routes and endings on that basis. It sorts out the unruly world of emotional bodies, constructs emotional identities both for people who are disabled and for people who are not, and models the feeling relationships that should exist between people on the basis of their corporeality. It can also reorganize those melodramatic bodies and their plotlines to produce new ways of thinking about ability and disability.

Significantly, the plotting of Victorian melodrama took place in an era in which disability and ability were less distinct as social states than they would be in the next century, in which a full-blown welfare state, systems of insurance and compensation, and subtler ideologies and more technologically sophisticated practices of eugenics evolved to organize and sometimes eliminate varieties of social bodies.

While literary and other texts collaborate and interweave, the literary holds a particular status within the web of nineteenth-century writing about disability. First, Lawrence's invocation of Milton, beyond reminding us that he is an educated man rather than a quack, supplements the inability of the other forms of discourse he uses to say anything powerful enough about blindness for his purposes as a speaker and writer. When he has recourse to emotion as a mode of articulating blindness, Lawrence turns to Milton. The literary is thus reinforced as the kind of mode we enter when we want to talk about feelings.

Second, literary texts invited more extended explorations of disability and its social meaning, partly because as a genre they thrive on conflict and crisis (not just resolution) in ways that other texts may not. Nineteenth-century literary works often articulate the differences between disabled and abled identities but also invite us to consider transgressing the boundary between them. Over time, many works blurred the clarity of melodrama's limited pool of emotional responses, the related distinction between abled and disabled bodies, and sometimes, the always tentative distinction between melodrama and other literary forms. In short, Victorian melodramatic literature's engagement of disability, ability, and feeling is dynamic and diverse, inviting more of our ongoing critical debates about whether melodrama is inherently conservative or subversive and demonstrating that the melodramatic mode enables both dynamics, even in the same work. In those novels that expanded melodrama's schematic of emotion to try different kinds of feelings on different kinds of bodies, the Victorian reader's imagination could be opened to picture different kinds of social and sexual relationships between the abled and the disabled, and the novels' endings did not always shut down such imaginings.

Finally, literary works were a major vehicle for the transfer of cultural values about disability from the nineteenth century forward, albeit through a limited set of texts and an equally limited imaginative terrain. Within the context of an uneven transmission of cultural beliefs, the undiminished strength of nineteenth-century constructions of disability has been achieved largely through the vehicles of literature and film.

Of the diverse range of Victorian representations of disability, reproduction, and production, only a few texts retained their popularity into the next century. These few came to function in their own and later times as shorthand for the experience of disability, from both abled and disabled points of view, becoming the definitive texts that trained readers and viewers in certain habits of feeling. While these texts may have been popular partly because they were useful in quelling topical concerns about disability, they remained cultural doctrine years after they had come unmoored from their historical anchors, and years after facts could have countered these concerns. While many Victorian theories of heredity are no longer taken seriously, works like *Les deux orphelines* have lost little of their cultural impact and continue to train abled and disabled audiences about how to feel about disability. While we may laugh at a sociological text that claims that people with disabilities are inherently more emotional and physically responsive than nondisabled people, we uncritically accept literary representations anchored to this assumption. Melodramatic literature thus preserves, in simpler form, complex cultural formations that responded to historical tensions about disability.

Specific uses of disability in melodrama—as the intense or too-real, or the unearned and unreal—corresponded to, bolstered, and were bolstered by other readings of the body specific to Victorian culture. Uncertainty about disability—whether it conveyed the intensely "real" potential for the transmission of defect, the quite different "real" of innocent suffering, or the falsity of malingering and "sturdy" begging—dovetailed nicely with melodrama's shifting reception as a conveyor of the emotionally intense or a receptacle for cheap tears. If the use of disability in melodrama was initially motivated by censorship, it took hold as a feature of the genre partly because it drew on and formalized an anxiety about reality and fakery with relation to disability that was exacerbated both by theories of heredity and by the need to distinguish "innocent" from "guilty" need in the aftermath of the New Poor Law. This historically motivated association would shape the "essential" or "natural" meaning of disability for years to come.

# 2

## Marital Melodramas

### Disabled Women and Victorian Marriage Plots

As darkness, too, favors the imagination, so, perhaps, her very blindness contributed to feed with wild and delirious visions the love of the unfortunate girl. . . . what wonder that in her wild and passionate soul all the elements jarred discordant; that if love reigned over the whole, it was not the love which is born of the more sacred and soft emotions? . . . There were moments when she could have murdered her unconscious mistress, moments when she could have laid down life for her. These fierce and tremulous alternations of passion were too severe to be borne long.

(Bulwer-Lytton 230–34)

Henriette: You have separated me from a poor child whose only help in life I am; whose misfortune commands the respect of criminals even worse than yourself. She is dependent upon me alone; without me she cannot take a single step, for she is blind!

OMNES: Blind?

Henriette: Yes, blind and alone! *(Trembling voice.)* Alone in Paris, without money, without help, wandering through the streets, sightless, homeless, wild with despair. *(Bursts into tears. Half aside.)* What will become of her? *(Again bursting out.)* She is blind! Gentlemen, do you hear me? She is blind!

Chevalier *(moved):* "Oh, this is too horrible!"

(Oxenford 21)

A useful understanding of the melodramatization of disability demands local analysis. What kinds of characters and plots show up often—or never? If certain disabled figures are indeed melodramatic, what purposes does the emotional excess they carry serve in the plot and in the larger culture? What is compelling about thinking of them on the terms melodrama offers us—emotional excess, visual display, and clear plot resolutions? One figure that can guide us toward answers to these questions is the recurrent melodramatic trope of a young disabled woman involved in a marriage plot to which she is denied access and the variations to that plot that allow her to marry. These Victorian narratives, fascinating in their own right, also give us a ground from which to approach the continuing difficulty mainstream culture has imagining disabled women as lovers, wives, and mothers. Each of these possibilities produced for the Victorians (and produces for us) a particular form of anxiety.[1] Such plots are exemplified here by five popular fictional works across a thirty-year span of the century: Sir Edward Bulwer-Lytton's *The Last Days of Pompeii* (1834), Charles Dickens's *The Cricket on the Hearth* (1846), Dinah Maria Mulock Craik's *Olive* (1850), Charlotte Mary Yonge's *The Clever Woman of the Family* (1865), and Dickens's last novel, *Our Mutual Friend* (serialized 1864–65).

These fictions are usefully approached with a sense of disabled women's double participation in cultural conventions of women and disabled people as "feeling bodies," particularly well represented by a late-century stage melodrama, D'Ennery and Cormon's 1874 *Les deux orphelines*. In various adaptations and translations, this Victorian work retained its popularity into the twentieth century. The play was performed for decades on both sides of the Atlantic, as well as in Moscow under Stanislavsky's direction; it was rendered multiple times in silent film. Because *Les deux orphelines* reprises the treatment of blindness and sexuality in earlier stage melodramas like John Wilkins's *The Blind Wife* (1850), it is not so much a new model of disability, ability, and marriage as the reinscription of a preferred model after decades of exploration. The fictions that precede it suggest the ways in which earlier writers use emotional excess to mark disabled women as unfit for marriage, and how later ones shuffle the plot's emotional and structural dynamics to give disabled women the traditional heroine's ending, minus the biological children. Readings of these fictions will prepare the way for speculations about the other cultural contexts that shaped these plots and finally favored the one in which a blind woman is the site of pathos, not eros.

## Feeling Bodies: Women, Disability, Melodrama

Writing of melodrama in the twentieth century, Tania Modleski asserts that

> [i]ntuitively . . . we ally melodrama with the feminine insofar as it is a genre quintessentially concerned with emotional expression. Women in melodrama almost always suffer the pains of love and even death . . . while husbands, lovers, and children remain partly or totally unaware of their experience. Women carry the burden of feeling for everyone. (331)

Michael Booth confirms the historical reach of Modleski's statement, asserting that "a cardinal rule of melodrama is that at some point, usually early in the play, the heroine begins to suffer" (24). It is her endurance and valor in the face of assaults to body and spirit that make the melodramatic heroine "the emotional core of melodrama and very often the storm centre of its action," generating most of the sentimentality and pathos that the genre is known for (30). Disabled characters have their own claims as "centre[s] of pathos," based on suffering that often exceeds that of the heroine (71).

Melodrama's designation of both women and disabled people as emblems and engines of affect was amply underwritten by other Victorian discourses. Women's identification with feeling, and particularly with suffering, received extensive treatment by nineteenth-century writers, enough to produce a host of irreconcilable contradictions. A wide range of Victorian thinkers, while they may have disagreed on everything else, connected women with an essential emotionality, a "greater affectionateness" and "greater range and depth of emotional experience" than was characteristic of men (Lewes 131). As the journalist W. R. Greg theorized this "marvellous faculty of sympathy and intuition," it was the product of a typical melodramatic heroine's experience of having "felt profoundly and suffered long" (149). Suffering and empathy also brought women together; Sarah Stickney Ellis, for example, asserted that "women . . . know that their sex is formed to suffer; and for this very reason, there is sometimes a bond existing between sisters, the most endearing, the most pure and disinterested, of any description of affection which this world affords" arising from "their mutual knowledge of each other's capability of receiving pain" (224).

As much as the capacity to respond to others' suffering was considered a mark of moral development and even of humanness, a marked moral ambiguity accompanied this construction of woman as a feeling body.[2] She might "transcend both nature and rationality by means of her spirituality and intuitive powers," or she might be "a pre-logical being, existing outside of rationality in a state of nature" (Pykett 164–65). While the first kind of woman was a moral and spiritual beacon, the second kind's childlike emotionality was potentially dangerous, particularly if it expressed itself sexually. While not all nineteenth-century writers subscribed to Aristotle's concept of woman herself as a deformity of nature, women's feelings, especially when they became sexual passions, could be framed as a moral defect. "Unwomanly" feelings, ironically, are themselves included in the characteristics of women generated by Victorian gender ideologies and a reminder of the eighteenth century's "gradual transformation of [a] sexualized image of woman as wilful flesh into [a] domestic ideal" (Poovey 10).

Feeling was central to Victorian discourses of disability as well. As Mary Klages explains in her study of disability in Victorian American culture, while Descartes and Locke had defined personhood in terms of the capacity for rational thought, eighteenth-century moral philosophers Thomas Reid, David Hume, and Adam Smith relocated humanness in the capacity to feel, and especially to feel compassion for the suffering of others. Within this context, people with disabilities could be theorized not only as suffering objects with a key role to play in the moral development of others, but also, given their capacity for feeling and compassion, as "empathic agents" in their own right.[3]

With its connection to physical responsiveness, however, sensibility (and particularly sentimentality, the gender-inflected concept into which it evolved) could associate a person not only with sympathy and moral development, but also with the "primitive" or the animal, who had never evolved beyond physical and emotional responsiveness to social feeling.[4] The capacity for emotion was thus as risky a basis for arguing the full personhood of those with disabilities as it was for arguing the moral superiority of women.

In the special case of melodrama, a genre that constructs its characters, its audience, and sometimes its author as creatures of feeling, characters who were both female and disabled had the potential to generate an extreme and complicated emotional charge. The dangerous connection between feeling and sexuality might transform emotionally expressive females in melodramas into figures for everything that was most alarming about women in general. Melodrama's use of a "twin structure" that pairs a disabled woman with a nondisabled one and gives them distinctly different physical, emotional, and marital futures may have offered a way to tap into emotional excess with all its interesting possibilities safely anchored to a few distinctive, visibly disabled female bodies with no danger of marrying. This is, arguably, the case with *Les deux orphelines*.

## Les deux orphelines

Adolphe Philippe D'Ennery and Eugène Cormon's *Les deux orphelines* opened in Paris and London in 1874. Its numerous English versions include John Oxenford's *The Two Orphans* (1874), N. Hart Jackson's *The Two Orphans* (1875), and Emanuel Gideon's *Blind among Enemies* (1885). After its success in the theater, the melodrama lived on in seven silent film adaptations, including D. W. Griffith's *Orphans of the Storm* (1921), which stars the Gish sisters.[5]

Louise and Henriette, sisters by adoption, are the orphans of the title. When these pretty country girls travel to Paris to seek a cure for Louise's blindness, they are almost immediately separated by the henchmen of an evil marquis bent on raping Henriette. Henriette is saved by De Vaudray, a good aristocrat who then falls in love with her, but Louise is taken in by the begging impostor La Frochard, who forces her to sing in the streets for alms. La Frochard's hale, lazy, and evil son Jacques leers at and abuses Louise, while her good, industrious, "hunchbacked" and "crippled" son Pierre pities and adores her (but is too timid to act). Meanwhile, De Vaudray's aunt, the countess de Linières, visits Henriette and becomes certain that Louise is the baby she abandoned on the steps of Notre Dame fourteen years ago after the death of the lower-ranked man to whom she was secretly married. Louise's valor, Henriette's determination, Pierre's sudden courage, and a host of startling coincidences reunite the blind girl with her sister and mother. As the curtain falls, we know that Henriette will marry De Vaudray, and that Louise will go home with her repentant aristocratic mother, whose doctor will try to cure her blindness.

*Les deux orphelines* renders a clear model of how melodrama puts disabled women into the marriage plot, underpinned by earlier French and British melodramas that equate sight with sexuality and mark blind women as unfit for marriage (Paulson 73). From the two sisters' arrival in Paris, they are pointed in divergent plot trajectories. Henriette is sexual prey for evil aristocrats, while Louise is a removable obstacle to sex. Henriette is promptly saved, while Louise is abandoned, a rejected and abject body whose erotic value is only realized by the "cripple" Pierre and his depraved criminal brother. While both sisters experience a range of misfortunes in the course of the plot, Louise's ordeal is the major scene of suffering and sadism. Her melancholy nature is well established before the abduction: she reflects that it might have been better to have died on the steps of Notre Dame, rather than to live to lose her sight and be "a cause of sorrow to all connected with me" (Gideon n.p.). In short order, her emotional pain is compounded with physical injury, as she is starved, made to beg, beaten, and kissed by the evil Jacques.

Louise and Henriette are twin heroines, then, with very separate work to do in the plot. Louise's job is to suffer abuse, rise up against it, and return to the arms of her sister and mother; Henriette's job is to be passively virtuous, resisting both rape and courtship until her sister's safe recovery allows her to marry. The story resolutely protects this divergence in the women's sexual roles. While Henriette is permitted to love not only her sister, but also her suitor, Louise is completely excluded from the world of sexuality.

*Les deux orphelines* is a key cultural text in which melodramatic contexts for blindness and marriage are reinscribed toward the end of the nineteenth century and passed on to the twentieth. I want now to offer a speculative genealogy of that moment of reinscription. The same basic "twin structure" undergirds the marriage plots of Bulwer-Lytton's 1834 potboiler *The Last Days of Pompeii* and Dickens's 1846 Christmas book *The Cricket on the Hearth,* but in these two fictions, emotional excess is eros as well as pathos. The blind women want exactly what their sighted friends want; while disability is still the main site of the plot's melodrama, the pathos of disability is the pathos of unrequited sexual longing. These fictions overdetermine the disabled woman's unfitness for marriage by characterizing her as hopelessly alienated from normal life and her desire invisible to the nondisabled. Most significantly, however, they represent her as too feeling, too expressive, and potentially too sexual for matrimony.

## The Last Days of Pompeii

𝔉rom the lurid visuality of sadistic pagan entertainments to the premature darkness of a sky filled with ashes, *The Last Days of Pompeii* enmeshes all its characters in a dense metaphoric fabric of visuality. Moments of witnessing (of a young man's murder and Christ's crucifixion) are followed by temporary blindness, literal or cognitive, and "evil eyes" are everywhere. (This emphasis on spectacle made *Pompeii* a natural to adapt for the melodramatic stage.)

Within the anticipation of the known disaster that will end the plot, which frames our experience of this novel, Bulwer-Lytton distracts us with the glorious Athenian Glaucus's courtship of the beautiful Ione, and the Egyptian priest Arbaces's attempts to ravish her. Moving in the interstices between the three characters, the blind girl Nydia, passionate for her master Glaucus, literally functions as slave, go-between, and rescuer of the marriage plot.

According to Bulwer-Lytton's preface to the 1834 edition of *The Last Days of Pompeii,* a casual conversation with an English resident of Naples attuned him to a blind character's potential to dramatize a world turned upside down by natural disaster:

> Speaking of the utter darkness which accompanied that first recorded eruption of Vesuvius, and the additional obstacle it presented to the escape of the inhabitants, he observed that the blind would be the most favored in such a moment, and find the easiest deliverance. In that remark originated the creation of Nydia. (x)

From a plot convenience, however, Bulwer-Lytton develops Nydia into the story's emotional engine. Like Louise, Nydia is identified by the plot as an emotionally extreme character because of her blindness. As her flower-selling song announces, blindness in the novel is a state poised between the living and the dead, even gesturing ominously toward the afterworld (rather than touchingly toward heaven, as in other melodramas). Nydia is "as one in the realm below" for whom "the living are ghosts" (9). Bulwer-Lytton registers Nydia's marginality as physical, spiritual, social, sexual, and moral. She is a foreigner to Pompeii (from Thessaly, "the witches' country"), stolen into slavery from her gentle parents, and though "still half a child," has features "more formed than exactly became her years" (10, 54). Although the other characters identify her as a permanent Vir-

Nydia of *The Last Days of Pompeii* (New York: Frederick A. Stokes, 1891). Photo courtesy of Dartmouth Medical School Photography and Illustration.

gin—"twice the age she is at present, she would be equally fit for Vesta,—poor girl' "—Nydia has nonetheless played the harp at Arbaces's orgies, and been exposed to all manner of sexual corruption (116).

Nydia's most important area of marginality, however, is her emotional excess, which inevitably suggests the volcano that is the chief aspect of Pompeii's mise-en-scène and, following the excavation of Pompeii and Herculaneum in the late eighteenth century, a recurrent image of troublesome emotion in nineteenth-century writing.[6] On the surface, Nydia is indeed as pure and sweet as several critics assert, but her noble rescues of the good and feckless principals mean nothing without her eruptions of passion for her master and malevolence for the woman he loves.[7] She jealously regrets having saved Ione's virginity, and wishes her dead; she almost does kill Glaucus, giving him a "love potion" that deranges him. Remorse follows passion, but Nydia's violent feelings always return.

The narrator insists that this is not about sex. "[I]n the wild heart of the Thessalian all was pure, uncontrolled, unmodified passion;—erring, unwomanly; frenzied, but debased by no elements of a more sordid feeling" (357). At the same time, the burden of Nydia's "fearful burning mood" is bodily as well as emotional, as her responses to Glaucus affirm; his voice leaves her "listening, blushing, breathless; with her lips parted, her face upturned to catch the direction of the sound" (151).

In fact, within the overt message of her blind purity, which seems to have convinced so many readers, Nydia alludes to an "unwomanly" sexuality that connects her more with nondisabled villainesses than with other blind women characters. The narrator specifically explains Nydia's moral instability as a perversion of her womanly nature:

> Nature had sown in the heart of this poor girl the seeds of virtue never destined to ripen. . . . the kindlier feelings, naturally profuse in the breast of Nydia, were nipped and blighted. Her sense of right and wrong was confused by a passion to which she had so madly surrendered herself; and the same intense and tragic emotions which we read of in the women of the classic age,—a Myrrha, a Medea,—and which hurried and swept away the whole soul when once delivered to love, ruled and rioted in her breast. (304)

This construction of Nydia clearly participates in Victorian discourses of woman and emotion, but says nothing about disability; in one sense, then, her passion decreases her exclusion from traditional women's plots, if it limits her to tragic and villainous positions within them.

If Nydia comes to the plot as part of the mise-en-scène, Bulwer-Lytton develops her into the unwieldy figure of a disabled woman with sexuality, mobility, and agency. In the end, however, he has no earthly place to put her. It is thus convenient to have Nydia vanish into the sea, crying, "There is no other Elysium for a heart like mine." She leaves the plot "mysterious from first to last," her passion unrecognized by any living characters (546). Glaucus raises a tomb to her in his garden, a memorial that "keeps alive . . . a tender recollection, a not unpleasing sadness, which are but a fitting homage to her fidelity, and the mysteriousness of her early death" (548). The plot's resolution depends on us forgetting (or failing to see, like Glaucus) Nydia's eros and enshrining her pathos, both of which are easiest if she is dead.

## The Cricket on the Hearth

Dickens finds a less extreme resolution to a similar problem in *The Cricket on the Hearth.* Like *A Christmas Carol, Cricket* was a Christmas book, published by Dickens to stimulate public awareness of social problems, invite charitable giving, and finance the needs of his growing family. *Cricket's* print version was more popular than *A Christmas Carol* during the nineteenth century; like *Pompeii,* it was adapted for the stage and became one of Dickens's public reading pieces, though one of the least popular.

The conflict, crisis, and resolution of *The Cricket on the Hearth* hinge on people's failure to see the truth about those they love. The cheery hearth in question belongs to carrier John Peerybingle and his young wife Dot. When Dot makes secret plans to reunite her friend May Fielding with May's long-absent lover, Edward Plummer, before May makes an unhappy marriage to the rich and misanthropic manufacturer Tackleton, the happy home is shadowed by deception and jealousy. Edward, disguised as an old deaf man, finds lodging in the Peerybingles' house, but when John, egged on by Tackleton, sees him remove his disguise and speak intimately with Dot, he believes Edward is a lover who will supplant him. John's suppressed but increasingly violent jealousy and Dot's growing fear that her husband has rejected her are the narrative's primary obstacles and dangers. The recognition of true love and the celebration of happy marriages, as embodied in May and Edward's reunion and the

Peerybingles' reconciliation, are the significant goals to which it pro-
gresses.

Given the structure and emphasis of the plot, Dot Peerybingle's logical "twin" is her peer, May Fielding. But instead, Dickens creates Bertha
Plummer, a third young woman with her own dreams of courtship and
marriage, and makes her more central to the plot than the virtually
absent, silent May. The French's acting edition of the play of *Cricket*
affirms this twinship—Bertha and Dot, like Henriette and Louise, are
dressed in "identical cottagers' dresses." "Blind Girl" Bertha, Edward's
sister, lives with her father in a tumbledown cottage where they make
toys for Tackleton. Structurally embedded in the center of the book, she
emerges from a miniaturized, fairy-tale frame of which the narrative is
self-consciously aware:

> Caleb Plummer and his Blind Daughter lived alone by themselves,
> as the Story-books say . . . in a little cracked nutshell of a wooden
> house. . . . you might have knocked down Caleb Plummer's
> dwelling with a hammer or two, and carried off the pieces in a
> cart. (182)

Bertha's father, the toy-maker, daily builds his own fairy tale of home
around her. As the narrator tells it,

> Caleb lived here, and his poor Blind Daughter somewhere else—
> in an enchanted home of Caleb's furnishing, where scarcity and
> shabbiness were not, and trouble never entered. . . . The Blind
> Girl never knew that iron was rusting, wood rotting, paper peeling
> off; the size, and the shape, and true proportion of the dwelling,
> withering away. The Blind Girl never knew that ugly shapes of delf
> and earthenware were on the board; that sorrow and faintheart-
> edness were in the house; that Caleb's scanty hairs were turning
> greyer and more grey, before her sightless face. The Blind Girl
> never knew they had a master, cold, exacting, and uninterested—
> never knew that Tackleton was Tackleton in short; but lived in the
> belief of an eccentric humourist who loved to have his jest with
> them, and who, while he was the Guardian Angel of their lives, dis-
> dained to hear one word of thankfulness. And all was Caleb's
> doing. (182–83)

As improbable as the deception is, this is a melodrama, and thus Bertha falls in love with Tackleton, imagining him kind and noble, with "a manly heart that tries to cloak all favours with a show of roughness and unwillingness" (190).

The open physicality of Bertha's affection for Tackleton immediately marks her as different from the stock Victorian heroine and probably destined for trouble. When Tackleton visits the Plummers' hovel, she holds and kisses his hand, thanking him for a rose tree she believes he has given her, then lays her cheek tenderly against the hand with "unspeakable affection and . . . fervent gratitude." Bertha becomes luminous when Tackleton, after muttering "Poor Idiot!" to himself, calls her to his side to ask a favor: "How bright the darkened face! How adorned with light, the listening head!" (188). The favor—that she include him in her weekly luncheon with the Peerybingles—moves Bertha to a state of "ecstasy," but immediately after, to one of startled shock, when Tackleton adds that he wants to bring May Fielding, whom he will marry.

Bertha's sense of bereavement of her dreams of love first finds "no vent in words," but later she begins to configure a new narrative about Tackleton, referencing the very "twin structure" into which she is written but has heretofore not perceived: she questions her father about May. When Caleb confirms that May is fair indeed, Bertha muses on May's hair, "darker than mine," musical voice, and comely shape, then describes the role she thought would be hers, which will now be filled by May:

> To be his patient companion in infirmity and age; to be his gentle nurse in sickness, and his constant friend in suffering and sorrow; to know no weariness in working for his sake; to watch him, tend him, sit by his bed and talk to him awake, and pray for him asleep; what privileges these would be! What opportunities for proving all her truth and devotion to him! Would she do all this, dear father? (191)

Significantly, Bertha imagines marriage as an opportunity to emerge from the cultural role of cared-for Blind Girl—about whom even the Peerybingles' dog is solicitous—and into that of nurturer of an aging husband.

When Caleb assures Bertha that May will fulfill this role, Bertha exclaims, "I love her, father; I can love her from my soul!" and lays "her poor blind face on Caleb's shoulder, and so wept and wept, that he was almost sorry to have brought that tearful happiness upon her" (190–91). Her distress has too much narrative promise, however, to be exhausted by this private scene. During the festive luncheon that follows, she once again weeps in front of her father, bemoaning "my hard, hard fate!" (201). While Caleb assumes that it is the "great affliction" of blindness that brings her sorrow, Bertha corrects him, and begs him to bring May to her so that she may unburden her feelings (201). In a classic melodramatic "falling" scene, Bertha grips May's hands, upturns "the blank sightless face, down which the tears were coursing fast," and delivers a fervent and strikingly passive-aggressive benediction on the marriage:

> "Every blessing on your head! Light upon your happy course! Not the less, my dear May"; and she drew towards her, in closer grasp; "not the less, my bird, because, to-day, the knowledge that you are to be His wife has wrung my heart almost to breaking!" . . . While speaking, she had released May Fielding's hands, and clasped her garments in an attitude of mingled supplication and love. Sinking lower and lower down, as she proceeded in her strange confession, she dropped at last at the feet of her friend and hid her blind face in the folds of her dress. (201–2)[8]

Bertha's scenes of distress over Tackleton's engagement form some of the story's most significant moments of crisis and emotional overflow. Until this point, she has functioned mostly as a plot nexus and a character whose supposed dependency and suffering, in keeping with eighteenth-century concepts of sympathy, have allowed others to reveal their worth (Dot and May shine through their kindness to her; Tackleton shows his full moral poverty by treating her callously). She turns into a problem the story can't solve, however, when she expresses her own feelings in floods of language and tears. Bertha's emotional intensity is, like her picturesquely gesturing hands and "blank sightless face," turned up as the tears flow down it, a convention of melodramatic representations of blindness. What breaks the convention and stalls the plot, however, is Bertha's pointed assertion that her agony is that of an unrequited lover: it is eros, not pathos (201). What's more, she had imagined herself a heroine with the same potential for love and marriage as her Dot or May, but now she understands what they are trying to tell her—that her disability precludes those outcomes.

Shortly after, Bertha repents her outburst and follows it up with a conciliatory one, holding her father's head to her breast. The narrative specifically tries to recuperate the problem of Bertha's desire by shifting it to the appropriate context of parent and child, but Bertha and Caleb's reunion has little of the simple relief of Louise's reunion with her mother at the end of *Le deux orphelines;* Bertha's thwarted desire for Tackleton makes a smooth return to her father's hearth impossible. When a wild and rollicking wedding dance produces what we would now call a Dickensian close, Bertha's joy is moved to the edge of that noisy room. She plays her liveliest harp tune, but does not join in the dance, a throng so democratic that it includes the reformed ogre Tackleton, cranky Mrs. Fielding, and even, according to John Leech's illustration, the cat and the dog.

Whereas Louise's happiness in reuniting with her sister and mother is central to the last scene of *Le deux orphelines,* the time of Bertha's significance is past by the close of Dickens's melodramatic story. At the same time, the resolution of her part of the plot is an unquiet one; when the narrative threads have finally been sorted out, Bertha lingers on the melancholy outside of the world of courtship and marriage. Her earlier moments of dramatic expression bring a sense of lasting disruption to *The Cricket on the Hearth* in part because they never culminate in either of the narrative fulfillments they seem to suggest: still greater misery, or triumph and joy (the fulfillment of Bertha's dreams, either in a transformed Tackleton or in some other man). Bertha's inclusion in the figurative blindness that besets so many characters in the story ironically emphasizes the fact that her blindness is different from theirs; she is the only one (except the narrator) whose suffering can't be genuinely cured by the domestic love that the plot promotes.[9] Since both her former dreamy self and the enchanted cottage of her father's invention are changed beyond recognition, the place she might return to is effectively gone, and there is no wedding in the future. Bertha's emotional excess is dangerous because it expresses this frustration and her wish to become a heroine in her own right, with her own story of courtship, love, and marriage. The resolution Dickens offers, of Bertha's cheerful return to her harp and her father, is never sufficient to neutralize her vocal, public expressions of desire and its mortifications.

It is hardly a surprise that the writers who envisioned more for disabled women characters than emotional excess and its outcomes were themselves women. In narratives by Dinah Craik and by Charlotte Yonge, a disabled woman's involvement in the marriage plot may indeed bring anguish and exclusion, but also strength, social power, and a surprising variety of fictional rewards. This much more optimistic placement of disabled women in culture is predicated on their being, or becoming, the polar opposites of the conventional melodramatic disabled heroines: if they suffer, or if they desire, these characters indicate it quietly and privately. While the narratives that house them retain the intensity and moral polarity of melodrama, in each of them the disabled woman is domesticated into a very different kind of heroine.

The emotional excess of Nydia and Bertha, along with its dangerous association with female sexuality, is shifted in Craik's *Olive* and Yonge's *The Clever Woman of the Family* to nondisabled women, who are either killed off or mortified and rehabilitated. The disabled heroines are models of meek, but not dull, restraint, and are rewarded for it with recognition, work, and the literal place—complete with husband and child—of the nondisabled heroine. In Yonge's *The Clever Woman of the Family*, the by-product of this empowerment of the disabled heroine is the explicit refusal of an unequal relationship of emotional charity and pity based on the assumption of the disabled woman's pathos and diminishment, and its replacement with a bond based on mutual affection and equality.[10] In essence, both Craik and Yonge make an experience of disability a necessary human transformation that qualifies both men and women for happy marriages.

## Olive

Disability is a recurrent interest of Dinah Maria Mulock Craik's fiction, and central to her best-known novel, *John Halifax, Gentleman* (1856), whose narrator is a male "invalid." *Olive* (1850) is a female bildungsroman complicated and enriched by the fact of the heroine's disability and the resulting exploration of the social consequences of beauty and "deformity." Born prematurely to a frivolous young beauty, Olive Rothesay's early years could not be farther from those of Tiny Tim or Bertha Plummer. While she is born wealthy, her parents' relationship is forever damaged by their responses to her disability and difficulty communicating about it. Initially delighted with her daughter, Sybilla Rothesay's joy becomes fear and resentment when a physician pronounces the baby "deformed."[11] The concept that her daughter is "doomed for life to suffer the curse of hopeless deformity" seems "a curse, a bitter curse . . . to the young and beautiful creature, who had learned since her birth to consider beauty as the greatest good" (14). Believing that her husband, on an extended trip to the West Indies, will also see the baby as "a deformity on the face of the earth, a shame to its parents, a dishonour to its race . . . [a] poor cripple," Sybilla conceals Olive's disability until her husband's return a few years later (14–15). It is only at that point that the reader, in the company of Captain Rothesay, receives a full description of Olive's person:

> Her limbs were small and wasted, but exquisitely delicate. The same might be said of her features; which, though thin, and wearing a look of premature age, together with that quiet, earnest melancholy cast peculiar to deformity, were yet regular, almost pretty. Her head was well-shaped, and from it fell a quantity of amber-coloured hair—pale "lint-white locks," which, with the almost colourless transparency of her complexion, gave a spectral air to her whole appearance. She looked less like a child than a woman dwarfed into childhood . . . . her lovely hair was arranged so as to hide, as much as possible, the defect, which, alas! was even then only too perceptible. It was not a humpback, nor yet a twisted spine; it was an elevation of the shoulders, shortening the neck, and giving the appearance of a perpetual stoop. There was nothing disgusting or painful in it, but still it was an imperfection, causing an instinctive compassion—an involuntary "Poor little creature, what a pity!" (23)

The novel is notable in its careful development of the social role of "deformed girl" or "cripple" and its purported emotional content. Craik also engages more directly the issues that Bulwer-Lytton and Dickens take as givens with scenes of Olive's adolescence and her involvement in the courtship rituals of her friend Sara, who is "twinned" with her in the early parts of the novel. Though Olive doesn't understand why her father mutters to himself that of course she will never marry, or why her mother insists that she will look prettier if she wears a fur mantle around her foreshortened neck, at her first ball, she grasps in the company of other young women the cultural name and place she has been assigned.

As Olive watches the other young people dance, she feels that "every one loved, or was loved, except herself" (65). Sara, the friend to whom she is passionately attached, articulates this universal human experience of isolation as one specific to disability. First, Olive overhears Sara laughing when another girl teases her that she should be jealous of Olive's friendship with Sara's lover.

> "Jealous of Olive—how very comical!" and the silver laugh was a little scornful. "To think of Olive's stealing any girl's lover! She, who will probably never have one in all her life—poor thing!" (66)

Later, when Olive tells Sara she overheard her, her friend offers these halting clarifications:

> "[I]t does not signify to me, or to any of those who care for you; you are such a gentle little creature, we forget it all in time. But perhaps with strangers, especially with men, who think so much about beauty, this defect—"
> She paused, laying her arm round Olive's shoulders—even affectionately, as if she herself were much moved. But Olive, with a cheek that whitened and a lip that quivered more and more, looked resolutely at her own shape imagined in the glass.
> "I see, as I never saw before—so little I thought of myself. Yes, it is quite true—quite true."
> She spoke beneath her breath, and her eyes seemed fascinated into a hard, cold gaze. Sara became almost frightened.
> "Do not look so, my dear girl; I did not say that it was a positive deformity."
> Olive faintly shuddered: "Ah, that is the word! I understand it all now." (66–67)

When the drunken Captain Rothesay calls his daughter a "white-faced, mean-looking hunchback," that much harsher remark is easier for the endlessly compassionate Olive to recognize as a melodramatic epithet uttered by an angry, drunken, disappointed man. Craik's dramatization of the social identity of disability consistently moves away from those terms, however (76).

The "twin structure" trajectory Craik invokes sends Olive off to become a successful painter and supporter of her widowed, blind mother, who finally recognizes Olive's value, a plot element of the purest melodrama. While Craik does not ultimately endorse Olive's sexual self-denial, she does articulate an engaging narrative of compensation, suggesting the benefits of life outside the marriage plot:

That sense of personal imperfection which she deemed excluded her from a woman's natural destiny, gave her freedom in her own. Brought into contact with the world, she scarce felt like a young and timid girl, but as a being—isolated, yet strong in her isolation; who mingles, and must mingle, among men, not as a woman, but as one who, like themselves, pursues her own calling, has her own spirit's aims; and can therefore step aside for no vain fear, nor sink beneath any idle shame. . . . Mrs. Rothesay trembled and murmured at the days of solitary study in the British Museum, and in various picture galleries; the long lonely walks, sometimes in winter-time extending far into the dusk of evening. But Olive always answered, with a pensive smile,

"Nay, mother; I am quite safe everywhere. Remember, I am not like other girls. Who would notice me?" But she always accompanied any painful allusion of this kind by saying how happy she was in being so free, and how fortunate it seemed that there could be nothing to hinder her from following her heart's desire. (127–28)

Sara offers additional evidence of the dangers of success at normative feminine roles. After a glorious debut, she marries young, is unhappy being a wife, and dies in childbirth; in short, she, like Captain Rothesay's illegitimate daughter Chrystal, a figure of sexuality and hysteria who commits suicide, is an excessive woman in the plot. For her part, the sensitive and sensible Olive struggles to overcome not the obstacle of disability, but her own acculturation into the idea that disabled women do not marry. She finds love and marriage with Sara's widower, and mothers Sara's child. By the novel's end, Olive's exclusion is reversed and her pain compensated, if not removed—a melodramatic ending, but hardly in the terms the earlier plots presented.

## The Clever Woman of the Family

Charlotte Mary Yonge, similarly, upends the disabled woman's role in melodrama.[12] Like *Olive*, *The Clever Woman of the Family* (1865) has the overt Christian message that disability is not an affliction but a blessing, but does not house that blessing in the Christian melodrama we will see in later chapters. Like Craik, she figures feminine disability as freedom from the professional and social limitations placed on a "normal" woman's body. Yonge also represents disability and mutual dependency as pervasive social goods, those which promote both the homosocial and more generally the social. While Craik kills off her excessive nondisabled heroines, Yonge rehabilitates one of hers and ultimately imagines a world in which nondisabled and disabled people are equal participants in the rewards of marriage and community life.

The novel follows the intertwined fates of the "clever" bluestocking Rachel Curtis and the wise Ermine Williams, who has used a wheelchair since her legs were burned in a domestic accident when she was twenty. The arrival of visitors from India—Rachel's widowed cousin Fanny Temple, her husband's aide Colin Keith, and Alick, Colin's younger cousin— brings about the meeting of Rachel and Ermine, Rachel's courtship by Alick, and the renewed courtship of Ermine by Colin. The latter relationship was forbidden by Colin's aristocratic father, who enlisted him in the regiment; Colin left for India after a visit to what he presumed was Ermine's deathbed. Colin and Ermine, neither knowing the other's fate, have never in their imaginations fallen out of love with each other.

Almost everyone in this novel has some sort of physical infirmity that requires another's care and help. The two heroes, Colin and Alick, are permanently wounded from the siege of Delhi; another character is blind; Rachel's mother is sickly. Mutual weakness and mutual nursing, moreover, characterize all the happy relationships in the book. When Rachel bemoans her dependency on Alick, Ermine consoles her with the idea that this dependency is not only inevitable, but also "will make you much more really useful and effective than ever you could have been alone" (283). The novel amply affirms the power of infirmity to draw people close, not only in parent-child or sibling relationships, but also in same-sex friendships (female and male) and in heterosexual courting couples, where it catalyzes rather than precludes marriages. As Sally Mitchell aptly observes, in Yonge's novels "the constellation man-woman-illness-pain often exudes an erotic tension," and disability, nursing, and interdependence are not bars to courtship but its bases (*Dinah Mulock Craik* 112). Ermine must finally take her own advice and acknowledge to both Rachel and Colin that the real obstacle to her marriage was the family disgrace, not so much her "helplessness." She finally allows that "if you like the old cinder, Colin, that is your concern" (Yonge 348–49).

Disability is also delineated, however, as bringing more private rewards. By removing Ermine from what she calls "the active work of life," her injury has forced her to support herself not by marriage or even, like her sister, by teaching, but by becoming a professional writer (78). Her disability and financial need combined allow the narrative to endorse her pleasure in publishing her essays under the pseudonym "The Invalid," while it marks Rachel's striving for publication and social reform (without the wisdom to do either well) as unwomanly and punishes her soundly. If Yonge's novel speaks of disability as a sort of cherished dependency, it dramatizes it as equally to be cherished as a liberating force, that which frees women from stultifying social roles without making them pay for the privilege.

Yonge releases Ermine not only from carrying the burden of the social expectations placed on Rachel, but also from "the burden of feeling." While Ermine's sister Alison describes the physical pain of the accident in appropriately emphatic language (Ermine threw herself onto a chemical fire in order to save her sister), even Alison admits that Ermine's "terrible suffering . . . was in the first years" and not the present (40–41). Alison confirms Ermine's declarations of happiness as well. The only point at which Ermine Williams' good cheer is figured as repressed suffering is when that pain is very briefly reexperienced, on the point of being relieved forever. After Ermine's wedding, Colin leaves to attend his dying brother; she has just come home to their house, which is decorated to replicate her childhood home and filled with gifts he has bought her during their long separation.

> No wonder Ermine laid her head on her hand, and could not retain her tears, as she recalled the white, dismayed face of the youth, who had printed that one sad earnest kiss on her brow, as she lay fire-scathed and apparently dying; and who had cherished the dream unbroken and unwaveringly, had denied himself consistently, had garnered up these choice tokens when ignorant even whether she still lived; had relied on her trust, and come back, heart-whole, to claim and win her, undaunted by her crippled state, her poverty, and her brother's blotted name. (358)

While nearly everyone else in the novel, including Colin, has cried in Ermine's arms, these are her first tears, coming in recognition of the fact that Colin has been as constant as she, has endured a "weary waiting" parallel to hers. If the reader cries as well, it is not the sense that Ermine is mutely suffering that brings on tears, but rather the scene's presentation of Ermine's mixed experience of keeping the pain alive, recognizing its value, and feeling its relief all at once. As Lady Temple assures her, "these ever-welling tears came from a source by no means akin to grief or repining" (358).

It is the nondisabled women in the book who suffer most visibly. Alison, who caused the fire that burned her sister, is the one who cannot recover:

> [H]er face missed the radiant beamy brightness of her sister's. . . . there was about her a look as if some terrible wave of grief or suffering had swept over her ere yet the features were fully fixed, and had thus moulded her expression for life. (37)

Alick's beautiful, witty, and flirtatious sister Bessie is in the plot only briefly before marrying Lord Keith (Colin's brother), whom she does not love, and dying in childbirth (after tripping over a croquet hoop). But Rachel is subject to the plot's most active mortification. The narrative blatantly excludes her from professional fulfillment (her announced goal in life), in a series of increasingly traumatic failures that begins with rejections from publishers and ends in a charitable project that causes a poor child's death. Rachel not only has to appear in front of an inquest, but also experiences a complete physical and emotional collapse, including a fainting episode:

> Rachel had despised fainting ladies, and had really hitherto been so superabundant in strength that she had no experience of the symptoms, or she might have escaped in time. But there she lay, publicly censured . . . for moral folly, and entirely conquered . . . by the physical weakness she had most contemned. (266)

Rachel essentially assumes the function of melodramatic sufferer in the story, that role which disabled women so often play.

The novel makes a scapegoat of Rachel not only for the joy of bringing her low, although there is a hint of that, but more importantly, to reiterate its message of the importance of acknowledged weakness to human relationships. And while a sort of parity is created in *Olive* by injuring nondisabled women and allowing Olive to excel at their failed roles, in *The Clever Woman of the Family*, Rachel's shame and infirmity elevate her to Ermine's status. When both women finally reap the traditional heroine's rewards together, the delay has been enriched by the friendship it produces.

In this novel, then, the erasure of emotional excess permits the homosocial to an extent none of the other works achieve. Nydia and Ione are impossibly separated not only by one's slavery, but also by the fact that Nydia both loves and would like to kill off her rival. While Bertha, Dot, and May are described as friends, the friendship's inequality is emphasized by Dot's charitable gifts to Bertha and Bertha's passive-aggressive rivalry with May. Olive's friendship is basically severed by Sara's marriage, and Sara's death is precisely what makes space for Olive's validation in the marriage plot.

While Rachel initially tries to include Ermine in her good works in the community, however, that false relation is not corrected by another unequal one in which Ermine patronizes Rachel. In some respects, Ermine functions as Rachel's mentor, seeing the younger woman as what she would have become "without Papa and Edward to keep me down"— and, it is implied, without her injury (95). Ermine's defense of Rachel, however, is presented as genuine, based on her enjoyment of their intellectual "scrimmages":

> When excited or interested, most people found [Rachel] oppressive; but Ermine Williams, except when unwell, did not find her so. . . . They seemed to have a sort of natural desire to rub their minds one against the other. (45)

Most of the characters in the novel initially expect the story of Colin and Ermine to be a tragic one, because Colin has returned only to find her unable to marry. Rachel, never considering that Colin's attentions to Ermine are anything but kindness, thinks he loves *her*. Ermine herself must learn to consider herself a marriageable woman; because she has been "always the cripple" with others, she is incredulous in the face of Colin's longing to wed her.

But Colin and the children see Ermine as whole rather than damaged or incomplete. Perceiving her as unaltered in person after their thirteen-year separation, Colin asks, "Why did they tell me you were an invalid, Ermine?" (60). Ermine struggles in vain to make him accept that her changed identity is "more than lame," that he has "kept [his] allegiance to the bright, tall, walking, active girl, and it would be a shame in the scorched cripple to claim it" (77). Her niece Rose, to whom "the contraction and helplessness of [Ermine's] lower limbs" were so familiar that "it never even occurred to her to pity Aunt Ermine," only begins to suspect there is reason for pity when Ermine entreats Colin to recognize her diminishment. Soon after, however, Rose decides not that Ermine is unfit for any aspect of life, but rather that Colin is "Aunt Ermine's true knight." Colin is frankly irritated by Ermine's suggestion that he become like her brother (94). Similarly, when Ermine's adopted son hears her mention his biological mother, he declares, "You are mother!" (365). All the adults in the novel ultimately endorse the children and Colin's concept of Ermine's appropriate social, economic, and sexual place.

To summarize, Bulwer-Lytton and the early Dickens construct disabled women as emotionally excessive women and explicitly mark them as unfit for marriage. Craik and Yonge, in contrast, construct their disabled women characters as emotionally controlled participants in the discourse of "passionlessness" Nancy Cott describes as a strategy for empowering women by disassociating them from sexuality. Excessive women do not marry, but "passionless" women do, even if they are disabled.

## Our Mutual Friend

In Dickens's last novel, *Our Mutual Friend,* his many explorations of disability and sexuality throughout the century culminate in adolescent needlewoman Jenny Wren, a dolls' dressmaker like Bertha Plummer, with whom she shares just about nothing except this occupation and disability. She is descended from at least two generations of alcoholic men, and the self-named parent figure to her father, a "bad child" whose bodily abjection Dickens makes much more vivid than Jenny's. She says, "I can't get up . . . because my back's bad, and my legs are queer" (271). As much as Jenny reiterates her body in these terms: bad back, queer legs, the parts of her that enter the text more energetically are those fulfilling the "weird sharpness, but not without beauty" Dickens wanted for her— her expressive chin, pointing needle-finger, and abundant golden hair, which she claims and delights in as an equally valid part of the identity she performs for the world (Johnson 2:1014).

Jenny not only re-creates the life-size world in miniature out of its scraps, dressing dolls for balls, weddings, and funerals, but also renders it, through language, in terms of its full potential, herself included. Unlike the other young women in this plot, she identifies herself as "the person of the house" (27). It is not just her centrality to *Our Mutual Friend*'s entire "world of verbalized consciousness," but also her disability that allows Jenny to rescue the very tentative, class-crossing marriage plot between her beloved friend Lizzie Hexam, a waterman's daughter, and Eugene Wrayburn, a lounging, jaded gentleman (Miller 304). After an assault by his rival nearly kills Wrayburn and leaves him disfigured, disabled, and dying, it is specifically Jenny who nurses his body, as well as articulating the word he cannot say—"wife." Dickens identifies Jenny as an expert on pain and disability—on being seen as "a child—a dwarf—a girl—a something—" (271). He links this experience, however, to the ability to remake individual relationships and, thus, the social world. Lizzie knows to rescue the mutilated, bloody, genderless thing that is Wrayburn after the assault, but Jenny can identify him afterwards as a man now fit for marriage (there is, of course, an echo of the blinding of Rochester in *Jane Eyre* in this plot, but Dickens does more with it). J. Hillis Miller suggests this connection between disability and generativity in an oblique way, as an authenticity and meaning derived from Jenny's contact with "the alien and inhuman . . . what from the human point of view is death" (315). Even more significantly, Jenny can imagine herself fit for marriage and speculate in detail about her future husband. Like any adolescent, she imagines marriage in terms of the relationships she knows. He will carry her work as Lizzie does, but won't be able to brush her hair the way her friend can. After a wrenching encounter with her father, she imagines how she will physically torture him if he is a drunkard. With her ability to conceive her future world poised as something in between dressing dolls and imagining both the best and worst things that adult humans can do to each other, Jenny's dreams of marriage are far more complex than what Dickens could imagine for his earlier dolls' dressmaker.

Jenny's melodramatic identity, then, is mixed. She surely evokes and is the handmaiden of pathos, but not so much in her rhapsodic, Christmas-book vision of children "not like me . . . not chilled, anxious, ragged, or beaten . . . never in pain" who used to come in "long bright slanting rows" to rescue her into a world of ease (290). Rather, Jenny's moments of melodramatic pathos emerge when she sees "a harmless bundle of torn rags" and recognizes these scraps of the world as her father. "My poor bad, bad boy! And he don't know me, he don't know me! O what shall I do," she cries, "when my own child don't know me!" (800). Her pathos is a sophisticated creation, set in relief by her usual irony and her father's display of false emotional excess, naming himself a "[p]oor shattered invalid" in an effort to persuade his daughter to forgive and finance his drinking (292).

Like Ermine Williams, Jenny connects human lives not as a pathetic object that clarifies others' worth, but through friendship; while the affect Lizzie imagines for their relationship is first charity and compensation, what it turns into, at least temporarily, is a homosocial bond that Dickens enjoys illustrating with sensually rich, almost Pre-Raphaelite scenes in which they let down and comb each other's hair:[13]

> [Lizzie] unfastened a ribbon that kept it back while the little creature was at work, and it fell in a beautiful shower over the poor shoulders that were much in need of such adorning rain. "Not now, Lizzie, dear," said Jenny; "let us have a talk by the fire." With those words, she in her turn loosened her friend's dark hair, and it dropped of its own weight over her bosom, in two rich masses. Pretending to compare the colours and admire the contrast, Jenny so managed a mere touch or two of her nimble hands, as that she herself laying a cheek on one of the dark folds, seemed blinded by her own clustering curls to all but the fire, while the fine handsome face and brow of Lizzie were revealed without obstruction in the somber light.
>     "Let us have a talk," said Jenny, "about Mr. Eugene Wrayburn."
> (402–3)

In this scene, Jenny brings Lizzie's desire into verbal being, participating in the birth of a courtship as someone with a right to be there. Her disabled body and abject family circumstances are part of her sharp beauty and enhance as much as limit her ability to imagine herself the heroine of her own marriage plot and a person of the house of love.

There is much more to be said about this novel. What are the relative weights of physicality, emotional expressiveness, and verbal expressiveness (or excess) as metonyms for sexuality and producers of Jenny's sexual subjectivity? To what degree does homosociality—either mingling hair like Jenny and Lizzie or rubbing minds together like Ermine and Rachel—facilitate or obstruct disabled characters' access to the normative heroine's plot? In *Our Mutual Friend*, at any rate, Jenny inhabits a version of the twin structure that is all the more memorable for its fragmentary and inconclusive use of melodrama. We do not know how to feel about Jenny Wren, and Dickens himself does not know where to place her. At the end, she is replaced in Lizzie's arms by Bella Wilfer, an able-bodied young woman who, like Lizzie, has reached matrimony through sorrows and mishaps (though hers are lighter and more comic). Jenny's dreams of marriage are supplied by a suggested romance with Sloppy, an intellectually disabled (and unfortunately named) young man. The insufficiency of these endings serves mostly to mark how complex a character she is.

Helena Michie and Hilary Schor both attend carefully to Jenny's relationship to the marriage plot. Michie argues that Jenny can articulate Lizzie's sexuality precisely because hers is protected from entering the social world: she is a child and "a cripple." Schor's stunning discussion speaks more expansively about what Jenny produces for the novel and what, through her, Dickens articulates that he could not in earlier works. Astutely tracing Jenny's genealogy in the Marchioness, Miss Mowcher, Rosa Dartle, and Esther Summerson, Schor argues that

> Jenny Wren's difference is her complete inclusion into the text's daughterly plots: not just . . . in an inappropriate love-match we are meant to admire . . . but her possible inclusion as erotic presence as well as textual oddity. The eccentric not only includes the erotic, but has made itself central. (204)

Providing a nuanced, attentive answer to Henry James's irritable question—"what do we get in return for accepting Miss Jenny Wren as a possible person?"—Schor argues that Jenny initiates a new heroine's story, too late for Dickens to do more with it before his death:

> [T]he weirdness of Jenny, the necessary singularity of the heroine with the bad back and the queer legs, seems to offer some other account of property and persons for Dickens. In that alternate account . . . the heroine has a house that is less bleak, and . . . she can sign her name to her own (however antic and crooked) story. (207)

Schor's discussion is an excellent example of scholarship that does the work of "disability studies" without ever calling itself such. What I would add to both Michie and Schor's wonderful and important essays on Jenny Wren is a more explicit attention to Jenny as a disabled woman, and more historicization of her as "a sign of social fact . . . realism's daughter" (Schor 198, 200). An ideal critical approach might be to merge their work with that of Goldie Morgenthaler, who argues that "hereditary relationships hardly exist" (175) in *Our Mutual Friend* and sees that absence as evidence of the end of Dickens's passion for biological inheritance. The Cleaver family is actually a fairly suggestive model of hereditary taint. Jenny's merging of the eccentric and the erotic is both fascinating in any context and central to her signification within Victorian culture.

## The Uses of Excess

I return now to the question of the status and function of disabled women characters, and the relative significance of what these texts say about "women in general" and what they say about disabled women, whose concerns are rarely included in such generalizations.

Is placing an "unmarriageable" woman in the midst of a marriage plot just narrative savvy, or to put it more harshly, a case illustrating the law that "sadism demands a story" (Mulvey 22)?[14] Is giving such a woman a happy resolution another example of good storytelling, a way of raising the warmth and relief of the ending? Beyond the long-standing entertainment value of cruelty and its cessation, in which literary representations of disability surely participate, what specific interests in women—and which women—inform these texts?

It is infinitely suggestive to interpret plots about "different" women as ways of modeling the "normal" woman's position in culture.[15] Sally Mitchell, for example, one of the first critics to investigate the function of disability in Victorian popular literature, reads the plethora of ill, disabled, and "weak or damaged human[s]" in fiction by nineteenth-century women writers as representative of the situation of women in general:

> Physical incapacity codifies the pain of helplessness, the lack of power and social position and financial ability and legal right to control the circumstances of one's life. (*Dinah Mulock Craik* 112)

In a culture that assumes impairment means helplessness, powerlessness, and widespread disenfranchisement, Mitchell's suggestion is plausible enough; perhaps more convincing are her observation that not only "crippled" heroes, but also a range of male protagonists who are feminized in various ways, are a feature of the novels of the sixties, and her assertion that "[t]he prevailing romantic fantasy was . . . a lover made in [the heroine's] own image and with her own virtues, rather than an incarnation of compensatory, opposite qualities." The "crippled or feminized hero" is both "a manageable object for the heroine's affections and an alternate persona, who provides the daydreamer with a gender role in which more interesting adventures are possible" ("Sentiment and Suffering" 38–39).

Alternatively or concurrently, as Helena Michie asserts, disabled women characters work as a safe haven in which women's desire can be expressed. By the same persuasive logic, these characters may also create an outlet for the expression of women's anger, a function Vicinus suggests was provided by another kind of "adjunct" heroine of early melodramas,

> a secondary figure, bordering on villainy, who embodied female rebellion . . . [and] permitted the author to leave the heroine an unsullied angel while still portraying women's energy and anger. ("Helpless" 133)

This framework certainly lends itself to analysis of many disabled women characters, including the passively aggressive Bertha and the manipulative, secretly furious Nydia.

Rosemarie Garland-Thomson suggests a more disturbing paradigm, in which women writers theorize nondisabled women's escape from the limitations of the female body by anchoring those limitations to someone who can be reified as "all body." Garland-Thomson discusses a mechanism similar to my "twin structure" in nineteenth-century American literature, in which "maternal benefactresses" and their physically disabled recipients are divided into "corporeal" and "incorporeal" figures. "By projecting the liabilities of femaleness onto the disabled women," she writes, "the novels open a narrative safe space where the maternal benefactress can create a moral society and a feminine liberal self unconstrained by the limits of embodiment" (*Extraordinary Bodies* 101). In both cases, the disabled woman is a crucial cultural mechanism, allowing significant cultural formations (nondisabled women's participation in American liberal ideology; Victorian ideologies of woman as disembodied, asexual "angel in the house") to grow unimpeded. All these variations suggest the particular utility of figures of disabled womanhood in enabling and enlarging cultural debates about "women in general."

But where does this leave disabled women? Of the critical works I mention above, only Garland-Thomson makes this question the primary focus of her inquiry. In light of the increased public interest in disabled people when these works were written, the aspects of many characters that resist reduction to statements about nondisabled women, and the inevitability of their saying something about disabled women simply by the fact of invoking them, all of these works demand concurrent or primary readings as cultural work directed at managing cultural concerns about blind, deaf, or otherwise physically "different" women.

Like actual women with disabilities, some of these characters have little in common with each other. What they share, however, is their placement in melodramatic courtship plots; their identification in terms of emotion, whether they express it or control it; and their implicit exclusion from biological motherhood.

If the courtship plot provokes the cultural and narrative problem of disabled women's passion, it also "handles" that problem. Inappropriate desire meets the structural cul-de-sacs of unresponsive beloveds and suicidal despair; it is deployed within the "safe" context of parent-child relations; and it is transformed into properly moderated womanly feeling. To the extent that writers characterize them as distanced from emotional excess and its dangers, disabled women characters become eligible for courtship and marriage. No matter how close they get to being traditional heroines, however, the bar to biological parenthood remains.

Victorian writers' varied methods of handling the questions "Will she marry?" "Who will she marry?" and "What about children?" are hardly conclusive evidence that they were concerned about disability and its transmission. The fact remains that these questions were articulated within a climate of scientific uncertainty that affixed itself with particular fervor to women's bodies—especially if they were physically impaired.

For us, adrift in our own time of scientific and ethical turbulence, Victorian concepts of how impairment might move from one person to another offer the pleasure of a scientific muddle distant enough—or so it seems—to laugh at. Disease and heredity each presented a theoretical challenge in which insufficient knowledge was filled in by fear, anxiety, or circular logic.

The concept that disease could cause some impairments was immeasurably complicated by conflicting theories about how people became ill. While the idea that "diseases were transmitted by contagion, and caused by micro-organisms . . . was not exactly new in the middle of the nineteenth century," resistance was strong for the first half of the century (Ackerknecht, *A Short History of Medicine*, 175). An anticontagionist or miasmist would argue that contact with cold air, harsh light, "the evil influence" of impure air, overcrowding, or some other environmental factor caused disease, particularly in individuals with a "scrofulous" or otherwise weak constitution ("Diseases of the Eye"). A contagionist would counter that the cause was contact with infectious material, but might also concede that the environmental factors provided an essential "predisposing cause," a necessary catalyst for the infection to take hold.

Flexibility and suggestiveness permeated discussions of illness and its transmission. For both contagionists and anticontagionists, the individual constitution presented an essential building block in the development of illness and impairment. Because doctors describe "strumous," "scrofulous," or otherwise "defective" constitutions with reference to symptoms that intermix the social, the behavioral, and the physical, however, terms describing constitutional types remain disturbingly capacious. Constitutional types, furthermore, are theorized as both hereditary and acquirable through overcrowding, unwholesome air, and poverty (Lawrence, Lecture XIV 2). Finally, the rhetoric of class difference that inflects descriptions of constitutional types and both sides of the contagion debates increases the vagueness of theories about the transmission of impairment-producing disease. In this context, any physical impairment had the potential to be perceived as transmissible by contact; by miasmatic air; by a combination of contact, environment, and individual constitution; or perhaps simply by the social class into which one was born.[16]

Blindness provides a particular case of one or two etiologies dominating the way in which disability is written about and thus the way in which the larger culture assigns it meaning. In Victorian medical writing, blindness is habitually written about in the context of disease (rather than in the context of accident, aging, or a host of other possible causes). This emphasis marks a professional and cultural priority. The dynamics of disease represented both an area of significant debate and a field in which Victorian physicians felt capable of making significant progress; thus blindness that resulted from trachoma or the contagious ophthalmias rather than accidents or aging was more compelling as a topic on which to lecture or publish. Luke Davidson argues that eye diseases were one of the centerpieces of the professionalization of medicine in the nineteenth century. A devastating epidemic of ophthalmia contracted by British soldiers on the Egyptian campaign of 1801 "galvanized British medical practitioners into an concerted investigation into the eye" and made the study and treatment of eye diseases an arena in which professional status was created (314). Practitioners used the particular status the eye thus acquired in nineteenth-century culture to generate a host of specialty hospitals, and used the medical journals to stage debates whose purpose was to distinguish educated practitioners from quacks.

The cumulative effect of this overdetermined interest in disease-related blindness is to make blindness a figure for disease itself, and particularly sexually transmitted disease. For anticontagonists, ophthalmias (eye inflammations, which could become serious enough to result in blindness) were caused by damp and cold, wind, indigence, predisposing constitutional factors like the mysterious scrofula, and social factors—in the case of infants, deprivation of "that constant attention and affectionate care, which a mother only can supply" (Lawrence, Lecture XI 628). Contagionists believed that many ophthalmias were transmitted by contact with infectious discharge. Both groups, however, reiterate a connection between blindness and venereal disease, whether they attribute gonorrheal ophthalmia to metastasis—that is, the suppression of purulent discharge causing the disease to move upward—or to eye contact with gonorrheal matter through "the great inattention to cleanliness among the lower classes," who are moreover given to collapsing "all cases of ophthalmic disease" into the term "sore eyes" and treating ophthalmias with ignorant and dangerous folk remedies—washing the eyes with urine, for example (Lawrence, Lecture XIII 851).

The connection between blindness and dangerous sexuality is maintained in the figures to whom the greatest innocence is attributed, newborn children—those "helpless objects who have fallen a prey to this destructive malady." One physician asserts that "the number of children every year disfigured, and rendered a source of unhappiness to their friends" by purulent ophthalmia is "prodigious" (J. Walker 885). Ophthalmia neonatorum, or babies' sore eyes, a gonorrheal infection, was in 1879 the cause of 25 percent of all childhood blindness in England and early in the twentieth century the largest single cause of blindness among children in the United States (Farrell 227). Driven to proliferate by a variety of medical concerns including public health and personal advancement, medical texts inscribed blindness as something transmitted interpersonally and sexually, not simply the product of disease but its permanent representative or metonym.

Hereditary transmission was also theorized in remarkably fluid rhetorics. The theory of maternal impressions or frights, which posited physical impairment as something that could be "caught" through the eyes and transmitted to an unborn child, may stretch our credibility far beyond its limits, but it was a commonplace belief among educated people at least through the 1850s. In *London Labour and the London Poor,* Henry Mayhew's collaborator Andrew Halliday criticizes the police for

> permitting certain of the more hideous beggars to infest the streets. Instances are on record of nervous females having been seriously frightened, and even injured, by seeing men without legs or arms crawling at their feet. A case is within my own knowledge, where the sight of a man without legs or arms had such an effect upon a lady in the family way that her child was born in all respects the very counterpart of the object that alarmed her. (Mayhew 4:433)

As the following letter to the *Lancet* from a "surgeon-aurist" demonstrates, ideas about hereditary transmission could encompass both direct "impressions" to the fetus via injury to the mother and mental impressions created by things the mother saw:

> The circumstances of a child being deaf on the same side as her mother, in consequence of the fall of the mother whilst in a state of pregnancy, is not extraordinary, when it is considered how many marks and peculiarities children frequently derive from the mother. At Dover, some years ago, a lady was frightened by a ferrit whilst in a state of pregnancy; the child, when born, had eyes precisely like that animal; every child after had the same kind of eyes, and they all became blind, or nearly so, about the age of puberty. (Wright 464)

The history of blindness published by the blind activist W. Hanks Levy in 1872 asserts that congenital blindness

seems usually to arise from a peculiar state of the nervous system
in one of the parents, but chiefly that of the mother. . . . Sometimes the affliction is ascribed to the mother having seen a blind
person before the birth of a child. (18)

Impressions are still frequently referenced in medical journals of the
1860s and 1870s as a debatable but not completely dismissible theory.[17]

The belief in maternal impressions represents a logical extreme
within Victorian concepts of heredity. Not only the general public, but
also most physicians, "assumed that heredity was a dynamic process
beginning with conception and extending through weaning" (Rosenberg 191). Not only physical traits like height and hair color, but also diseases like syphilis and addictions like alcoholism, were considered truly
hereditary in the nineteenth century; an ill parent would produce a "viti-
ated sperm or ovum" and finally offspring with "defective" constitutions,
if not the parent's particular illness (Lomax, "Infantile Syphilis" 24).
Both acquired weaknesses and the particular state of the parents' bodies
and minds at the moment of conception were believed to influence the
formation of the unborn child—causes usually described in vague and
suggestive language rather than the clinical terms modern readers might
expect.[18] Holmes Coote, a surgeon writing in an 1860 issue of the *Lancet*
on congenital "deformities," scoffs at the theory of impressions, asking,
"What would become of the human race were the fancies of every
excitable and pampered woman to influence and modify the important
processes going on during pregnancy?" He suggests, however, that most
cases of "club-feet" and "club-hands" are due to "dynamic influences"
transmitted over generation, themselves the result of "individual imperfection, or the transgression of some natural law" (400–401).

If the parents were weak or "defective," according to followers of
degeneration theory, each successive generation of ill parents would be
weaker still, with infertility the only factor that would eventually stem the
progression.[19] As the physician and neopsychiatrist Henry Maudsley
described it,

Certain unfavourable conditions of life tend unquestionably to
produce degeneracy of the individual; the morbid predisposition
so generated is thus transmitted to the next generation, and, if the
unfavourable conditions continue, is aggravated in it; and thus is

# INTERMARRIAGE:

## OR

### THE MODE IN WHICH, AND THE CAUSES WHY,

## BEAUTY, HEALTH, AND INTELLECT,

### RESULT FROM CERTAIN UNIONS, AND

## DEFORMITY, DISEASE, AND INSANITY,

### FROM OTHERS ;

#### DEMONSTRATED BY

DELINEATIONS OF THE STRUCTURE AND FORMS, AND DESCRIPTIONS
OF THE FUNCTIONS AND CAPACITIES,
WHICH EACH PARENT, IN EVERY PAIR, BESTOWS ON CHILDREN,—
IN CONFORMITY WITH CERTAIN NATURAL LAWS,
AND BY AN ACCOUNT OF CORRESPONDING EFFECTS IN THE
BREEDING OF ANIMALS.

## WITH EIGHT ILLUSTRATIVE DRAWINGS.

### BY ALEXANDER WALKER.

## NEW YORK:

### HENRY G. LANGLEY, 8 ASTOR-HOUSE.

#### 1844.

Title page of Alexander Walker's *Intermarriage* (New York: Langley, 1844). Photo courtesy of Dartmouth Medical School Photography and Illustration.

formed a morbid variety of the human kind, which is incapable of being a link in the line of progress of humanity. (609–10)

As a Victorian cultural sign, disability pointed not only backward, to parental transgression and defect, but even more urgently forward, to future generations. Victorian medical and social science reshaped the biblical category of "unclean" into the social-scientific category of the dysgenic or degenerative. The belief that "Beauty, Health, and Intellect Result from Certain Unions, and Deformity, Disease, and Insanity from Others," as Alexander Walker's influential 1838 text *Intermarriage* so memorably capsulizes it, retained its urgency throughout the century and beyond. The development of a eugenicist discourse is marked by hereditarian writing's increasing emotionalism and increasingly social emphasis. Rosenberg locates the turning point about at midcentury: before the 1840s, hereditarian explanations for human differences both served as "one of the necessary elements in the endlessly flexible etiological model that served to underwrite the social effectiveness of the late eighteenth- and early nineteenth-century physician" and were used to promote moderate behaviors, yet "there were no calls for eugenic marriage laws, for sterilization of the criminal and retarded" (202). An 1864 piece in the *Lancet* reflects the change after midcentury:

> The old should not marry with the young, nor the strong with the weak and debilitated. People with marked hereditary taints should pause ere they run the risk of transmitting their endowments to a long line of suffering successors. The strong and the healthy should beware that it be no act of drunken or insensate folly which records the honour of paternity they have gained. At the moment of conception does the mysterious virtue of the creative force transmit not only an impression of the physical being of the parents, but likewise the moral physiognomy . . . that lies beneath its surface. The impoverished life, the tainted blood, the mental and moral flaws, become the dowry of the descendants.

Included in this dowry are "scrofula, epilepsy, insanity, albinoism, deaf-mutism, idiocy, and defective vision," which are read as "the various impairments of the offspring arising from the influence of too frequent admixture of the same blood" ("Intermarriage and Its Results" 69).

The fear of heredity is, if anything, worse by the end of the century. Evelyn Hunt's late-century piece "The Cry of the Unborn" sums up both the connections and the overall pessimism that could be attached to them:

> We look around and see the sickly girl uniting herself with an equally sickly man. We know that in the families there are fatal tendencies to horrible disease. We see cousins marrying, we know how fatal this will prove to their helpless offspring . . . . And even worse. Heredity. We may call it a catch word, cant, what we will. It exists, nevertheless, and the time has come when it can no longer be ignored. In the smiling, innocent baby may be the fatal taint that will wreck it, body and soul, in spite of all education and environment can do. (Qtd. in Spongberg 161)

Throughout the century, then, within a fabric of uncertainty and anxiety about bodily conditions and their potential to circulate, disability is reconfigured from a show of divine judgment and Providence to a visible indicator of medical and social pathology. These contexts suggest the utility of representing women with disabilities as prepubescent children or as models of womanly self-discipline, especially in light of the powerful and dangerous primacy of the mother's body in Victorian theories of impairment and its genesis. The same medico-socio-scientific context explains the excitement of positing disabled women as desiring women, and the necessity of thwarting that desire before it results in reproduction.

As potential signs of both disease and sexuality, disabled women characters functioned not only in parallel ways to "fallen" women in Victorian literature and culture—as containers for the most dangerous qualities associated with all women—but even as stand-ins for fallen women. As Mary Spongberg argues in *Feminizing Venereal Disease*, in the early nineteenth century all women were conceptualized as diseased, if in varying degrees, as a result of medical research into the transmission of venereal disease and doctors' belief that women were the more significant source: "the male body came to represent the standard for health, the female body came to be seen as an aberration from the norm" (5). As the century progressed, however, medical science (particularly anthropology) created a "gulf between the upright woman and the fallen woman" in which

"the prostitute's body continued to be seen as the representative sexu-
alised female body, but it increasingly was also seen as a site of abnormal
indulgence" (6). As doctors theorized visible physical anomalies by which
one could recognize the prostitute and distinguish her from the upright
woman, the prostitute's body came to stand in for disease itself, and to
function as a cultural "cordon sanitaire that differentiated good women
from bad" (14). The signs of the diseased woman, further, included
blindness, deafness, paralysis, "deformity and disfigurement," and other
forms of physical disability (169). Victorian cultural suspicions of not
only disease, but also sexual fallenness, lurk under erasure within "twin"
courtship plots.[20]

Ironically, while the stigmatized source of disease and defect seems
to be endlessly protean, shifting from all women to prostitutes to disabled women, there is no apparent change in the cultural authority of
stigma; the proliferating categories of devalued human difference seem
rather to mutually reinforce and reinscribe each other. Figuring a disabled woman as a container for dangerous sexuality, however, may not
let the prostitute or the "woman in general" off the hook, but may
rather place her on a proliferation of new hooks, with each addition
increasing the cultural suspicion attached to all kinds of women. The
chain could easily be continued; while I have focused on twin plots as a
way of representing disabled women's relationship to marriage, some
such fictions suggest that "excessive" affection between women is
another danger that motivates the expulsion of the disabled woman
from the center of the plot.[21]

Even cast by medical (and social scientific) culture as the embodiment of disease and its sexual component, physically disabled women
were much more difficult to remove from the plot than traditional fallen
women, perhaps because physically disabled women were also emblems
of the counter-ideology of sympathy/charity, which cast them as figures
of innocent suffering. As Harlan Hahn observes, while disability has historically been "associated with what might be termed a 'subversive sen-
sualism' reflecting a curiosity and fascination that is frequently infused
with erotic impulses," physically disabled people have also been imbri-
cated in a "supposedly more civilized tradition of charity and help that
has seemed to transform disabled adults into sexless beings" (27). The
relatively difficult placement of characters like Nydia, Bertha, and Jenny,
as well as the more comforting situation of characters like Olive, Ermine,
and Louise, negotiate this same complex cultural terrain.[22]

**From an essay on congenital orthopedic dislocations, *British Medical Journal* (1865).
Photo courtesy of Dartmouth Medical School Photography and Illustration.**

The melodramatization of disabled women in courtship plots may have
looked like a safe way to work through nondisabled women's desire, to
imagine the happy realms of able-bodied love by warning of the miseries that lay outside it, or simply to add a double shot of feeling to a
plot. The larger cultural context, however, suggests that these plots

were equally useful as a way of exploring issues about disability itself. To bring a disabled woman of reproductive age into a courtship plot, and to have her fulfill her role of emotional outlet in terms of heterosexual longing, is neither to produce a random figure of pathos and irony nor to evoke an essential truth about disability; whatever else stories like *The Last Days of Pompeii* and *The Cricket on the Hearth* do, they raise the specter of a historically provocative figure, not a timeless image of a woman barred from marriage through the fundamental difference of disability. The comforts of characters like Olive Rothesay and Ermine Williams, whatever they suggest about the situation of "woman in general," are equally grounded in historical context, as is the provocative, sharply beautiful ambiguity of Jenny Wren.

The disabled women in courtship plots confirm that the melodramatization of disability, especially in fiction, generates complex cultural meanings. While nineteenth-century literary works do gravitate toward casting people with physical impairments as "essentially alien, absolute others . . . something more or less than human," it is simply inadequate to say that disabled characters are all sinners or saints, and leave it at that (Fiedler 2–3). Literary texts as a whole posit physical disability as a condition producing a range of subject positions within an emotional and moral universe (and even within a productive economy). While many characterizations of physical disability are clearly designed to accommodate the fears and desires of nondisabled people, not all of them seem likely to relieve or satisfy those feelings. As useful as Leslie Fiedler's dyad of pity and fear has been to describe nondisabled people's attitudes toward disability, Victorian literature reminds us to add—at the very least—a third term, desire.

The expansion (and sometimes contraction) of the place of a disabled woman within melodramatic plots obviously enacts the expansion and contraction of the genre itself. While all these works preserve the emotional heart of melodrama by creating one or more characters who express or evoke more emotional outpourings than anyone else in the plot, the fiction of Bulwer-Lytton and Dickens specifically articulates disabled women's emotional excess as sexuality rather than infantile or spiritual emotionality. The fiction of Craik and Yonge shifts the function of expressing excess emotion away from a disabled woman to a nondisabled one. Dickens's last novel disperses, ironizes, and complicates that excess, making it into a verbal performance that announces disability and its ties to pathos and eros while affirming its centrality to humanness itself.

Because all of these works honor the melodramatic contract not to evoke more controversy than the ending can resolve, they are able to introduce and attempt to "normalize" a number of potentially startling notions about disabled women. These include her potential to be a professional writer or artist; her ability not only to love, but also to be loved back, in the context of heterosexual mating rituals; and most significantly, her ability to mother a child, if not to bear one. The fact that these narratives have been less resilient than *Les deux orphelines*, which returns a blind woman to pathetic isolation from the marriage plot, should not make us discount them.

The next chapter examines disabled women's possibilities for love, sex, and marriage as written into fiction by Wilkie Collins, a contemporary and frequent collaborator of Dickens who shared his affinity for melodrama and his interest in disability, but whose innovative representations of disabled women were targeted by critics (and not only Victorian ones) as examples of the author's moral, aesthetic, and even physical deformity. In Collins's hands, the safe space of melodrama is changed beyond recognition through a combination of clinical detail and radical messages about disabled women's sexuality. *Poor Miss Finch*, published two years before *Les deux orphelines*, offers a lively last look at why the latter's plot was the one that lasted.

# 3

## "My Old Delightful Sensation"

### Wilkie Collins and the
### Disabling of Melodrama

> Where Collins got the idea for a deaf-mute heroine is conjectural.
> He had the chronic invalid's fascination for mental and physical defor-
> mities. (Ashley 37)

Wilkie Collins was one of the two most prolific producers of disabled
characters in Victorian literature, along with his friend, colleague,
collaborator, and competitor Charles Dickens. While critics and biographers have narrated Collins's interest in disability as purely personal, the
manifestation of his own experiences with chronic illness, or as evidence
of his reliance on melodramatic claptrap to get a plot moving, his own
statements about representing disability have much more to do with an
interest in antimelodrama and realism. Collins specifically positions his
two major disabled heroines, Madonna Blyth in *Hide and Seek* (1854) and
Lucilla Finch in *Poor Miss Finch* (1872), as direct challenges to melodramatic modes of representing disability. He remarks in an end note to
*Hide and Seek,*

I do not know that any attempt has yet been made in English fiction to draw the character of a "Deaf Mute," simply and exactly after nature—or, in other words, to exhibit the peculiar effects produced by the loss of the senses of hearing and speaking on the disposition of the person so afflicted. . . . the whole family of dumb people on the stage have the remarkable faculty . . . of always being able to hear what is said to them. (355)

In the dedication to *Poor Miss Finch*, similarly, Collins asserts,

More than one charming blind girl, in fiction and in the drama, has preceded "Poor Miss Finch." But, so far as I know, blindness in these cases has been always exhibited, more or less exclusively, from the ideal and the sentimental point of view. The attempt here made is to appeal to an interest of another kind, by exhibiting blindness as it really is. (5)

Collins thus announces his interest in disability not simply as a life experience or aesthetic theme, but as an issue of representation. Taken together, his remarks and the hard-to-reconcile critical responses to his disabled characters help us approximate the unwritten rules for representing disabled women at this point in the century, and the ways in which two highly melodramatic novels manage to offend those conventions.

In his work with disabled women in marriage plots, Collins both shores up and dismantles conventions. He takes apart the "twin structure" by creating two successful novels, *Hide and Seek* and *Poor Miss Finch*, whose disabled heroines have no nondisabled sisters or friends who illustrate the disabled women's unfitness—or fitness—for marriage. Further, while the deaf heroine of *Hide and Seek*, Madonna Blyth, does not finally marry the man she loves, the problem is not disability or excess emotion but incest. Lucilla Finch, the heroine of *Poor Miss Finch*, survives a series of melodramatic plot twists including eye surgery and deception by two male twins; but when she marries, she is wilfully and happily blind. As a blind woman, she bears two children and ends the plot a happy, wealthy, married mother.

As these details should suggest, Collins goes farther than any other writer of the period in his willingness to test melodramatic plotting as a framework for exploring disabled women's ability to love, marry, and bear children. Like *The Last Days of Pompeii* and *The Cricket on the Hearth*,

Collins's novels construct disabled women as figures of eros rather than pathos. Like Craik, Yonge, and the later Dickens, Collins imagines disabled women as potential wives and mothers. Remarkably, however, Collins does both at once, creating a disabled woman who not only expresses sexual passion but also survives this display of excess to reap the traditional heroine's rewards of courtship and marriage—as well as articulating disability as a state of sexual delight and becoming a biological mother. Even more remarkably, in the context of nineteenth- and twentieth-century literature and culture, this disabled heroine is a blind woman, a figure other writers posit as so radically removed from "normal" life that even when they attribute desire to her, it is almost by definition unrecognized and unrequited.[1]

## Hide and Seek

In his earliest representation of female disability, *Hide and Seek*'s deaf heroine Madonna Blyth, Collins collapses two conventional and usually mutually exclusive roles for disabled women in melodrama by constructing Madonna as an object of both pity and desire. More significantly, Collins constructs Madonna as not only a sexual object, but also a desiring subject, leading toward a shocking conclusion toward which the novel gestures, but does not reach.

*Hide and Seek* is a mystery novel about parentage, developed through the adventures of Madonna and Zack Thorpe, two young people who are unknowingly half-siblings. Zack, the vigorous, picaresque hero, finds relief from his Evangelical father and his stultifying bourgeois home when he meets the painter Valentine Blyth and his family, including Blyth's spinally impaired wife Lavinia and their lovely adopted daughter Madonna, who is deaf. The arrival in the plot of a rough woodsman returned from the American West—actually Madonna's uncle—begins the unraveling of Madonna's mysterious past (and ultimately the dismantling of her nascent romance with Zack).

From her first appearance in the novel, Madonna is objectified primarily in erotic terms. The only romantic heroine in the plot, she is characterized as a sexual object *before* she is identified as deaf; if much of the novel eroticizes deafness, it also develops Madonna as a sexual subject.

The narrative frame that introduces Madonna associates her with the realm of the "consolations" a married man seeks, ironically, in response to his wife's disability. We first learn the history of Valentine Blyth, an energetic artist who fell in love with Lavinia, a woman with a history of "spinal malady," and married her against his family's wishes. When the illness returned, Lavinia and Valentine "nobly" hid "the shock" of her disability from each other, but she insisted that Valentine "seek consolation, where she knew he must find it sooner or later, by going back to his studio" (24).

The next chapter resituates the reader in the fictional present and the aforementioned studio. While "consolation in the studio" is not necessarily a euphemism for sex, Collins encourages that reading by describing the entrance in the studio of a "mysterious resident" in the Blyth household, "a Young Lady" who is "in no way related" to either Blyth and who is "deliciously soft, bright, fresh, pure, and delicate." This object of neighbors' "prying glances . . . and lamenting looks" gives the reader pause, as of course Collins intends her to do. The narrative goes on to detail the physical beauties of this mysterious young woman, articulating them in a specifically sexual context, as a series of men praise her "incomparable blue eyes" that inspire elopement fantasies and her "sweet lips smiling at her dimpled chin, / Whose wealth of kisses gods might long to win" (34, 35).

It is only after she has been thoroughly characterized as an object of desire and one whose connection with Valentine Blyth is both mysterious and intimate that the novel clarifies their relationship as that of father and daughter. Established for the reader as a mysterious and sexually desirable woman, Madonna is developed in a flashback chapter as a deaf—and desirable—child. Seeking amusement while on a painting trip, Valentine goes to a country circus, where he "discovers" her. Deafened in an equestrian act, the girl is now exhibited in front of the circus crowd as

THE MYSTERIOUS FOUNDLING!
AGED TEN YEARS!!
TOTALLY DEAF AND DUMB!!! (40)

While the performance involves some simple "conjuring tricks," the real spectacle is clearly the combination of the child's beauty and her affliction (43). While Blyth does not murmur "Deaf and dumb!" like the rest of the crowd, he is even more stimulated than they are by the sight of her, and provides a small spectacle in himself:

> From the moment of the little girl's first appearance, ample recreation had been unconsciously provided . . . by a tall, stout, and florid stranger, who appeared suddenly to lose his senses the moment he set eyes on the deaf and dumb child. . . . Mad and mysterious words . . . poured from his lips. "Devotional beauty," "Fra Angelico's angels," "Giotto and the cherubs," "Enough to bring the divine Raphael down from heaven to paint her." (43)

Blyth's artistic appreciation is posed against the crowd's desire for spectacle, but as soon as the child is face-to-face with him, his "artistic" response is followed by a rapture of sentimentality:

> Ah, woful sight! So lovely, yet so piteous to look on! Shall she never hear kindly human voices, the song of birds, the pleasant murmur of the trees again? Are all the sweet sounds that sing of happiness to childhood, silent for ever to *her*? From those fresh, rosy lips shall no glad words pour forth, when she runs and plays in the sunshine? Shall the clear, laughing tones be hushed always? the young, tender life be forever a speechless thing, shut up in dumbness from the free world of voices? Oh! Angel of judgment! hast thou snatched her hearing and her speech from this little child, to abandon her in helpless affliction to such profanation as she now undergoes? (44)

This passage seems to issue from the narrative itself rather than Blyth's consciousness, as if the book had fallen to its knees in the face of such pathos. In light of the scene that follows, however, this sentimental deluge begs to be considered as an advance denial of any suspicions of prurience in the next moment, in which Blyth and the child share a moment of magical mutual connection.

> Her pretty lips smiled on him as they had smiled on no one else that night; and when she held out some cards to be chosen from, she left unnoticed the eager hands extended on either side of her, and presented them to Valentine only. He saw the small fingers

trembling as they held the cards; he saw the delicate little shoulders and the poor frail neck and chest bedizened with tawdry mock jewelry and spangles; he saw the innocent young face, whose pure beauty no soil of stage paint could disfigure, with the smile still on the parted lips, but with a patient forlornness in the sad blue eyes, as if the seeing-sense that was left, mourned always the hearing and speaking senses that were gone—he marked all these things in an instant, and felt that his heart was sinking as he looked. (44–45)

Overcome with emotion, Blyth kisses the girl's hand and rushes out of the circus. It is clear, however, that "[i]f ever man was in love with a child at first sight, he was that man" (46).

In short order, Blyth decides to rescue this "injured, beautiful, patient little angel" from the circus and the abusive circus-master, Jubber (50). While child-rescue narratives are a staple of Victorian literature, this one hyperbolizes not only the spiritual nature of the savior-man and the violent degradation of the abuser, but also the physical connection between the "good man" and the beautiful, tawdrily dressed girl he smothers with kisses.[2] The effect is to amplify and make blatant the erotic context all manner of "rescue" texts (educational and medical ones, for example) posit for attractive disabled girls.[3]

Deafness itself is constructed as a state of sensuality as well as pathos, partly through Collins's use of nonfiction. John Kitto's autobiographical *The Lost Senses* (1845) is his major source for the details of the child's deafening, treatment, and characterization and some of the ideas behind its dramatic scenes. Collins tinkers with Kitto's already-melodramatic narrative to craft a melodrama of the female body. For example, the fact that Kitto's voice after the fall that deafened him was "so greatly altered as to be not easily understood" (20) in *Hide and Seek* becomes a phenomenon rich in resonances of anxiety regarding little girls and how they should sound. The first time Madonna speaks after her fall, says her foster mother Mrs. Peckover, her voice "sounded, somehow, hoarse and low, and deep and faint, all at the same time; the strangest, shockingest voice to come from a child, who always used to speak so clearly and prettily before" (71). This voice, which Mrs. Peckover first thinks is a joking attempt to imitate Jubber, alarms her so much she spills the tea she is carrying. When Mrs. Peckover is urged by the doctor to "treat her severely" in order to keep her speaking aloud, it is not only Madonna's obvious misery upon being asked to speak, but also "the shocking husky moaning voice that . . . didn't belong to her" that make Mrs. Peckover give up the attempt (75–76).[4]

The disturbing effect of Madonna's deafness on those who are close to her seems based in part on her new behavior's violation of gender codes: she loses not only her pretty temper, but also her pretty voice. She is no longer docile and sweet, and she sounds as if she is imitating an unsavory adult man. What is "shocking" about the husky moaning voice is not clear, but it is impossible for a modern reader to ignore its suggestion of sexuality—a potentially alarming idea in connection with a ten-year-old girl, but one that the narrative keeps reiterating.

Other descriptions of Madonna's experience develop deafness as a state of physical responsiveness that can only be considered "dangerous" in the context of Victorian ideologies of woman. For example, using a passage in which Kitto elaborates (through an experience of disgust, ironically) the aesthetic sense deafness produced in him, Collins writes Madonna into a sensual rapture in the presence of nature:

> All beautiful sights, and particularly the exquisite combinations that Nature presents, filled her with an artless rapture, which it affected the most unimpressible people to witness. Trees were beyond all other objects the greatest luxuries that her eyes could enjoy. She would sit for hours, on fresh summer evenings, watching the mere waving of the leaves; her face flushed, her whole nervous organisation trembling with the sensations of deep and perfect happiness which that simple sight imparted to her. (94)[5]

Finally, Collins's dramatization of some of Kitto's incidental remarks produces scenes that specifically use a mix of disability and sexuality to move the plot forward. Kitto states, "It must be obvious . . . that being in darkness must be peculiarly irksome to the deaf, as this nearly throws out of exercise all the perceptive faculties, and, for the time, reduces the patient as nearly as possible to the deplorable state of one who is *both* deaf and blind" (57). Collins dramatizes this condition in one of the novel's most memorable (and sadistic) scenes. As she searches for a lost item in a dark room, Madonna's candle suddenly is extinguished. The reader perceives, by reading the words and looking at the illustrations, that a hidden man has blown it out, but Madonna does not. The transformation of a logical aversion to darkness into a scene in which a young

Frontispiece to Harper edition of *Hide and Seek* (1898). Photo courtesy of Dartmouth Medical School Photography and Illustration.

woman is not only "overcome by the most violent terror but also being watched by an ominous stranger," melodramatizes disability by putting the "helpless and unfriended" in danger, but suggests—before we know the man's identity—that the danger is sexual (280).

While many of Collins's changes to Kitto have the effect of positing the deaf woman as the catalyst for others' sexuality (like Louise in *Les deux orphelines*), Madonna is also constructed as a sensual being inclined to look and desire. Specifically, she looks at Zack Thorpe, who the narrator tells us

> was handsome enough to tempt any woman into glancing at him with approving eyes. He was over six feet in height; and, though then little more than nineteen years old, was well developed in proportion to his stature. His boxing, rowing, and other athletic exercises had done wonders towards bringing his naturally vigorous, upright frame to the perfection of healthy muscular condition. . . . He trod easily and lightly, with a certain youthful suppleness and grace in all his actions, which set off his fine bodily formation to the best advantage. (99)

The passage makes it clear that it is Zack's body that Madonna examines, and suggests elsewhere that his animal good health is probably the only thing about him that would recommend such admiration. Madonna's reactions to Zack's presence are similarly coded as erotic.

> A bright flush overspread the girl's face. . . . Her tender blue eyes looked up at him, shyly conscious of the pleasure that their expression was betraying; and the neat folds of her pretty grey dress, which had lain so still over her bosom when she was drawing, began to rise and fall gently now, when Zack held her hand. (99)

Collins makes Madonna's desire indistinguishable from that of a hearing woman, and when Mrs. Blyth suggests to Madonna that "you must like [Zack] very much, love," Madonna does not reply; rather, like any other well-bred young woman, "her treacherous cheeks, neck, and bosom answered for her" (115).

Soon after this point, the novel retrenches abruptly from its representation of a disabled woman's sexuality, or at least removes the context in which she can express it. There are no other romances afoot, no able-bodied women to usurp Madonna's role; and the happy Blyth family stands as an endorsement of disabled women's ability to be exemplary wives and mothers. Madonna even visits Zack's bedroom to tend him during a fever, often the harbinger of an approaching romance, albeit not necessarily a marriage. Before anything further can develop, how-ever, the novel reveals that Zachary Thorpe Sr. is Madonna's biological father, and the careless cause of her biological mother's ruin. The two young people are whisked apart without ever having occasion to con-front their situation together, leaving us in breathless retrospect to imag-ine a second story that might have been—one even more ill-fated than that of Thorpe Sr. and Madonna's mother, and the basis of an even more sensational novel. In fact, by abandoning the incestuous narrative trajec-tory (but presenting it as somewhat narrowly missed all the same), Collins manages to have it both ways. He (amazingly) appeases critics like Geraldine Jewsbury, who were incensed by the references to sexual-ity in his earlier *Basil* (1852) and were pleased that in *Hide and Seek* he had "ceased walking the moral hospital." At the same time, he gives read-ers the *frisson* of imagining, on their own time, the sensational story that doesn't take place.

While the romance never materializes, it is important to note that what officially disables it is the specter of incest, and *not* Madonna's deaf-ness. In fact, both the unfolding mystery of Madonna's parentage and the threat of incest displace deafness itself as a center of melodrama. A more suspicious reading, however, might propose that incest is brought in as an emergency measure to permit Collins to escape a real resolution of the situation between Madonna and Zack. Reluctant to back away from his attempts to create an innovative portrait of both deafness and disabled women's ability to play traditional feminine roles, but con-cerned about critics' castigation of the morality of his previous novel, he resorts to a different order of "melodramatic machinery" to resolve the conflict. By shifting the focus to incest, Collins still evokes a concept with associative links to deafness through Victorian theories of intermarriage and impairment.[6] Incest, however, has a moral clarity the issue of a deaf woman's marriage lacks. With the unambiguous horror of brother-sister marriage filling the stage, Collins never has to resolve the more compli-cated issue of disability, sexuality, and marriage.

## Poor Miss Finch

**N**early twenty years later, Collins wrote another novel with a young disabled heroine, but this time her emotional and erotic excesses lead to the traditional happy endings of marriage and motherhood. Lucilla Finch, of *Poor Miss Finch,* is allowed what even nondisabled Victorian heroines are usually denied, an assertive, abundantly expressed sexuality that does not result in prostitution, religious conversion, tragic death, or all three. Her desires are both reciprocated and approved within the society of the novel, making her rare among disabled women characters and unheard of among blind ones.

In his preface to the novel, Collins articulates his belief that it will correct previous fictions' sentimentalized portraits of blind characters by "presenting blindness as it really is" (5). In the novel proper, however, this supposed vehicle for mimesis is embroiled in what one critic calls "the most implausible plot in English fiction," one befitting Collins's fame as progenitor of the sensation novel (Bedell 19). Lucilla Finch, a young, middle-class woman who has been blind since early childhood, falls in love with Oscar Dubourg, a man who later develops epilepsy from a head injury and then turns blue from the treatment. As luck would have it, Lucilla has an inexplicable but violent prejudice against dark colors—in clothing, but especially in persons.

Oscar's desire to hide his transformation from Lucilla until after they are married is so strong that when his twin, confident, nonblue brother comes to town, Oscar tells Lucilla that Nugent is the blue man. This backfires when Nugent brings in an oculist who cures Lucilla's blindness; her first vision is of Nugent, who has fallen in love with her and sabotages his brother by pretending to be him. Nugent manages to bring Lucilla to the verge of the altar before she is rescued. The novel ends in the brothers' reconciliation, after which Lucilla and Oscar marry and have two children; Nugent goes on an Arctic expedition and freezes to death.

*Poor Miss Finch*'s parody of melodramatic and sentimental stereotypes begins as early as the title and dedication. "Poor" is habitually appended to "blind woman" in both fictional and nonfictional texts, where it serves as a code word for the extremity of her physical and economic dependence. The novel's title cues us to expect the usual sad and sentimental portrayal of a blind woman, and Collins's remark in his dedication that "it is . . . possible for bodily affliction itself to take its place among the ingredients of happiness" seems to build on this expectation of a morally uplifting account of acceptance of life's misfortunes, an obligatory theme for Victorian texts about disability.

Thus prepared, we begin the novel proper in the company of the narrator, Madame Pratolungo, who summarizes her thoughts on becoming Lucilla's companion in terms of clichés: "Young—lonely—blind. . . . I felt I should love her" (14). The person known by the local villagers as "Poor Miss Finch" lives in the oldest part of a house formerly a convent, with "one great pleasure to illumine her dark life—music" (14). She first appears as "a solitary figure in a pure white robe" who looks like a Raphael Madonna, except for her "poor, dim, sightless eyes" (27, 29). It appears that Lucilla, perhaps even more so than the previous Madonna, will present disabled femininity in the classic melodramatic terms of pathos and spirituality.

This pretty tableau of the sweet, dependent blind woman is immediately and comically disrupted when Lucilla recoils from her new companion, convinced she is wearing something dark. The contrasts continue. Lucilla is both physically and financially independent; she wanders guideless about her small town, but she also bankrolls her father and his ever-growing family (Lucilla's stepmother and step-siblings). Whereas the plot's suspense in *Les deux orphelines*, *The Cricket on the Hearth*, *The Last Days of Pompeii*, and *Hide and Seek* hinges on scenes in which the disabled woman is victimized, Lucilla is only victimized when she regains her sight.

Collins's treatment of the issue of emotional and specifically erotic excess presents the most striking disruption of the patterns of the other literary works. By her second meeting with Oscar, Lucilla's behavior toward him is "so bold" that it terrifies Pratolungo: "Instead of her blindness making her nervous in the presence of a man unknown to her, it appeared to have exactly the contrary effect. It made her fearless" (64–65). Later, Lucilla explains that she distinguishes Oscar and Nugent only by "something in me [that] answers to one of them and not to the other. . . . When Oscar takes [my hand], a delicious tingle runs from his hand into mine, and steals all over me" (232). No "passionless" heroine, Lucilla's expressed eros is fully reciprocated, at least to the extent that her timid lover is able.

The specifics of Lucilla's emotions and behavior suggest that Collins is playing in pointed ways with conventions of seeing, nonseeing, and desire. While she is blind, Lucilla's sexuality (like her prejudice) has a distinctly specular aspect to it, albeit imagined specularity. Lucilla is obsessed with making Oscar a mental object, visualizing him in all his material specifics. In addition, when Pratolungo questions Lucilla's choice of lover, Lucilla responds by ordering her companion, "Look!" She directs her fiancé to sit by her, put his arm around her waist, tell her he loves her—"Out loud!"—and kiss her. When Oscar is too embarrassed to comply, Lucilla kisses him. While Pratolungo comments that Lucilla, "strong in her blind insensibility to all shafts of ridicule shot from the eye, cared nothing for the presence of a third person," Lucilla seems, in fact, to make aggressive use of that third person to witness and react to her sexual commitment to Oscar (274).

Her sexualized showing and forcing Pratolungo to look offer a meaningful reversal of a repeated scenario in the nineteenth century and our own time in which the blind woman is the unknowing object of aggressive looking.[7] Lucilla, shockingly, not only desires but also displays herself as a desiring subject. Her exhibitionism shifts the power relations in the stereotypical scene of looking and desire.

A similar reversal occurs in terms of literary conventions about blindness, cures, and sexuality. Regained sight is usually the only circumstance in which blind nineteenth-century women characters become sexual and marry; William Paulson observes that in eighteenth- and early nineteenth-century French popular theater, "the 'awakening' to sight offer[s] a particularly propitious moment for emotional or erotic relations" (73). The cataract surgery that oculist Herr Grosse performs on Lucilla was in the French dramas cast as "a literal ocular equivalent of defloration" (82). In direct contrast, Lucilla's regained sight is something the novel firmly associates not with new sexuality but with the loss of "the delicious tingle," so much so that she shuts her eyes to try to "renew [her] blindness" and regain the excitement (511). When this fails, she wonders if "the loss of my sense of feeling [is] the price that I have paid for the recovery of my sense of sight" (511–12). Grosse confirms this, saying that "all those thrill-tingles that she once had when he touched her belong to [another] time. . . . it is a sort of swop-bargain between Nature and this poor girl. . . . I give you your eyes—I take away your fine touch" (625).

The fact that Lucilla is seeing and embracing the wrong man after her surgery seems incidental; the effective message of the novel is that blindness is a state of sexual desire that sight removes, rather than the

**Lucilla and the Dubourg twins in Harper edition of *Poor Miss Finch* (1873). Photo courtesy of Dartmouth Medical School Photography and Illustration.**

reverse. This is emphasized by the fact that she is blind again when her original lover, and her sexuality, return:

> For one awful moment, when she first felt the familiar touch, the blood left her cheeks. Her blind eyes dilated fearfully. She stood petrified. Then, with a long, low cry—a cry of breathless rapture— she flung her arms passionately round his neck. The life flowed back into her face; her lovely smile just trembled on her parted lips; her breath came faint and quick and fluttering. In soft tones of ecstasy, with her lips on his cheek, she murmured the delicious words:
>
> "Oh, Oscar! I know you once more!" (643)

At this point, Collins's assertion in the dedication that "bodily affliction" can be one of "the ingredients of happiness" takes on an entirely new meaning. Lucilla herself, after she is told of the fraud on her, still says that it is her blindness, not the return of the real Oscar, that "has given me back my old delightful sensation" (645).

Lucilla Finch, like Madonna Blyth before her, is initially framed by the image of a Raphael Madonna.[8] Like so much else in *Poor Miss Finch,* this reference acquires substantial irony by the story's close. While many readers would probably have preferred that a blind heroine never become a mother in any way, even virgin birth, the novel ends with Lucilla's marriage and two biological children.

While many subversions take place in the novel, it is not, overall, a parodic work; nor is it a work of "pure" melodrama. Rather, it is an unstable mix of melodrama turned on its head and medical discourse toyed with. Whereas Collins's use of documentary sources in *Hide and Seek* was relatively reverent, in *Poor Miss Finch* he evokes both literary and nonliterary "codes" of representing blindness much more ironically, as well as drawing from a wider range of possibilities.

While *Poor Miss Finch,* like *Hide and Seek,* is interested in medical diagnoses and treatment, the later novel often employs such details to achieve a form of insider humor about serious concerns of Victorian medicine. For example, Oscar's epilepsy is treated with silver nitrate, the same substance used to prevent "babies' sore eyes," the congenital ophthalmia caused by the mother's venereal infections, that substantial source of infant blindness in the nineteenth century. Elsewhere, there are enough reminders of congenital and hereditary blindness to create suspicion, including the fact that Lucilla's mother is dead, like so many other mothers of disabled women in fiction. The subplot of Lucilla's stepmother's awesome fertility and its consequences further develops this atmosphere of irreverent reference to hereditary weakness (as well as to the miasmist discourse of disease with its emphasis on air, moisture, and dirt). Mrs. Finch is a "damp woman. . . . [n]ever completely dressed, never completely dry; always with a baby in one hand and a novel in the other," and the Finch household is a swarm of children, fourteen in all, in "dirty frocks," including one of "deficient intellect" (24). Despite these relatively playful allusions to the transmission of impairment, however, there is no discussion of the status of Lucilla's children's eyes. This is a contrast to the only other fiction I know of in which an impaired woman gives birth, Dickens's Christmas story "Doctor Marigold," in which a deaf woman's baby's risk of impairment is invested with pathos and suspense and in which the outcome—the birth of a hearing child to two deaf parents—is a good example of narrative fiction palliating the concerns about hereditary "defect" raised by Victorian medical science.

The oculist's association with both the "clinical" and the "melodramatic" aspects of the novel is similarly hard to pin down to any unitary position. For all the "Actual" that accrues to Herr Grosse—so much so that readers asked Collins for his real name so that they could consult him about their eyes—the medical framework in which he places blindness is essentially thrown out the window by the conclusion; Lucilla says "Thank God, I am blind," and refuses any further interventions. Grosse's function in the novel both honors his melodramatic role as the gateway to marriage, and subverts it, as the cure removes Lucilla's "thrill-tingles."

Finally, while *Poor Miss Finch* is indeed a sensational novel, with a dizzying series of crises and complications (some raised and never really resolved, like the twins' association with a murder), Lucilla's marriage and motherhood are completely normalized; the novel never broaches the question of whether or not a blind woman should marry (though it does posit that question in reference to Oscar once he has developed epilepsy). The fact of Lucilla's ability to fall in love and be loved back is also presented as not worthy of special comment. This presents a striking contrast to the novels of Dickens and Bulwer-Lytton, in which certain women's exclusion from marriage is treated as a given, and those of Craik and Yonge, which address the issue of disabled women's marriage seriously and directly before affirming the conditions under which it can take place. The only question Collins makes significant is that of *whom* Lucilla will marry.

Blindness and blueness notwithstanding, the most sensational thing about this novel may be how conventional a heroine Lucilla Finch finally is. Her transformation into a married mother from a single, financially independent woman who wanders into town alone and meets strange men can be read as a retrenchment to a familiar ideology of woman and domesticity, a closing down of the wildness the character originally has. It's impossible to evaluate this plot resolution on such terms, however, without considering the exclusion of disabled and particularly blind women from these traditional plots and their benefits as well as dangers.[9] Given the climate of anxiety and suspicion about disability and reproduction that shored up this exclusion, a "domestic story" about a blind woman having babies is a real Victorian sensation.

If the fiction of Dickens and the other writers did not exactly produce disabled heroines "safe as houses," it nonetheless functioned as a site in which relatively controversial material about both disabled and nondisabled women could be explored without alarming readers and critics. The popular and critical acclaim that met such explorations and permitted them to have a cultural impact relied on the novelists' practice of anchoring radical notions about disability and sexuality to the relatively stable and formulaic genre of melodrama. These other writers created a balance between their innovations of the place of a disabled woman and their concessions to her traditional role, creating, for example, disabled women who express passion but are given no place to deploy it in the marriage plot, or married disabled women whose sexuality and reproductive potential are carefully downplayed.

Collins, in contrast, compromises not only the safety of disabled women as containers for the issue of women's emotions, but also melodramatic literature as a site of expansion and exploration of disabled women's place in culture, by failing to make any firm concessions to either "realism" or melodrama. His representations of disabled women are a hash of sentiment and science, saintliness and bold sexuality; they alternate between honoring the melodramatic contract and tearing it to bits.

Such differences may well have contributed to divergent critical receptions of Collins and Dickens despite their investment in similar literary modes and interest in "different" bodies. Collins's disabled characters have been criticized both as aesthetic failures and as the perverse products of mental and physical infirmity. If Walter de la Mare includes "disfigurements" in his appreciative catalogue of Collins's "machinery of melodrama," Andrew Lang terms *Poor Miss Finch*'s use of blindness and disfiguration "manifest and grotesque 'machinery'" (96; 27–28). For twentieth-century critic Julian Symons, Collins's treatment of physically disabled characters exemplifies his inferiority to Dickens:

> He had already introduced a deaf-and-dumb heroine into one story, a blind hero into another. It was felt that a writer who used such material for the most part without thought of his readers' moral improvement, could not be regarded seriously. Dickens had the same taste for the grotesque . . . and had survived similar criticism, but Collins was not, like Dickens, a genius. (10)

While many critics attacked Collins's use of disabled characters as a detour from realism, others disliked them for being too real. An anonymous critic in *Saturday Review* characterizes *Poor Miss Finch* as "a surgical and medical novel" and offers a candid and interesting explanation of how these qualities weaken the fiction:

> Now we are willing to admit that passions sufficiently intense, and situations sufficiently sublime, may be born of pain and physical afflictions. We know that Poor Miss Finch's special burden of blindness has lent itself before to the noblest purposes of poetry and romance. But then those authors who have turned it to their professional purposes have idealized it gracefully, resting lightly even on the sightless eyeballs, dealing with the thoughts and following the mournful fancies of a mind driven to prey upon itself. Mr. Wilkie Collins recognizes this in his preface, and takes credit for handling the subject of his choice in an original and more natural manner. He undertakes to interpret faithfully what others have misrepresented for artistic purpose—to represent a blind person acting and speaking she would really act and speak. . . . [W]e have little doubt that Mr. Wilkie Collins has made his blind girl more faithful to nature in thought, act, and speech than Lord Lytton's Nydia. What then? Fidelity is, after all, not the foundation of all fiction . . . we prefer the work of art that suggests to us bright impressions and graceful fancies. (2 March 1872, 283)

A contemporary review queries petulantly, "[W]hat is the aim of this story? That the blind should marry the dark-blue? There is then an excellent opening for some novelist, distracted for a plot, to write about the love of the color-blind for the jaundiced" (unsigned review, *Nation*, 7 March 1872, 159).

Algernon Swinburne extends the significance of Collins's disabled characters to the figurative body of the writer. They are at once symptomatic of his literary "incapacity" and an aesthetic "crutch":

> [T]he remarkable genius of [Collins] for invention and construction and composition of incidents and effects was limited by an incapacity and dependent on a condition which cannot but be regarded as seriously impairing his claims to consideration as an artist or a student. He could not, as a rule, get forward at all without the help of some physical or moral infirmity in some one of the leading agents or patients of the story. (589)

The most fascinating strain of Collins criticism makes the writer's body material, positing a realm of defect that encompasses the writer's physical as well as aesthetic health. For John Ruskin, Collins's portrayal of physical disabilities in *Poor Miss Finch* represented the nadir of the "whole cretinous school" of "lower fictitious literature" he dubbed the "literature of the Prison-house" or "Fiction mécroyante" (276–79). Ruskin's "Fiction Fair and Foul" (1880) rails against fiction full of illness and violent death. Physically diseased, "deformed," and ignobly dead bodies are symptomatic of diseased and deformed genres, produced by morally and physically ill writers to cater to the tastes of morally and physically diseased urban readers deprived of the healthy stimulation of natural beauty and thus addicted to low literature.

Ruskin attributes the "truncated and Hermes-like deformity" of Nigel Dubourg's frozen hands at the end of *Poor Miss Finch,* for example, to "the grotesque and distorting power" of brain disease and other types of "personal weakness" experienced by the authors of "foul" fiction (278–79):

> [I]n Dickens it . . . gives Quilp, Krook, Smike, Smallweed, Miss Mowcher, and the dwarfs and wax-work of Nell's caravan; and runs entirely wild in *Barnaby Rudge,* where, with a *corps de drame* composed of one idiot, two madmen, a gentleman-fool who is also a villain, a shop-boy fool who is also a blackguard, a hangman, a shrivelled virago, and a doll in ribands. . . . It is this mutilation, observe, which is the very sign-manual of the plague. (279)

Ruskin's view was extreme but not unique. Walter Phillips quotes another critic who makes an explicit link between sensation fiction and disease:

> Precisely as certain diseased conditions of the body give rise to a craving for unnatural food, so do certain morbid conditions of mind produce an appetite for literary food which a sound mental organization would reject. Individual instances of such morbid affections are fit subjects of study for the physican only. (27)

Twentieth-century critical biographies of Collins continue to lean on authorial illness and trauma, or else eccentricity, as primary causes of disabled characters. Collins not only experienced chronic pain from eye, limb, and digestive ailments, but also was configured differently than either his century or ours thought a man should look. Sue Lonoff, whose readings of Collins's disabled characters are exceptionally astute, crafts a persuasive biographical argument for them, asserting that his

> interest in such topics is certainly rooted in his personal history. He himself was oddly proportioned. . . . His forehead bulged noticeably on one side. His head was large, while his feet were so tiny that the smallest pair of women's slippers fitted him comfortably. Short, unathletic, and inclined to be plump, he became, as the years passed, a semi-invalid, dependent on laudanum but never visibly out of control of his habit. . . . His family was preoccupied with matters of health and, in a period when physical illnesses tended to be common and recurrent, more liable to infirmities than most. (158–59)

Catherine Peters, similarly, suggests that

> perhaps Wilkie's fascination with physical disabilities and their effect on the psyche, repeatedly used until it became a hallmark of his fiction, was originally triggered by his own physique. . . . The terrifying scene in which [Madonna Blyth] is left deprived of the sense of sight on which she relies . . . gains its impact from the author's imaginative identification with her handicap. (142)

These arguments are compelling but also leave a lot unsaid. Wouldn't anyone with a body be interested in writing about bodies that go out of the bounds of the "normal," as our bodies all do in small and large ways throughout our lives? As interesting and relevant as Collins's body is, why does it so often fill the page, obliterating the space that could be used to explore other questions? Further, why have we not devoted as much energy to Dickens's chronic illnesses as fictional catalysts?

Perhaps it was "genius" that unmoored Dickens's characters from the biography of his body. From another angle, the relative seamlessness of Dickensian disability melodrama made (and continues to make) readers happy. Characters like Bertha Plummer and Jenny Wren are unquiet and sharp, but never discordant enough to keep the fiction from a satisfying close. They trouble "graceful fancies," but only temporarily. At the end, above all, they keep their proper distance from the able-bodied marriage plot, whereas Collins's characters do not.

# 4

# An Object for Compassion, An Enemy to the State

## *Imagining Disabled Boys and Men*

The distinction between abled and disabled bodies in Victorian culture (and our own) was produced partly in terms of the distinction
between men and women and beliefs about what "naturally" characterized each gender; the place where the two distinctions overlap is often
the place where the meaning of disability is created in most influential
and resilient ways. For example, if what distinguishes men from women
is that the latter stay home and produce children while the former go to
a workplace and make money, the disabled woman's difference is often
imaginatively marked by her working (or roaming the street for alms), by
the difficulty of her having her own home, and by the "impossibility" of
her marrying and having children. The disabled man's difference, correspondingly, is that he either is tied to the domestic sphere or else
roams the streets without a regular workplace, and that he does not, in
the eyes of the public, "make" (earn) money but begs. This chapter
examines texts directed at the situation of boys and men with disabilities.

Leslie Fiedler's admission that he has "wept . . . and will . . . weep again" (13) over *A Christmas Carol* evokes Dickens's own admission that he "wept and laughed, and wept again, and excited himself in a most extraordinary manner in the composition" of the Christmas book (Johnson 1:466). It also reminds us how often we get to engage in serial weeping about disability through the particular catalyst of crippled children. Tim not only revives every Christmas season, but is also remade in countless appeals from twenty-first-century nonprofits and charities. While Tiny Tim has come over time to embody melodramatic excess as cheap sentiment (using a "cripple" to make someone cry and give money), Tim in his own time was more a figure of pure pathos, an afflicted, innocent child.[1]

The relief that Tim survives might be immeasurably complicated, however, by the fictional adulthoods we can imagine for him. After Tiny Tim, the world of disabled adult males in Victorian literature is peopled by a host of terrifying, leering old men with avarice, deception, and a smoggy sexuality hovering about them—men with monosyllabic names like Quilp, Hyde, Stagg, and Pew, who bilk money from good people; ogle, stalk, and knock down little girls; and terrify young boys. There are a few benign alternatives that no one but a Victorianist is likely to remember, like Dickens's Master Humphry and Collins's Sir Patrick Lundie. This representational gap corresponds to an emotional one: while Tiny Tim, at least in his own time, primarily figures emotional excess as the intensity of pure pathos, the adult characters represent the excess of bilked emotion, imposture, and inauthenticity. Between them, the two kinds of characters map out a melodramatic universe whose poles are pathos and fakery and their companion pieces, sympathy and outrage.

The innocent afflicted child and the begging impostor (as I will tag them) do not encompass the entirety of representations of disabled masculinity in Victorian literature, but, like the disabled woman of marriageable age, they are both recurrent and resilient. Prominent figures in the landscape of disability as the Victorians imagined it, they remain significant cultural figures of disability in our own time. What was compelling and useful about these opposed representations, and what was the unimaginable middle that separated them? Understanding the contexts and potential uses of this melodramatic representational cluster requires exploration of the historical layers of cultural representations of disability. After a reminder of some key Dickensian figures of affliction and fakery, I examine educational texts, the most enthusiastically motivated site of images of innocent afflicted children. Social work texts offer a background on the general problem of work and dependence in the Victorian era, as well as disability representations within that framework. Finally, the popular journalism of Henry Mayhew shows exactly where and how the binary of innocent boys (pathos) and wicked men (imposture) breaks down, and what lies in the space between them.

The relationship between the literary and the nonliterary is both reiterative (the same kinds of victims and villains show up in both) and collaborative: the gaps in literary representations are potentially explained by the nonliterary. On the basis of these texts and the complex emotional terms in which they engage disability, we can theorize the attractions of the melodramatically clear figures of the afflicted innocent and the begging impostor, and the fearfulness of the middle they exclude, the disabled worker.

As Adam Smith articulates it in *The Theory of Moral Sentiments* (1759), sympathy is a tricky business, as likely to end in detachment and anger as it is in connection and compassion:

> As the person who is principally interested in any event is pleased with our sympathy, and hurt by the want of it, so we, too, seem to be pleased when we are able to sympathize with him, and to be hurt when we are unable to do so. We run not only to congratulate the successful, but to condole with the afflicted. . . . it is always disagreeable to feel that we cannot sympathize with him; and, instead of being pleased with this exemption from sympathetic pain, it hurts us to find that we cannot share his uneasiness. If we hear a person loudly lamenting his misfortunes, which however, upon bringing the case home to ourselves, we feel, can produce no such violent effect upon us, we are shocked at his grief; and, because we cannot enter into it, call it pusillanimity and weakness. (13)

As played out in Dickens's novels, for example, the dynamics of sympathy can be similarly fraught, as when Scrooge cannot feel sympathy, or when the narrative undermines the suffering of those who ask for sympathy, as in the case of Jenny Wren's father. When a sympathetic encounter produces satisfaction for all involved, however, there is often a disabled child at its center.

"And how did little Tim behave?" asked Mrs. Cratchit. . . .

"As good as gold," said Bob, "and better. Somehow he gets thoughtful, sitting by himself so much, and thinks the strangest things you ever heard. He told me, coming home, that he hoped the people saw him in church, because he was a cripple, and it might be pleasant to them to remember on Christmas Day, who made lame beggars walk, and blind men see."

Bob's voice was tremulous when he told them this, and trembled more when he said that Tiny Tim was growing strong and hearty. (45)

Tiny Tim, glad to be looked at in church on Christmas Day, thus invests pleasure both in the act of looking at disability and in the experience of being looked at as a disabled figure. But the nature of the pleasure of the onlookers is not initially clear. He is a reminder not only of the Christ of miracles, but also of the pervasiveness of disability in the world they inhabit. If the pleasure is to remember Christ's power to heal bodies, that pleasure is juxtaposed to the experience of seeing someone whose body has not been healed, whose "limbs [are] supported by an iron frame" (44). Scrooge, however, does not see this ambiguity but only the extremity of little Tim, who may not live, and his equally "little" father Bob. It is this version of "seeing" Tim that catalyzes his change of heart and reconnection with society.

The character Smike in *Nicholas Nickleby* presents a somewhat more complicated example and suggests the demographics of sympathy's breakdown. Smike is an inmate of Dotheboys Hall, a "school" in Yorkshire for boys whose physical impairments Dickens makes transparent to their social misery:

Pale and haggard faces, lank and bony figures, children with the countenances of old men, deformities with irons upon their limbs, boys of stunted growth, and others whose long meagre legs would hardly bear their stooping bodies, all crowded on the view together; there were the bleared eye, the hare-lip, the crooked foot, and every ugliness or distortion that told of unnatural aversion conceived by parents for their offspring, or of young lives which, from the earliest dawn of infancy, had been one horrible endurance of cruelty and neglect. (88)

Of all these children, Smike is the most abject. A putative orphan, he is left at the school as a small child and treated as school slave and whipping boy when his "friends" stop paying for his support. While his disabilities are vaguely drawn, it seems clear that they are emotional and intellectual as well as physical—he actually is the "shattered invalid" Jenny's father claims to be. Nicholas, a new teacher at the school, befriends Smike and defends him against a beating from the schoolmaster, Squeers (a one-eyed man, the other half of the disabled male dichotomy). He beats the schoolmaster himself, and leaves the school. When Smike joins him, Nicholas pledges himself to the other boy, telling him, "My heart is linked to yours" (256).

Smike's suffering and need catalyze the ethical aspects of Nicholas's bildungsroman: if Squeers's brutal beating of Smike initially produces Nicholas's rage, rebellion, and beating of Squeers, it is his ongoing experience of Smike's vulnerability and illness that makes Nicholas into a caring man, fit for adult relationships. Angus Easson's wonderful discussion of affect, gesture, and "affectedness" in *Nicholas Nickleby* points out that Nicholas and Smike (and Tim Linkinwater and the invalid boy who lives across from him) are tied together in a dynamic of tears indicative of moral worth.

The same tears facilitate social unity. While Easson does not articulate it as such, weeping over afflicted boys is also productive of adult men's homosocial bonding; Tim Linkinwater and Nicholas are drawn together in their ability to weep at affliction. Smike and the unnamed invalid, the objects who facilitate this development and bonding, do not develop a similar connection; they will not need it, as neither survives.

Even more than *A Christmas Carol, Nicholas Nickleby* offers an example of how disability and the homosocial relate, though less evolved than the dyad of Jenny and Lizzie and far distanced from the community in *The Clever Woman of the Family*. Both Lizzie and Rachel initially want to help (or "compensate") Jenny and Ermine, but that charitable goal (based on unequal relationships) changes into a more mutual, homosocial bond. Part of the deeper pathos of *Nicholas Nickleby* comes from the homosocial bond's failure between Nicholas and Smike. While Nicholas can move on into the world of work and marriage, Smike, with his exhausted body and ashamed love for Kate Nickleby, must be left behind (the fact that he needs to be killed off to do this invites comparisons with the courtship plots of chapter 2). Smike inhabits the closing lines of the book, when a group of happy, healthy, and loved children come to weep at his grave; but there is no "bildung" for boys like Smike.

Dickens's disabled boys, then, both figure emotional extremity (pathos) and produce emotional growth and connection in others, while always remaining outside the world of adulthood and homosocial and other bonds based on equality.

Dickens's disabled men are similarly important to the emotional effects of the plot, but indicative of the other form of excess, that which conveys a suspicion of false emotion and trickery, the invasion of emotional "technique" into the sacred realm of charity. These men, like Tim and Smike, are often men of marginal social status; their work, if it can be called that, ranges from minor fraud to outright blackmail. *Our Mutual Friend*'s Silas Wegg sells ballads and other small goods from a street-stall, but his major business is to extract money from the newly rich Noddy Boffin, which he does on the false pretence of being the "literary man *with* a wooden leg" that Boffin believes him to be. Authentically missing one leg (and searching for his amputated limb, a minor comic thread), Wegg is deeply false in every other regard; "he ranged with that very numerous class of impostors, who are quite as determined to keep up appearances to themselves, as to their neighbors" (97). Wegg's humiliation at the end of the novel stops short of the revenge exacted on its other villains, Rogue Riderhood and Bradley Headstone, but is nonetheless a moment of sadistic humor the narrative seems to relish:

> Sloppy . . . deftly swung him up like [a] sack of flour or coals. . . . A countenance of special discontent and amazement Mr. Wegg exhibited in this position, with his buttons almost as prominently on display as Sloppy's own, and with his wooden leg in a highly unaccommodating state. . . . Mr. Sloppy's instructions had been to deposit him in the road; but, a scavenger's cart happening to stand unattended at the corner. . . . Sloppy found it impossible to resist the temptation of shooting Mr. Silas Wegg into the cart's contents. A somewhat difficult feat, achieved with great dexterity, and with a prodigious splash. (862)

If Tim and Smike elicit an ennobling sympathy, Wegg (and Squeers, Stagg, Pew, Quilp, and others) elicits a righteous outrage that seems less easily theorized as moral development, unless we can term it a sense of social conscience. The extended exploration that follows is an attempt to find the utility of sympathy and rage as products, within a web of social issues.

> Few there are, if any, who have entered the walls of this Institution without emotion, at the sight of so many of their fellow-creatures deprived of that blessing, without which, *every other* appears empty and insignificant; and although the gloom of their once lonely and dependent condition is happily cheered . . . still present to the mind is the lamentable conviction of their dark and benighted state, for which no relief can be found on this side of the grave. (*School* n.p.)

In the broad strokes of Victorian texts, the melodramatic figure of the afflicted child was any incapacitated and dependent—and thus, honestly deserving—disabled person. The begging impostor (or "sturdy beggar," in the language of the Elizabethan poor laws) was a disabled person whose economic resilience was the product of corruption and whose bodily condition did not signify complete and utter incapacity.

Deborah Stone has persuasively argued that in the nineteenth century there developed a "'disability category' with enough shared cultural meaning to serve as a defining characteristic for public welfare programs" (26). The creation and reproduction of figures that inspired polar responses to disability, I argue, contributed to the development of this disability category. In contrast to other classificatory gestures that appear in nineteenth-century texts about disability—lists of types of "afflicted" children eligible for aid, for example—this one enacted a relatively simple refinement of the larger concept of "affliction" into two emotional subdivisions with the emotional clarity of melodrama. As nineteenth-century texts construct them, an innocent, suffering child unquestionably deserves pity, tenderness, and financial support, and a duplicitous, avaricious, and probably malingering beggar is blatantly undeserving of any of these. In terms of melodramatic excess, they correspond to pathos and inauthenticity.

These two figures, I will argue, anchored and stabilized the shifting economy of emotions that characterized discussions of physical disability. They offered a way to classify not only the feelings that might be inside people who were disabled, but also the complex emotions that might surge within the nondisabled people who read about, saw, or knew them. In theory, at least, conceptualizing all disabled people as one or the other allowed nondisabled people to enjoy unalloyed pity toward the innocently dependent and unalloyed outrage toward the guiltily dependent, despite the fact that their feelings toward all disabled people (and all dependent people) were probably mixed.

As Mayhew's *London Labour and the London Poor* exemplifies, however, the afflicted child and the beggar ultimately failed in their melodramatic promise of emotional clarity. The child and the beggar were hard to distinguish emotionally, intellectually, structurally, spatially, and institutionally, as their textual relationships illustrate. While afflicted children are predictably more common to educational texts, and beggars are indigenous to the writings of social reformers, the figure of the beggar shadows educational texts as a probable fate of graduates of schools for blind or deaf people, given public resistance to employing people with disabilities. Similarly, hasty references to innocent affliction appear in warnings against begging impostors, as if the writer was trying to remember that not all disabled people are villains. Both written texts and the institutions that produced them reflect a structural inability to keep children and beggars apart.

Beggars and children are also hard to separate because they are often defined in terms of each other. Most texts present the beggar as a detestable person because he is a travesty of childhood, a vile simulacrum of a sweet and loved incapacity that children—especially children with disabilities—are believed to embody. The nadir in scandalous treatment of afflicted children, correspondingly, is to make them into beggars.

Rather than simply linked opposites, however, children and beggars share at least one defining characteristic; they are simultaneously isolated from, and yoked to, the working world. An afflicted child's utter dependence is central to the tender feelings he evokes; its cause is posited as physical insufficiency. The same dependency in an adult beggar spurs disgust and outrage, because *even if he is blind or otherwise physically impaired,* the cause is constructed as moral failure. But while afflicted "children" of all ages were imagined as part of a sacred nonworking realm, and beggars as mired in a profane one, both were defined by their distance from the productive economy.

Indeed, disabled people's status in the emotional economy, as "objects for compassion" or "enemies to the state," was shaped in large part by their status in the monetary economy. It was the instability of that position—the fact that all "dependents" in a troubled productive economy were perceived as *both* pitiable and detestable—that made the division of disabled people into innocent children and guilty beggars so engaging and yet so untenable.

## Poor Neglected Little Ones: The Education of Disabled Children

The framing context for innocent afflicted children in our own time might well be the hospital. In the Victorian era, while it was also the era in which specialty hospitals like the Great Ormond-Street Hospital were developed, the school might be the more frequently engaged context, corresponding to the tremendous energy devoted to the education of disabled children during the century.[2] Although Elizabeth Gilbert noted in 1874 that "children constitute but a small proportion of the Blind, as about nine-tenths of the thirty thousand Blind in the United Kingdom become so above the age of twenty-one," disabled children—blind ones in particular—remained the preferred figures of disability in the Victorian imagination (*COR*, 11 November 1874, 321).

The education of children with sensory disabilities had become a topic of popular interest in the late eighteenth century, prodded as much by philosophical speculation about the cognitive capacities of people born blind or deaf as by humanitarian feelings. Numerous private asylums and schools were founded from the 1790s on. Statutory provisions for the education and maintenance of disabled children (and some adults) followed much later in the century.[3]

Controversy permeates the history of disabled education. As well as heated debates over specific issues like oralism versus Sign, or Braille versus Moon type, educators addressed the question of whether disabled people (particularly the blind and deaf) could learn at all. Both the content and the methodology of disabled education became increasingly vexed issues in relation to the work students might do once they completed their education or vocational training. In the case of blind children, educational debates encapsulated popular tension between sympathy for people whose social place was so narrowly prescribed that it presented no threat to the established order, and anxiety that these social and economic roles could change and ultimately affect the roles of the nondisabled.

Educational writing played a critical role in constructing disabled children as emotionally resonant figures, using the melodramatic mode as an effective way to promote individual institutions or particular causes. Like Tiny Tim and Smike, the neglected child who is mentally and emotionally susceptible to the power of charity and education is central to such fund-raising narratives. This emotionally legible, provocative figure was a critical tool for gathering tangible support for the day-to-day operations of the Victorian "special" institution, much as "Jerry's kids" and the March of Dimes poster children are the centerpieces of twenty-first-century fund-raising campaigns. The irony and problem of both eras is that even a genuine desire to support independent lives for disabled people is often bankrolled by the emotional capital of abjection and gratitude rather than that of employment and pride.

Educational writing uses the before-and-after structure of learning to produce a melodramatic narrative of startling reversals and transformations. As it is strategic for writers to demonstrate, the emotional state of disabled children before they are educated is constructed as one of deprivation and sadness, guaranteed to stimulate tears. Learning transforms these "poor neglected little ones" into busy and happy pupils. The School for the Indigent Blind in Surrey assures visitors that

> they will not find the pupils (of a class, hitherto, considered as doomed to a life of sorrow and discontent) sitting in listless indolence, or brooding in silence over their own infirmities, but they will behold them animated in their amusements, during the hours of recreation, and cheerfully attentive to their work, during those of employment. (*Account* 8)

Work is important not so much for its economic benefits as for its emotional power,

> the effect which habits of industry are found to produce on their feelings and conduct. It is . . . difficult to point out any two situations in life, more opposite to each other, than the condition of a blind person with his faculties benumbed by sloth, and his spirits depressed by the consciousness of his infirmity, and that of the same individual, engaged in regular employment. (*Account* 5)

An emotional transformation is even more central to descriptions of deaf children (and adults) before and after education. The Asylum for

Indigent Deaf and Dumb Children in Surrey is dire in its representation of the "mute sorrow" and "misery of dumb ignorance" that characterize deaf children before they are "rescued from their melancholy situation, and raised to the rank of rational beings" (*Historical Sketch* vii, viii). Without the knowledge of spoken or written language, "they . . . remain in a state of deprivation and ignorance, bordering upon, and often terminating in, confirmed idiotism. And if, by a peculiar energy of mind, some few of them may be roused to partial exertion, they are mostly found to be suspicious, discontented, and sullen" (*Historical Sketch* iv).[4]

After their training, graduates will be

> enabled to participate in the general intellectual advantages of human nature; to communicate their thoughts as social and intelligent members of the community; to understand what is said or written by those with whom they associate; and to partake of the blessed instructions and glorious hopes given to mankind in the Sacred Scriptures. (*Historical Sketch* xii)

If there is no education, however, the consequences can spiral out to the entire nation, as "the uninstructed Deaf and Dumb must be causes of unceasing sorrow to their afflicted parents and friends, and in most cases useless and burdensome, often dangerous and injurious, members of Society" (*Historical Sketch* iv).

The significant advertising function of most of the texts I have cited so far elucidates, in part, the recurrence of such urgently emotional representations of children with disabilities. The argument must be poised between two ideas: deaf people will be utterly miserable, idiotic, and even dangerous, if uneducated—but they are eminently educable, more so than ever believed. If the miseries of deafness are infinite, so are the benefits of education.[5]

The School for the Indigent Blind in Liverpool's solicitation for a new chapel must be carefully worded, as it is strategic to represent its pupils as *still* dreadfully afflicted in order to make the reader to appreciate the significance of the proposed chapel. If the blind students remain preoccupied with "the lamentable conviction of their dark and benighted state, for which no relief can be found on this side of the grave,"

> [h]ow merciful and kind, then, to direct their thoughts BEYOND IT!—Though shut out from the Light of the Sun, let the LIGHT OF THE GOSPEL shine upon them. . . . Let the BEAMS OF DIVINE TRUTH

irradiate the darkness of their understanding, and the COMFORTS
of RELIGION will refresh their precious souls!—Is there any mode
of CHARITY like unto this?

A final salvo of sentiment closes the plea:

> [F]or this GLORIOUS OBJECT . . . *your* compassionate assistance is
> now implored.—Extend a helping Hand to raise their drooping
> Hearts,—to cheer their gloomy paths,—by affording those blessed
> words of never-failing comfort, which will be *abundantly adminis-*
> *tered* to them in that SACRED EDIFICE. (*School* n.p.)

The visual extremism of the text reiterates its verbal excess, adding a
nonverbal semiotic overlay that heightens the effect, as music does in
melodramatic performances. The text also evokes the tableaux of melodrama, in which, at the close of a scene, the characters freeze in attitudes
of supplication, grief, or joy amid a set replete with rainbows, meteors,
and other heavily symbolic features (like those beams of Divine truth)
that communicate the scene's significance.[6]

Finally, like all forms of melodrama, these fund-raising texts construct each person as a feeling body. Beyond the afflicted pupils and
even more important than them, the benevolent public are presented as
creatures defined by their earnestness and sensitivity, whose sympathetic
behavior the appeal confidently outlines. The new chapel is "a Cause
which comes home to the Bosom of every one susceptible of the feelings
of humanity" (*School* n.p.).

Even longer texts, with a less urgent promotional function and a
more complicated focus, rely on the tools of melodrama to represent disabled children as figures of pathos. Thomas Anderson's *Observations on*
*the Employment, Education and Habits of the Blind* (1837) has its own particular cause to advance, the superior benefits of asylums over schools. In
many ways Anderson writes against the afflicted-child image. Though his
students are mostly young people, he calls attention to adults with families, those "almost overlooked" people who form a substantial percent-
age of all the blind, and urges their "large, very large claim upon our
sympathies" (36). He also attacks the popular conception of blind people as sufferers:

> They certainly are, as a body, the most habitually cheerful of
> mankind. How it comes to be so, I cannot tell, and I have no wish

to theorize. I cannot designate the blind, as is almost universally
done, "the unhappy," "the melancholy," "pitiable," and so on. I
know nothing more erroneous, or more opposed to the feelings
of by far the greater majority. They cannot endure such terms
themselves. (78)

The Paris Blind School and other European "raree-shows," he argues,
cater to these attitudes, exemplified by a visitor to his institution who
viewed various examples of handiwork done by blind girls:

> She, by half articulated ejaculations, showed what was passing in
> her mind, but I believe none of us were prepared for the astound-
> ing climax which followed, when . . . she said, in the hearing of
> all—"Well!—*poor* things!—do they *ever speak?*" The effect was
> almost instantaneous, and I was glad to get her outside the room
> door, to allow vent to the burst of laughter which immediately fol-
> lowed her exit. (79)

This and other anecdotes in Anderson's book are so energetically
opposed to existing stereotypes that he runs the risk of replacing the
mythology of the afflicted blind with a countermythology of the incredi-
bly jolly blind person, which points out the difficulty of working outside
of emotional constructions of blindness.

Like the other writers, Anderson describes in glowing terms the
power of education to transform "dark" lives into happy and lively ones,
but his melodramatic gloom frames not the lives of those who never
come to the asylum, but rather the future prospects of even successful
graduates:

> I am quite aware of how it "strikes a stranger" when they enter a
> school for the blind:—"Well, this is delightful—who would have
> believed it! How very nicely they get on!—and such a blessing to
> be enabled to do for themselves—how cheerful, how happy!" No
> feeling mind can look on such a scene without indulging in such
> thoughts. But, let that stranger—and I would also invite the direc-
> tors of such institutions—look forward to a few years, when these
> young people will all have been dispersed to their several villages,
> crowded lanes, or hovels! . . . The charm is gone. . . . the excite-
> ment and benevolence called forth while perambulating the

extensive and comfortable premises of a *school* are one thing, while those called forth by viewing a succession of those very pupils, after they have left the institution, are quite another. (10–11)

Anderson imagines pupils leaving school only to "take their places by the highwayside, and beg at the corner of the streets, with the pangs of dependence sharpened to torture by increased sensibility" (19). His critique of disabled education, like the fund-raising solicitations, relies on the sentimental capital of the afflicted child (and tries to extend it to the afflicted adult as well).

The most important thread in all these texts is the consistent use of affect to articulate disability. Even educators like Anderson, who recognized and opposed emotional typologies of disability, ultimately relied on them to represent blind people. With emotional constructions of impairment so deeply woven into Victorian culture, the real problems with vocational training for disabled people were most likely perceptual and attitudinal rather than logistical. The frustrated comments of blind activist and educator W. Hanks Levy, the director of the Association for Promoting the General Welfare of the Blind, indicate that popular resistance to material evidence about blind people derailed many efforts to change educational programs. Levy writes in 1872,

> The principle on which all institutions for the blind had been established contained two fallacies . . . it was assumed that the majority of the blind lost their sight in infancy; and it was also taken for granted that if they were instructed in youth, they would be enabled to provide for their own maintenance without further assistance. Both these assumptions were erroneous, statistics having proved that the blind generally lost their sight as adults and not as children; and an examination into the history of those blind who had been at institutions having shown that after leaving such establishments, they were obliged to earn their daily bread by begging in the streets, or were compelled to enter a workhouse. (471–72)

Despite the abundant public interest, charitable dollars, and statutory support devoted to the cause of disabled education in the course of the century, what persisted in the public imagination—as reflected by contemporary writing—is a concept of disability as dependency and misery. This popular investment in images of "afflicted children" contributed significantly to educational programs' continuing failure to transform "poor neglected little ones" into independent, working adults.

## Innocent Needs and Guilty Ones: Disability and Charity

The remarkable tenacity of emotional representations of afflicted children, alongside public disregard for the much larger issue of disabled adults and their needs, cannot be explained solely within the context of their constant reproduction by educational writings and educational policies. Part of the afflicted child's importance was derived from social developments that were more concerned with poor adults, and yet informed the way that all disabled people (and all "dependents") were perceived in nineteenth-century British culture.

Poverty and its relief were central issues in Victorian Britain in part because physical and economic distress were both visible and perceived as endemic and incurable. Relief, however, was not the only concern of public and private social agencies. In part because of the competing concern of repression of the undeserving who asked for help, social workers were determined to classify the distressed. Were they appropriate recipients of out-relief, or workhouse paupers? Were they fit objects for state aid, or for private charity? Most crucially, did they *deserve* to be helped? Despite early reformers' faith that a trained observer could readily discern a person's place within this moral and socioeconomic system, most poor people occupied a position of taxonomic and moral ambiguity in the minds of those who were concerned with systems of poverty relief.

Under the Elizabethan poor laws, the people of each parish were taxed in order to provide work for the able-bodied unemployed and "competent sums for relief of lame, blind, old and impotent persons" (Mayhew 4:395). "Indoor" *relief* came in the form of "poor houses . . . for the reception of the impotent poor only," whereas punishment for the able-bodied paupers who refused to work took place in places of correction or jails (Mayhew 4:395). In theory, at least, the "House" under the Elizabethan laws was a refuge for the physically and mentally disabled rather than a site of punishment and stigmatization; an asylum, not a "workhouse Bastille."[7]

Because the poor laws were administered in a highly decentralized fashion, however, policies varied from parish to parish. Over time, many Victorian social reformers believed, poor-law provisions were misapplied and even abused. The fourfold increase in the poor rates between 1780 and 1820 was considered clear evidence of the system's inadequacy, not a sign of increased need.

Many reformers believed that the root problem was a need for uniform procedures for classifying and treating the needy. Under the Poor Law Amendment Act of 1834 (the New Poor Law), a centralized system was put in place, complete with new restrictions on relief. The policies for which the Act became infamous were stricter eligibility requirements for outdoor relief, and the "workhouse test":

> An ablebodied man seeking relief had to receive it in the workhouse, or not at all. "Less eligibility" meant that relief in the workhouse was made as uncomfortable as possible by irksome regulations, few social amenities, poor food and a general and deliberate encouragement of gloom and despondency. (Young and Ashton 47)

Poor Law Commission secretary Edwin Chadwick had intended to use separate constraints and separate dwellings to house other classifications of paupers, such as children, the old, or the disabled. Like so many of the new law's reforms, however, this design was derailed by economics; all-purpose workhouses were cheaper. By 1852, "children, lunatics, incorrigible, innocent, old, disabled were all mixed together" in English workhouses (Young and Ashton 127). The desire to save money effectively submerged the proposed system of classification and left a highly charged dichotomy in its place. The needy were either eligible or ineligible for out-relief, and this generally meant that they were either blamelessly poor or guiltily so.

Until it met its goal of decreasing the destitute population and not merely the number of people assisted by the poor rates, the new system implied an increased burden for the charities, who responded extravagantly to the challenge. By the mid-1880s, "the income of London charities was greater than that of several independent governments, exceeding the revenues of Sweden, Denmark, and Portugal, and double that of the Swiss Confederation" (Owen 468). As the Poor Law Amendment Act essentially proclaimed state aid as a form of punishment rather than simply a last resort for all the needy, the flood of charitable aid was earmarked for the "deserving poor."

This division of funds, however, was not judged successful by all observers. Population growth and urbanization, at least in theory, precluded the personal relations that would allow individual donors to decide whom to help and how. If the New Poor Law was criticized for its excessive harshness, many charities were attacked for their laxity, particularly in terms of researching the entire character of those they sought to relieve; too many recipients were undeserving.

These beliefs catalyzed the development, over the century, of a new social role of intermediary or gatekeeper, positioned between donors and recipients, and a corresponding emphasis on casework and other "scientific" procedures to research recipients and organize and administer aid. The Charity Organisation Society, founded in 1869, epitomized this program to revise the operations of both the Poor Law and charity. The founders of the COS believed that "the mass-misery of great cities arose mainly, if not entirely, from spasmodic, indiscriminate, and unconditional doles, whether in the form of alms or in that of Poor Law relief" (Owen 217). Its two most immediate precursors were the Society for the Relief of Distress (established in 1860 in response to the social fallout from a recession) and the London Association for the Prevention of Pauperism and Crime. A less obvious, but significant, earlier influence was the Mendicity Society, formed in 1818 "to protect noblemen, gentlemen and other persons accustomed to dispense large sums in charity from being imposed upon by cheats and pretenders, and . . . to provide, on behalf of the public, a police system, whose sole and special function should be the suppression of mendicancy" (Mayhew 4:399). The key concepts of relief and repression, as well as the tension between them, survived in the Charity Organisation Society's proper name—the London Society for Organising Charitable Relief and Repressing Mendicity.

Among the major principles of the COS were decentralization, thorough understanding of cases, and an explicit relationship between public and private assistance; sharing the philosophy of the famous Goschen Minute of the Poor Law Board (also produced in 1869), the society believed that state aid was for the truly destitute and that charity was for all others. Like the Poor Law's attempts to classify the poor, however, this project served not so much to endow charitable assistance with the objectivity and organization of science as to reinscribe the concept of dependence as an innocent or guilty state.[8]

Despite the recurrent emphasis on "scientific" classification methods,

reformers were often less concerned with statistical evidence of need
than with deciphering the moral content of material facts. The primary
goal of case research seemed to be learning how to feel about the person
in question and using that information to position him or her in the
relief system. In fact, at the heart of the desire to classify was the need to
sort out and justify passionate mixed feelings toward dependent members of society.

Emotional extremism was a characteristic of various Victorian reform
groups (as it often is of welfare reform debates in our own time in the
United States). Social reformers early and late in the century often subscribed to a harsh form of individualism, in which they devoted more
energy to the credo of self-affliction than to that of self-help, attributing
all wretchedness to individual rather than social causes. For their part,
the texts of charitable groups and individuals often make the prospective
"helped person" secondary to the personal satisfactions of sympathy and
charity. What launched social reformer Josephine Butler into her energetic career, she asserts, was becoming

> possessed with an irresistible desire to go forth and find some pain
> keener than my own . . . as my heart ached night and day. I had no
> clear idea beyond that, no plan for helping others. . . . My sole
> wish was to say to afflicted people, "I understand: I too have suf-
> fered." (26)

Both midcentury attitudes and fiction participated in this "cult of benevolence," whose products were not only a performative and "excessive"
emotionalism, but also an increase in the "indiscriminate alms-giving"
reviled by the COS (Houghton 273–74; Rooff 25).

As attractive as a melodrama of cruel poor-law reformers and benevolent donors might be, Walter Houghton's suggestion that both emotional stances were fueled by ambivalence toward the poor seems more
to the point.[9] Although reformers were generally more energetic in vili-
fying the undeserving, and the benevolent more rhapsodic about the
innocently afflicted (disabled people, for example), contemporary texts
document the close coexistence of calls for repression and celebrations
of pity. Rather than putting excessive sympathy and harshness in
opposed camps, it may be more productive to see both emotional
responses as interconnected responses to widespread indigence and
integral parts of the cultural work that addressed it.

As elaborated by various influential Victorian writers, the theory of charitable relief is more than anything an attempt to classify, justify, and organize mixed feelings toward the needy, and only later to classify and organize the bodies and material requirements of the needy themselves. Descriptions of the charitable transaction position both independent and dependent people as participants in a highly charged economy of real distress, manufactured distress, relief, and repression. Mixed feelings are sorted out and justified by directing them at two different objects, the innocent and the guilty.

London magistrate Patrick Colquhoun's widely circulated *A Treatise on Indigence* (1806), for example, distinguished between innocent poverty and guilty indigence. The former resulted from unpreventable circumstances, like disability; the latter, from "preventable" behaviors like immorality and drunkenness. Innocent poverty should be "propped up" with social work and relief; guilty indigence should be punished.

The ideas of Scottish evangelical minister and political economist Thomas Chalmers, whose influence on the COS was considerable, illuminate the mechanics of the charitable relationship and its relationship to the concept of "excess." Private charity was for Chalmers a beautiful and sacred aspect of human relations, increasingly imperiled by social change. Chalmers was concerned with benevolent individuals' tendency to give indiscriminately simply to relieve their desire to express sympathy. A donor needed constant vigilance against the temptation even an undeserving object represented, for "the most undeserving are likely to obtrude themselves" (*Problems of Poverty* 347).

If the undeserving are the most stimulating spectacles, then the truly deserving never present themselves to the eye at all, or at least do not "obtrude" themselves. The model has the attraction of returning control over the charitable transaction to the donor, whom it gives the authority to judge whom to help among a set of docile or even invisible subjects, and to ignore the clamor of those who by their insistence mark themselves as undeserving, even fraudulent. Further, as being seen or heard is usually a prerequisite of being helped, Chalmers's model enables the fantasy that there are no deserving poor, and thus no help is required.

Not only do the undeserving present a stimulating spectacle to potential donors, but also, according to Chalmers, the sight of a rich donor stimulates the undeserving to become even more compelling an object for charity; it "inspires avarice in the mind of a poor man, and causes him, by a little more profligacy or a little more destitution, so to excite pity, that a permanent pension may be available" (321). These ill effects rebound, moreover, onto the donor:

> When he saw his gifts being squandered on the undeserving, or used for luxury and perhaps vice, his heart was hardened. The press would give publicity to heart-rending accounts of distress and money would pour in, but subsequent appeals had to be accompanied by even more spectacular stories of misery to make the public respond. This was known by the professional poor, who deliberately set out to manufacture sores and other distresses. (Young and Ashton 94–95)

What Chalmers articulates, then, is a highly visual, highly emotional economy in which excesses on each side—the donor's unconsidered benevolence and the recipient's increasingly histrionic performance of his or her body and plight—result in hardened hearts, manufactured sores, and a need for increasing stimulation to achieve the relief of the (now cheapened) charitable transaction. Statutory provisions also profaned the charitable bond. In Chalmers's mind, a presumption of basic rights and "the sight of a bottomless pocket in the public fund" would remove all incentive for self-help (Young and Ashton 73).

These influential theories on indigence and charity organized mixed feelings about the dependent into pure pity or pure suspicion, and classified recipients as deserving or undeserving. This binary structure was purposeful and specific cultural work; it offered a promise, however illusory, that the limitless and uncontrollable situation of unemployment and poverty would become manageable if only the undeserving were winnowed out. Reformers' and social workers' tendency to establish more and more recipients as undeserving, and to include disabled people among them, indicated not only a new perspective on disability and work but also a strong desire to reduce the extent of social responsibility for human needs (if not the extent of the needs).

While most Victorian social reformers reference them obliquely or not at all, people with disabilities, particularly visible ones, were both crucial to the emotional economy of suffering and relief and by definition problematic figures of innocent need. On one hand, visibly disabled people may have presented compelling figures for the widespread human suffering of the century. Traditionally viewed as the "unquestionably deserving" element among the financially dependent because they were assumed to be dependent in all other ways as well, they were often placed at the center of fictional and nonfictional narratives of suffering and charitable relief. As innocently afflicted objects, they inspired a flood of tender feelings and alms that redounded to the donor's credit, yielding the double satisfaction of having followed in Christ's footsteps and received the heartfelt gratitude of the feeble recipient. In terms of the credo that the truly deserving were neither seen nor heard, visible disability might constitute a way of being seen without being regarded as "obtruding" oneself, and of communicating without offensive clamor through the silent, modest speech of an impaired body. The visibly disabled neatly corroborated the prevailing philosophy of the COS that the deserving were identifiable.

Further, as people who deserved the unstigmatized help of outdoor relief or charity, they marked the origin of charitable feelings (as the able-bodied who refused to work marked the point at which charitable feelings broke down). In terms of melodramatic conventions, they enacted the delightful tonic of pure pathos. In short, people with visible physical disabilities were compelling advertisements for charitable giving and state aid.

Disabled people could not represent "innocent indigence" in general, however, because popular opinion and the poor laws both positioned them outside the generality of the poor. That is to say, they were seen as outside the working economy because physically incapable, and outside the increasing scrutiny and suspicion (formalized in the New Poor Law) of the needy. They were theoretically exempt, along with the ill and the insane, the elderly and the orphaned, from the strict eligibility requirements for outdoor relief that governed the able-bodied, and thus were theoretically due "a minimalist form of state provision" in the form of limited financial support (Lonsdale 28).

These provisions, however, often failed to hold up. Susan Lonsdale writes that disabled people were frequently admitted to the workhouse instead, in part because

> the Poor Law administrators were concerned that if a better and more amenable system [of outdoor relief] was provided for some recipients such as those who were chronically sick and disabled, then this would pave the way for people pretending to be ill. (29)

Indeed, people whose disabilities were not readily apparent, like deaf people, often fell under suspicion of malingering. Ironically, the fact that a person who is physically disabled is not *a priori* ill or incapable made it even more likely that overzealous Poor Law Guardians would see capable disabled people as workhouse paupers and assign them to an environment in which specialized training was as hard to come by as specialized care, despite the aims of Chadwick and other reformers.

Even people with visible, easily "authenticated" disabilities were not always treated as "those . . . classes of suffering humanity, whose claims upon our sympathy no one will call into question" (Anderson 3 n. 1). In terms of Victorian middle-class beliefs, which attributed misfortune of all kinds to personal moral failure rather than social circumstances, they could be seen as bringing about (or exacerbating, through improvidence) their physical impairments. Lonsdale observes that although disabled people were often admitted to the workhouse "benignly, as a form of asylum," once they were in the House, most poor people with disabilities bore a burden of blame and guilt for their individual condition (29). And even if the New Poor Law had succeeded in establishing specific, nonpunitive workhouses for people who were disabled and destitute, the incredible diversity of disabilities and the people who experienced them would have made it far from simple to establish who should inhabit them. Classification on the basis of physical impairment presented as much of a puzzle as any other attempt to classify the poor. Then as now, the meaning of "disabled" was very much open to debate, and the diverse capabilities of disabled people made it inappropriate to simply categorize them as "ill," "impotent," or "incapable," the usual terms under which poor laws included them.

As they could not be generalized as paupers nor always appropriately grouped with the ill and impotent, and no third category formally recognized their specific situations, disabled people existed on various conceptual fringes and were often subsumed into systems designed with the general poor in mind. This mainstreaming left them liable to lose the exempt status they had been granted for centuries, but without any new provisions from the "scientific" system proposed by reformers. Put "inside" (often literally, inside the workhouse) without provisions to accommodate their disadvantages, they were in effect given equal access to suspicion and destitution.

Charitable efforts to help people with physical disabilities were much more vigorous than statutory provisions, if not always measurably more effective. From 1799 to 1899 the number of known societies and institutions for the blind in Great Britain jumped from 4 to 154 (Rooff, 177). These included residential asylums and homes for the aged and infirm, home visiting societies, home teaching societies, schools for children, and vocational training centers and workshops for adults. Disabled people created some of the more resilient nonstatutory programs, notably Elizabeth Gilbert and W. Hanks Levy's Association for Promoting the General Welfare of the Blind (1856) and the British and Foreign Blind Association (1865), founded by a group of blind men headed by Dr. Thomas Rhodes Armitage. Educational and social programs for deaf people were somewhat less extensive.

The work of the Charity Organisation Society had a significant impact on social programs for people with physical disabilities because of its emphasis on education and training and on researching the actual situation of disabled people. The society created a Special Committee on the Blind whose membership included several blind activists for blind people (Gilbert, Armitage, Francis Campbell, William Moon, and Henry Fawcett), and whose activities were a regular feature of the *Charity Organisation Reporter*. The *COR* also reported on national and international developments in education and training for disabled people. The society catalyzed the creation of the Royal Commission on the Blind, Deaf and Dumb, etc. in 1889 and the Education Act for disabled children in 1893–94, as well as transforming some purely formal provisions for disabled people into active measures for their welfare (transferring, for example, the duty to educate disabled people from the Poor Law Guardians to the boards of education).

Ironically, however, the COS and other charitable agencies' ability to imagine disabled people as part of the productive economy produced a surprisingly harsh outlook toward them. The *COR*'s article "Is a Blind Man Able-Bodied?" illustrates the situation. It reports that the Bridgenorth Guardians have discussed this question at length in regard to "a certain blind man, who had attempted to get his living out of the house by making mats, but failed" (1 July 1880, 162). The man was ultimately refused out-relief. While in so many texts blindness is assumed to mean total incapacity, here disability is defined both on the basis of visual impairment and by the man's relation to the productive economy. This interesting and potentially progressive outlook, however, results in a suspicion that a recipient may not be qualified for the outdoor relief to which his disability theoretically entitles him. Even *failing* as a worker moved this person from one category of disabled person to another, and his effort, ironically, disqualified him for the less stigmatized variety of state aid. It is unresolved whether or not the man's experience made him a fit object for charity, or simply for the House.

If disabled people are not utterly dependent, these texts argue, they may not be unequivocally "deserving" of financial assistance.[10] At the same time, utter dependency has lost its innocence, as a letter from a Poor Law Guardian about "the terms on which the Guardians would be likely to co-operate with a Blind Pension Society" demonstrates. The commingling of terms quantifying financial status and those evaluating personal worth suggests that by 1874 complete dependency, even among blind people, is both *required* and at the same time an indelible moral blot:

> Our guardians will not grant more than 2s. This added to an income of 3s. [from a pension] is only sufficient to keep a person in a position to beg. . . . *Destitute cases will be left to go into the house. Worthy people must have an allowance made up to support them.* I know charity can do this. . . . It will do so when it feel the necessity, and leaves off patching up desperate cases with 1s. doles. (*COR,* 8 July 1874, 283)

A belief in individual, rather than social, responsibility for misfortune has clearly been extended to disabled poor people, as the *COR* "Difficult Cases" feature (a sort of social reform puzzler) illustrates. In one issue, the object of scrutiny is

> A.B., aged 55, wife, aged 27, two children, aged 10 and 8. A.B. was a commercial traveller, and bore an excellent character. His health failed him four years ago, and he has not earned anything for two years. He is now blind and paralysed. They have lived on savings and selling their goods, and have had help from former employers. The wife is doing her best to maintain the family by millinery, but having to look after the husband and children, she cannot earn enough for their support. They have no relations able to assist. What is to be done for them? (19 October 1876, 143)

One reader offers the following surprisingly harsh assessment of A.B.'s situation:

> [T]he first point that occurs to me is that there is likely to have been improvidence in the case, as commercial travellers earn large sums, and no mention is made of the amount of savings or of insurances or clubs. Secondly, the fact of the man having married a girl of 16 is not in his favour. . . . if there has been improvidence the husband should go into the workhouse, and then, but not till then, . . . the wife should be put in the way of supporting herself and children independently. (26 October 1876, 146)

If there has been no improvidence, the correspondent asserts that the COS should give the family a weekly allowance immediately, but it should end when the husband can be removed from the family and sent to an institution for the blind.

A second reader also delves into A.B.'s habits and domestic situation, again with a caseworker's eye for improvidence:

> He is 55 and his eldest child is 10. Was he married before? If so, did he have a family, and have they all died? Or was he a single man till 44? Unless he had very heavy expenses, could not a commercial traveller, single till 44, or married without a family, with an excellent character—that is, in good situations—provide well for old age for himself and small family, even with sickness? What were his earnings and mode of life? (26 October 1876, 146)

One wonders, finally, what constitutes a deserving case. The following description of an appropriate candidate for a tiny pension of £5—surely the smallest supplement to a subsistence income—suggests that an individual with no dependents and no material needs might be the ideal recipient:

> PENSION FOR A BLIND PERSON.—A nomination for a pension of £5 from "the Charities to the Aged Blind, distributed by the Clothworks' Company". . . . Qualifications.—Applicants must be fifty years of age, of sober life and good morals: have been totally blind for three years; not be entitled to any estate, annuity, salary, pension, or income for life, to the amount of £20 a year; nor be an

inmate of a Workhouse or public institution; nor publicly solicit
or receive alms. (*COR*, 17 May 1877, 87)

Levy's assertion in 1872 that "a pension really to . . . keep the recipient
from seeking alms, or entering a workhouse, should not be less than £26
a year," puts the amounts in perspective (495).

While the new expectation that disabled people could help themselves brought about a harsh response when they failed, an alternate perspective attributed only sinister capabilities to them. The following
writer bemoans the inability of any of the metropolitan charities to help
a "person of good character . . . stricken with blindness":

> I am informed by those well able to judge that the shortcoming
> arises in the first instance from the fact that Nature, in depriving
> these [blind] unfortunates of one faculty, has endowed them with
> another, viz., a special aptitude for obtaining cumulative relief; so
> that a few experts are, in fact, exhausting the resources of a num-
> ber of societies, while those of their brethren who are less self-
> asserting meet with the same answer that I have recorded above.
> (*COR*, 11 November 1881, 222)

This letter exemplifies the spread of suspicion about the "undeserving"
to all people with disabilities; even if a physical impairment looks valid,
the argument goes, it may be supplemented by an invisible advantage:
one more instance of the difficulty of distinguishing mendicity from
mendacity.

The problem of whom to help, and how much to give, was further
encrypted and entangled by the issue of social class. *COR* writers frequently suggest that only disabled people from the lower middle and
middle class are fit objects for charity. According to Wilkinson, for example, poor-law support is for "chronic cases of destitution or physical
inability among the poorer classes," and charity is for "the totally unpro-
vided for who belong to a higher grade" (*COR*, 5 January 1876, 2). Later
that year, he complains that disabled people of the lowest classes are
clogging institutions that should house their betters:

> Under the present system those admitted into charitable institu-
> tions were treated as charity-paupers, and thus the whole lower
> middle class and upper artisan class, who would gladly contribute

to the charities *and who deserved charity,* did not obtain it, the totally destitute being preferred to them. (*COR,* 23 February 1876, 38; emphasis added)

This echoes the complaint, in a survey of charities for blind people four years earlier, that "if the charitable were not traded upon by a variety of hangers-on upon the skirts of charity, abundant means would be available for doing everything that is really necessary" (*COR,* 3 July 1872, 123). Further, it associates the lower classes with the obtrusive, undeserving variety of disabled people, those who divert charity from its proper objects.

The COS emphasis on the social class of disabled people is one more way of managing the concept of innocent or guilty dependence. Those who belong to the lower classes, it is implied, *are* responsible for their own situation and could have prevented it—perhaps not the unexpected misfortune of physical disability, but the poverty that disability pushed into destitution. But the real function of this use of class as arbiter of innocence or guilt is to organize the ambivalence that any disabled person might arouse, especially when that person was no longer viewed as utterly helpless.

Ironically, both disabled people who seek assistance, and those who actually achieve independence and thwart the "disabled role" that they are still expected to play, are targets of suspicion. The worst nightmare was no doubt the National League for the Blind, which put to the test Elizabeth Gilbert's recommendation to charities to "let the blind themselves be consulted, and have as much voice as possible in the measures adopted for their welfare" (*COR,* 11 November 1874, 321). The league, whose slogan was "We desire work rather than beggary," was formed in 1898 by a group of blind industrial workers. It was vocal in its critique of charity, asserting that too much money was paid to sighted managers and for administrative expenses and demanding "scientifically administered" state aid rather than "the piecemeal action and insufficient resources of the voluntary agencies" (Farrell 153–54). Model "charitable objects," then, might not necessarily be those who moved beyond charity, and were certainly not those who engaged it critically from an insider perspective.

The potential for self-sufficiency clearly invoked a series of weighty changes in a needy and disabled person's status: from someone innocently dependent to someone guiltily so; from one of "those who can not work" to one of "those who *will* not work"; from a tenderly regarded object of charity to a nonproductive and thus worthless member of the national workforce. The paternalism of the past, in which disabled people were seen as loved, even sacralized, incapables, was replaced by a new paternalism that accorded them the potential to work, but judged them failures or slackers if they still needed help, and tried to control the terms of the independence they did achieve. Ironically, both disabled people's illegibility within the New Poor Law and the attention they received from private agencies subjected them, like their nondisabled peers, to scrutiny and suspicion.

For those social reformers who saw charity as a compact whose sanctity derived in part from its taking place "outside" the productive economy, the relocation of disabled people "inside" the economic world in some sense profaned them.[11] No longer lilies of the field, under special divine protection, they were increasingly liable to be characterized as one of "the minor streams which ultimately swell the great torrent of pauperism" (Royal Commission xii). Chalmers's belief that "[m]en will become voluntarily poor, but they will not become voluntarily blind or deaf, or maimed, or lunatic" no longer seems to be shared by his descendants later in the century (*On Political Economy* 419). While disability might still be taken for a sign of divine anger, or parental sin, it now carried the additional taint of individual responsibility, at least when it was combined with poverty.

While one might imagine that the idea of blind, deaf, or otherwise physically disabled people as working members of society would have produced a score of new representations of self-sufficient disabled adults, I found very few. The following "case reports" were produced by the Association for Promoting the General Welfare of the Blind:

> "A." became blind when a child; he was educated in two blind schools, but from want of work was obliged to beg through the country with his wife, who was also blind, and three young children. He is now supplied with constant work by the Association, and the whole family is thus rescued from vice. "B." lost his sight in infancy, and was an inmate of a workhouse for several years, where he had the character of being generally insubordinate. Proper instruction and employment, however, have not only

made him docile, but have also transformed him into a really useful member of society. . . . "D." was a foreign sailor, who lost his sight in the English service. He became entirely dependent on charity, and must have sunk lower and lower had he not been rescued by this Association, which now supplies him with work to the extent of 16s. per week. "E." became blind while a servant; her dependent position exposed her to great temptation. She was, happily, rescued by this Society, and now supports herself by the labour of her hands. (Levy 474–75)

These brief narratives, with their equal emphasis on the sorrow that could have been and the happy ending, use the same melodramatic strategies of the school reports. They narrate the successful as recipients of a rescue.

The more prevalent narrative of post-COS disabled people is the impostor alert, illustrating a public preoccupation with imposture and malingering:

A BEGGING IMPOSTOR.—The Brighton Charity Organisation Society reports that the French beggar named Charles A——, who is very near-sighted and pretends to be "stone-blind," has recently left Brighton. . . . "He says that he was invalided from the 6th Carabineers in 1866, on a pension of 9d. a day for two years, that he has been in the Institution for the Blind, Avenue Road, Regent's Park, where he learned basket making. Since he has been in Brighton, a period of five months, there is no doubt that he has got his living by begging. His plan is to go about with a stick, and to make his way with great apparent difficulty, to the houses of the charitable; but immediately he gets into Edward Street (a very low neighbourhood) the difficulty vanishes, and he walks about just like other people. A few evenings ago our Agent saw him in a beerhouse, drinking his ale and *reading* the newspaper. After hearing that he was being inquired about, he burnt a quantity of letters, &c., and hastily quitted the town." (*COR*, 10 June 1874, 269)[12]

The general effect of the belief that disabled people can work is to produce a recurrent concern with *moral*, rather than physical, incapacity, and continued allusions to the emotionally clear figure of the begging impostor.

## The "Anergetic" Portion of Society

The elision of the working disabled adult in most Victorian representations of disability is produced in part by the deep ambiguity that clouds at least two of its terms, work and disability. Henry Mayhew's *London Labour and the London Poor,* a massive collection of interviews with the lower classes of London, has work as its focus and classifying muse, but for all that never completely resolves the question of what work is, especially in relation to physically disabled people. This problematic and clearly anxiety-laden issue occasions a series of fascinating anatomies of the afflicted child and the begging impostor, and the conceptual and emotional ambiguity that clouds their relationship.

One of the most remarkable and valuable aspects of Henry Mayhew's *London Labour and the London Poor* is the record it provides of lives doubly slated for public invisibility by poverty and physical impairment. Further, this "history of a people" does seem to issue, as Mayhew claims, "from the lips of the people themselves" in the form of individual autobiographical statements that give "a literal description of their labour, their earnings, their trials, and their sufferings, in their own 'unvarnished' language" (1:xv).[13] As many critics have noted, the text's elision of many interviewer questions encourages readers to imaginatively merge with the "speakers," which means, in the case of disabled interviewees, that Victorian readers might identify, however briefly, with people who were probably distanced from them not only by social class but also by bodily configuration. Yet the interviewer questions and framing narratives persist as integral parts of the disabled people's stories.

Mayhew and his collaborator Andrew Halliday drew on their backgrounds in popular literature and, apparently, on the methodology of the nascent profession of social work. Working environs, homes, and "modes of life" are all subject to Mayhew's scrutiny. His "casework" with disabled people is unusually extensive (and intrusive), at times taking the character of an enthusiastic personal research into the "habitudes or idiosyncracies" of disabled people, especially blind ones (1:393). He questions them regarding their day and night dreams, what they would give to be "normal," and in some cases whether or not they have ever wished they were dead. Positioning himself as a sort of paramedical practitioner, he solicits detailed narratives about the causes of impairments and records in detail the bodily configurations and behaviors of his interviewees (a particularly disturbing dynamic in the case of blind peo-

ple). In one instance, physical research accompanies his linguistic prob-
ings. He asks a blind man to feel items of similar different-colored substance to see if he can distinguish them; he even presses the man's eye to
check for a response (1:401).

Above all, Mayhew is—like most Victorian social workers—a diagnos-
tician of the degrees of suffering, earnestness, and moral worth that
attend each interviewee's life, and fiercely concerned with distinguishing the innocent from the guilty, a distinction he often characterizes as
that between those who are forced to take to the streets or even to beg,
and those who by disposition or breeding simply hate to work and love to
rove. His initial remarks about each subject usually contain an explicit or
implicit appraisal of these qualities and provide a sort of emotional crib-
note for the reader, indicating how we should feel about the account we
are to hear. The nutmeg-grater seller, for example, is

> an example of one of the classes *driven* to the streets by utter
> inability to labour. . . . of the sterling independence of some of
> these men possessing the strongest claims to our sympathy and
> charity, and yet preferring to *sell* rather than *beg*. . . . I have made
> all due inquiries to satisfy myself as to his worthiness, and I feel
> convinced that when the reader looks at the portrait here given,
> and observes how utterly helpless the poor fellow is, and then
> reads the following plain and unvarnished tale, he will marvel
> like me, not only at the fortitude which could sustain him under
> all his heavy afflictions, but at the resignation (not to say philos-
> ophy) with which he bears them every one. His struggles to earn
> his own living (notwithstanding the physical incapacity even to
> put the victuals to his mouth after he has earned them), are
> instances of a nobility of pride that are I believe without a paral-
> lel. (1:329–30)

The story of "the most severely-afflicted of all the crossing-sweepers" is
another prime example:

> Passing the dreary portico of the Queen's Theatre, and turning to
> the right down Tottenham Mews, we came upon a flight of steps
> where an old man, gasping from the effects of a lung disease, and
> feebly polishing some old harness, proclaimed himself the father
> of the sweeper I was in search of, and ushered me into the room
> where he lay a-bed, having had a "very bad night." (2:488)

For this man, as well as the others whose suffering Mayhew deems authentic, he produces a beautifully crafted melodramatic frame. We assume that the first picture of "affliction" will be the main site of pathos; the fact that he is mobile and his son is in bed increases the magnitude of the suffering we imagine present in the sweeper himself. When we finally meet the sweeper, we hardly need to be prompted to feel that "the sight of his weak eyes, his withered limb, and his broken shoulder (his old helpless mother, and his gasping, almost inaudible father,) form a most painful subject for compassion." The coup de grâce, as it were, is Mayhew's description of the man himself:

> The sweeper, although a middle-aged man, had all the appearance of a boy. . . . his manners and his habits were as simple in their character as those of a child; and he spoke of his father's being angry with him for not getting up before, as if he were a little boy talking of his nurse. (2:489)

This sweeper, the "utterly incapacitated" nutmeg-grater seller, the "wretched spirit-broken and afflicted" blind needle-seller, and many others, approximate the same figure of afflicted innocence that was the centerpiece of Victorian writing about disabled education. Predictably enough, Mayhew lavishes sympathy on these deserving cases, modeling the assessment the reader is supposed to make.

Elsewhere, however, Mayhew's attitude toward his disabled interviewees is much less clear, as exemplified by his treatment of blind street-sellers. His first treatment of them is by exclusion, when he asserts that his heading "Of the Beggar Street-Sellers" includes

> only such of the beggar street-sellers as are neither infirm nor suffering from any severe bodily affliction or privation. I am well aware that the aged—the blind—the lame and the halt often *pretend* to sell small articles in the street . . . and that such matters are carried by them partly to keep clear of the law, and partly to evince a disposition to the public that they are willing to do something for their livelihood. . . . Such, though beggars, are not "lurkers"— a lurker being strictly one who loiters about for some dishonest purpose. (1:363)

The apparent problem is how to talk about beggars when there are two types, the innocent and the guilty. Mayhew comes up with the discreet solution of absolving the innocent of the term *beggar,* while making sure that the reader understands that this is really what they are, but that in their case begging is not offensive.

While disabled street-sellers constitute the majority of the group whom Mayhew judges innocent enough to escape the term *beggar,* later sections suggest that his feelings are far from settled on the subject. His introduction to the "character, thoughts, feelings, regrets, and even the dreams, of a very interesting class of street-folk—the blind" is actually an extended justification of permitting blind people to beg (1:395). This opening focus not only establishes begging as the primary activity associated with blind people, but also raises again the problem of distinguishing good blind beggars from bad ones.

Mayhew's first premise is that poverty and exhaustion can cause even able-bodied people to "fall from misery to mendicancy," and that if this is so,

> there must be some mitigating plea, if not a full justification, in the conduct of those who beg directly or indirectly, because they *cannot* and perhaps *never could* labour for their daily bread—I allude to those afflicted with blindness, whether "from their youth up" or from the calamity being inflicted upon them in maturer years. (1:395)

The argument both builds on and undermines the "afflicted child" figure, as it predisposes the reader to look at blind people as not only physically weak, but also morally indolent as a result. The presumption that blind people are completely incapable of physical work is central to his justification of begging; it brings with it, however, the suspicion that they are also incapable of moral effort.

The concept of "indirect" begging, further, puts a new complexion on his admiration for some disabled street-sellers' attempts to "earn an honest crust." The interviewees he accords so much respect—whom he characterizes as those "forced to become street-sellers as the sole means of saving themselves from the degradation of pauperism or beggary"— have apparently *not* completely saved themselves (1:342). And begging, despite Mayhew's attempt to partly excuse it, is an activity about which his feelings are decidedly mixed. This ambivalence emerges in the very words he chooses to assert that "the blind have a right to ask charity of those whom God has spared so terrible an affliction, and . . . whom—*in the canting language of a former generation of blind and other beggars*—'Providence has blessed with affluence'" (1:395; emphasis added). Within this claim that begging is permissible, Mayhew not only invokes a stereotyped blind beggar unlikely to inspire a sympathetic response from readers, but further casts suspicion on this figure by alluding to his "canting" lament. Suspicion of beggars is further inscribed by his hurried qualification, that this "right to solicit aid . . . is based on their helplessness, but lapses if it becomes a mere business, and with all the trickiness by which a street business is sometimes characterized" (1:395–96).

Mayhew's central conviction that blind people exemplify "those who are not able-bodied. . . . those who *cannot* work. . . . those to whom nature has denied even the capacity to labour" places an impossible strain on his attempts to accommodate the variety among the blind people he meets (1:397). If blind people are incapable of work, their activities in the streets of London must be either outright begging or a cover story for the same. The idea of begging, however, evokes not only the childlike, deserving dependency of the blind people he seems to cherish, but also the deceitful self-sufficiency he finds so scandalous in others.

Mayhew's vigorous attempts to distinguish the afflicted child from the beggar are repeatedly thwarted by the interdependency of the two figures. His effort to shift the focus to the social causes of blind beggars merely maps out the connection between the two. Blind people's exemption from the workhouse, and the workhouse test, is all too often purely theoretical, which drives them to beg to avoid the House. Ironically, however,

> The blind beggar, "worried by the police," . . . becomes the mendacious beggar, no longer asking, in honesty, for a mite to which a calamity that no prudence could have saved him gave him a fair claim, but resorting to trick in order to increase his precarious gains.
>
> That the blind resort to deceitful representations is unquestionable. One blind man, I am informed, said to Mr. Child the oculist, when he offered to couch him, "Why, that would ruin me!" And there are many, I am assured, who live by the streets who might have their eyesight restored, but who will not. (1:396)

The overt benevolence of Mayhew's thesis—that harsh social policies like the workhouse system force innocent dependency into guilty dependency—is repeatedly undermined by a stronger message of indeterminacy and suspicion regarding dependency itself. When one sees a blind beggar on the streets, there is no way of telling whether what one sees is innocent or guilty mendicancy, an afflicted child or a begging impostor. Mayhew makes his own warning to the public—to "distinguish between those determined beggars and the really deserving and helpless blind" and not "to allow their sympathies to be blunted against all, because some are bad"—practically impossible to follow (1:396).

While Mayhew's ambivalence is most striking in regard to blind people, he displays similarly mixed feelings toward the crippled crossing-sweepers and anyone else he considers to be following an "*apparent* occupation" rather than a real one. By turns, he calls their activity an "excuse . . . for soliciting gratuities without being considered in the light of a street-beggar" and "the last chance left of obtaining an honest crust" (2:465). He seems to consider the industry of the disabled street-sellers and street-workers a symptom of their noble refusal to become parish paupers, and is often lavish in his sympathy for the hardships they suffer. At the same time, judging as he does that their work is *not* really work, he also sees it as social vampirism, as indicated by his later characterization of *all* nonworkers as parasites whose "distinguishing characteristic [is] the extreme irksomeness of all labour to them" (4:3).

Disability in *London Labour* thus wavers between the pathetically struggling needle-seller, who nobly asserts that "the workhouse coat is a slothful, degrading badge," and the blind bootlace-seller/beggar whose narrative follows Mayhew's "introduction" to blind people. The latter, a graduate of the "low lodging-houses," has achieved his independence on terms that ally him with "the *natives* of the streets—the tribe *indigenous* to the paving-stones—imbibing the habits and morals of the gutters almost with their mothers' milk" (1:344, 320).

By volume 4, in which disabled people appear as a component of "the Non-Workers, or in other words, the Dangerous Classes of the Metropolis," the afflicted child has all but disappeared (4:v). In Mayhew's taxonomy of the workers and nonworkers of Britain, for example, people characterized by "physical defect . . . the old and the young, the super-annuated and the sub-annuated, the crippled and the maimed" are as much constituents of the "anergetic" part of society as those whose "defect" is moral. Physically (and mentally) disabled persons, as well as vagrants and thieves, are all "human parasites living on the sustenance of their fellows." When Mayhew writes, "The industrious must labour to support the lazy, and the sane to keep the insane, and the able-bodied to maintain the infirm," he makes an inescapable connection between the lazy, the insane, and the infirm, the same connection that hovers over most Victorian discussions of dependency, regardless of the source. Structurally, the connection appears as the double listing of blind and crippled people under "Those Who Cannot Work" and "Those Who Will Not Work" (4:3).

Halliday's discussion of "Beggars and Cheats" energetically reiterates Mayhew's ambivalence toward disabled people. He asserts that those "Bodily Afflicted Beggars" who have not yet been "cleared [off] the streets" by the Mendicity Society are mostly "blind men and cripples," and that by and large they "are really what they appear to be— poor, helpless, blind creatures, who are totally incapacitated from earning a living, and whom it would be heartless cruelty to drive into the workhouse, where no provision is made for their peculiar wants" (4:431).

His catalog of the seven varieties of "beggars who excite charity by exhibiting sores and bodily deformities," however, begins and ends with beggars who falsify their afflictions. The first group, for example, "those having *real or pretended* sores, vulgarly known as the "Scaldrum Dodge," broadcasts the equivalence of disabled beggars and impostors that is the governing thesis of this section of the text (4:432; emphasis added). The other six categories, with the exception of the last one, sound like "legitimate" disabilities:

> 2. Having swollen legs. 3. Being crippled, deformed, maimed, or paralyzed. 4. Being blind. 5. Being subject to fits. 6. Being in a decline. 7. "Shallow Coves," or those who exhibit themselves in the streets, half-clad, especially in cold weather. (4:432).

Halliday's exposition of each category, however, either declares all its members impostors "wholly without exception" or indicates that they are, at the very least, dangerous eyesores. For example, he wishes the police would interfere more often with some of "the more hideous" of the crippled beggars, as

> [i]nstances are on record of nervous females having been seriously frightened, and even injured, by seeing men without legs or arms crawling at their feet. . . . I have frequently seen ladies start or shudder when the crab-like man I have referred to has suddenly appeared, hopping along at their feet. (4:433)

And while he expresses surprise that there is no institution for cripples, who are "certainly deserving of sympathy and aid; for they are
utterly incapacitated from any kind of labour," his very next sentence
begins, "Impostors are constantly starting up among this class of beggars" (4:433). His one interview with a crippled man, titled "Seventy
Years a Beggar," elicits a narrative of a man who began as an able-bodied
impostor beggar and only broke his leg at age thirty (in a drunken accident). This "career beggar," put to the trade by his mother, regales Halliday with stories of the high life he lived until "the new police and this
b– Mendicity Society . . . spoilt it all" (4:432). The effective message is
that there is no real difference between impostors and those entitled to
beg; in general, they are part of the same immoral culture of mendicity.

The final note of the chapter, which constitutes the last section of
text in *London Labour and the London Poor*, is a tocsin regarding all dependency: "It is the office of reason—reason improved by experience—to
teach us not to waste our own interest and our resources on beings that
will be content to live on our bounty, and will never return a moral profit
to our charitable industry" (4:448). It is in this context of suspicion bolstered by economic "reason" that *London Labour* leaves the generality of
disabled people.

*London Labour*'s material on disabled people is so much absorbed by
the question of begging that it is all too easy to forget that these discussions occur in the face of many new beliefs about disabled people's ability to work. I want to return now to the issue of work and Mayhew's
difficulty with it in relation to disability.

The guiding spirit of *London Labour and the London Poor* is the desire
to classify people in every conceivable relation to the idea of work.[14]
Most of Mayhew's disabled informants are engaged in ceaseless activity
of some kind, directed toward survival outside of the workhouse. In addition to the people he interviews, who are mostly street-sellers or crossing-
sweepers, he hears of others pursuing various forms of industrial and
other labor. The blind bootlace-seller reports on blind people of his
acquaintance who turn polishers' or cutlers' wheels or mangles; blow
forges for blacksmiths; chop horses' chaff; make baskets, chair bottoms,
rope mats, or shoes; or play church organs. Mayhew himself, although
he interviews no deaf people, encounters two apparently capable deaf
women. One "poor creature" is a robust and cheerful "dustie" with
impaired sight as well as hearing, who does "the labour of the strongest
men" (2:178). The other is a pensioner of a crossing-sweeper who calls

her a "poor cretur, who's deaf as a beadle; she works at the soldiers' coats, and is a very good hand at it, and would earn a good deal of money if she had constant work" (2:478–79). And even the crippled nutmeg-grater seller, for Mayhew the acme of pathetic incapacity, has apparently operated a successful business in the past. To read Mayhew's remarks, however, there is not a worker among them. They all represent the "anergetic" portion of society, that imagined group which aroused in the Victorians (as it does in many of us) both compassion and outrage.

Mayhew's conviction that disabled people cannot work leads him into various unsatisfactory resolutions to the problem of what to term their pursuits, especially when those activities produce an income or are pursued by people who fail to approximate the image of pathetically afflicted, utterly incapacitated children. In the case of blind musicians, he denigrates the products of their activity, classifying musicians as "the skilful and the blind," and asserting that the latter constitute "the rudest class of performers" (2:159). The proceeds of this activity he stigmatizes as alms: blind performers, who use their music "not . . . as a means of pleasure, but rather as a mode of soliciting attention," are given money "in pity for their affliction rather than admiration of their harmonies" (3:159). This does not address various suggestions that the music cannot be completely unpleasant—for example, the fact that some of his interviewees make a part of their living working for hire. As troublesome as the presumption of incapacity is to maintain, however, Mayhew stands by it. His conviction that disabled people *cannot* work is as purposeful as the COS's presumption that they *can*. Both result in the reproduction of images of disabled people as afflicted children and beggars. While Mayhew may have ignored new beliefs about disabled people, beliefs to which the COS subscribed, both were responding to the problem of widespread unemployment, a crisis so severe and perplexing that it seemed unable to accommodate the employment needs of a "subgroup," especially one long considered out of the running for jobs. In light of the widespread unemployment of nondisabled adults, the concept of a working blind or deaf person simply represented an insurmountable problem to social reformers and the general public alike.

An emphasis on two disabled "types" defined by their inability to work allowed nondisabled people to focus on charity and repression, ignoring the much greater, but much more complicated, need for education, training, and employment for disabled adults. The representational gap between Tiny Tim and Silas Wegg supported and was underwritten by this elision. The ideological uncertainty that permeates Victorian fiction about disability worked together with contemporary nonfiction, in which the already unstable meanings of work, class, and gender are additionally inflected and complicated by cultural constructions of disability. The resulting disequilibrium reminds us of the necessity of defining the key words we use so freely, and of marking how particular contexts inflect and change them. It also affirms the power of disability—as a cultural construct, if not necessarily as a lived experience—to overturn and deconstruct our unexamined assumptions about all bodies and their differential social, sexual, economic, and overall cultural value.

# 5

# Melodramas of the Self

*Auto/biographies of Victorians
with Physical Disabilities*

A satisfactory autobiographical narrative—mental, spoken, written—can function as a critical form of self-preservation during the disruptions or transformations of self that are sometimes produced by bodily and other changes, disability included. Perhaps more significantly, autobiography can articulate a personal counternarrative of identity that is different from the stories the dominant culture tells about your experience. As nineteenth-century disabled people represented their lives, those narratives of self were inevitably fashioned with reference to the melodramatic conventions that permeated cultural constructions of disability.[1]

What was the relationship of figures like Bertha Plummer, the "debauched blind beggars" of the *Charity Organisation Reporter,* or Tiny Tim—who likes to be looked at as a reminder of Christ's miracles—to the lived experiences of people with physical impairments? How did nineteenth-century people who were blind, deaf, or otherwise physically impaired navigate the pervasive cultural discourse of their radical and largely negative difference from able-bodied people? How do their life stories interact with the emotional economy of disability, and with popular stereotypes of disability? Where do we see compliance with cultural master narratives about disabled roles, and what benefits does compliance produce? In what contexts can we identify direct or indirect resistance to these inscribed roles—and what seems to make resistance possible? Finally, how do socioeconomic class, gender, and other contexts shape the stories people with disabilities tell about their lives? Answers to these questions are provisioned here by means of various forms of life narratives, whose subjects are Henry Mayhew's disabled interviewees; celebrated writer and intellectual Harriet Martineau (1802–1876); religious writer John Kitto (1804–1854); Cambridge professor and Liberal MP Henry Fawcett (1833–1884); and activist and philanthropist Elizabeth Gilbert (1826–1884).

A mediated and multivocal quality, in some case a literal feature of the circumstances that produce the narrative, marks all of these life texts. Mayhew's narrative frame regularly precedes and then threads alongside the recorded words of his interviewees, a guideline that emerges and then disappears, providing a fascinating interplay between interviewee and interviewer. While Martineau and Kitto write their own life stories, only Kitto specifically focuses on his deafness to do so, and does it, moreover, in the context of a cultural history of deafness and blindness; Martineau tells more about deafness in her "Letter to the Deaf," which mixes narrative and exposition, than she does in her autobiography. Both writers draw on multiple reference points and cultural obligations to write their lives, including literature, religion, and gender. The life stories of Fawcett and Gilbert must be pieced together from a combination of their published statements about disability, autobiographical statements recorded by their biographers, and the biographies that were written shortly after their deaths. While mediation and multivocality are hardly features restricted to life writing about disability, they are possibly more significant and striking features of this genre, given how highly charged the issues of representation and access to self-representation have been for the disability community. These features also remind us that pure autobiography is a construct; finally, there may be no way to isolate individual "voices" from the multiple cultural discourses of embodied identity in which they participate.

The discussion here in no way enacts a systematic study of Victorian life writing about disability; instead, it gestures speculatively towards the kind of questions we might have asked of such texts, but heretofore have not. Within those limits, however, three noteworthy features emerge. First, Victorians with physical disabilities habitually locate themselves in relation to melodramatic figurations of disability. Regardless of the differences that are the forgotten hallmark of disability experiences, including socioeconomics and access to support services; education; gender; and timing and nature of impairment, all of these people display an engagement with the master narratives of "affliction" written by their larger culture. While there is considerable variation in how they engage the afflicted child, the begging impostor, and the unmarriageable woman—from outright resistance or compliance to a complicated position in between—none of these people articulates his or her life "outside" these representations. Affect or its explicit refusal are the major registers on which experience and prospects are articulated, and the plots emphasize extremity, whether of emotion, events, or both.

The second, much more significant commonality is that within the constraints of cultural "fictions of affliction," each person uses narrative and rhetorical strategies to transform his or her cultural position into a source of power, even if the power is tenuous and provisional.

## London Labour and the London Poor

Reading *London Labour and the London Poor,* we may become less and less sure of how to feel about disability, in part because the question is so complex for both Mayhew and the people he interviews in 1849–52. The interviews often enact a critique of the idea that disability is an emotionally charged state, though this is far from their explicit aim. Both Mayhew and the interviewees discuss physical disability in terms of many melodramatic conventions, including the concept of disability as occasioning both emotional intensity and a sense of "excess." As the differences among the collaborative producers of these autobiographies illustrate, however, it is impossible to establish what exactly is emotionally excessive treatment of physical impairment, especially when the impairment is someone else's. In their material facts, the lives many of the interviewees are unremittingly miserable. At the same time, however, the narrative accounts of these lives are often surprising for their *lack* of emotion, given the facts.

This absence of an expected affect becomes especially noticeable when Mayhew establishes the narrative as a melodramatic story of affliction and then the subject of the story counters with an account grounded in material facts rather than feelings, or a story that mingles unhappiness with joy and accomplishment. A fascinating interplay ensues, between Mayhew's diagnosis of a person's degree of suffering, the interviewee's own treatment of the facts of his or her life, and the reader's response.

Mayhew had a background in popular theater, and his chief collaborator, Andrew Halliday, wrote extensively for the popular stage, among other things adapting *David Copperfield* and collaborating on a farce entitled *The Census*. This last item, like the entries in *London Labour* themselves, underscores the fact that Mayhew and Halliday, like so many other writers of their day, lived and wrote in the interstices of multiple disciplines.

The concept of identity as performance is evoked in Mayhew's interviews, perhaps complicated by his familiarity with the conventions of the melodramatic stage. His interview with an able-bodied street reciter is illustrative, offering both a perspective on melodramatic acting and a reminder of the performative, specular, and perhaps erotic aspects of charitable transactions. Mayhew first sees the street reciter with his partner, a boy with "a priggish look" whose "manner was 'cute'" and who "pushed himself saucily forward." Mayhew prefers the "modest" reciter, who "seemed to slink back":

> He was an extremely good-looking lad, and spoke in a soft voice, almost like a girl's. He had a bright, cheerful face, and a skin so transparent and healthy, and altogether appeared so different from the generality of street lads, that I felt convinced that he had not long led a wandering life, and that there was some mystery connected with his present pursuits. He blushed when spoken to, and his answers were nervously civil. (2:151)

Mayhew's description of the boy, and the reactions imbedded within it, evoke not only the conventions of melodrama—this girlish, mysterious innocent only needs to be mute to completely fit a stereotype—but also those of social reform. The boy's reluctance to "obtrude" himself, as Chalmers would say, and his appearance of having come from a respectable background, combine with his beauty and health to make him attractive; he is in many ways a model of the "deserving" recipient, one without any immodest appearance of need.

The theatrical performance that follows does not seem to diminish Mayhew's appreciation for the boy, perhaps because it reveals his lack of subtlety as an actor. It is *only* when he begins to recite that the boy's diffidence and girlish voice are replaced by

> a deep stomachic voice—a style evidently founded upon the melo-dramatic models at minor theatres. His good-looking face . . . became flushed and excited during the delivery of the speech, his eyes rolled about, and he passed his hands through his hair, combing it with his fingers till it fell wildly about his neck like a mane.
>
> When he had finished the speech he again relapsed into his quiet ways, and resuming his former tone of voice, seemed to think that an apology was requisite for the wildness of his acting, for he said, "When I act Shakspeare [*sic*] I cannot restrain myself,—it seems to master my very soul." (2:151–52)

Mayhew knows the melodramatic stage well enough to identify (possibly with dry humor), this performance as derived from the *minor* theaters. That, along with the boy's apology for being overcome by Shakespeare, confirms his belief that the first, shy persona is *not* acting but authentic behavior.[2]

The absence of this certainty in many of his interviews with disabled people, especially the blind seller of bootlaces, is a source of troubling ambivalence for Mayhew; he does not know how to feel about people whose feelings he cannot classify as either true or false. The fact that he, himself, evokes the melodramatic to signify to readers that he finds a speaker truly deserving only underscores the possibility that the accoutrements of the melodramatic stage can be used in service of imposture or authentic suffering, and that the final effect depends on the quality of the performance.[3]

The crippled street-seller of nutmeg-graters exemplifies the gap between Mayhew's melodramatic frame and the interviewee's sense of what kind of story his autobiography is. He seems absolutely to merit Mayhew's assessment of exceptional suffering, given the accumulation of abuse to body and spirit he has experienced. The man's own narration

of these events, however, seems at times *anti*-melodramatic. For example, his mother, a woman of "weak intellects" who bore him out of wed-
lock, paid a fellow servant to take care of him after her marriage, and saw
him only once a year (or less) until her death. The seller's explanation
of what could certainly be called abandonment, however, is nonjudg-
mental and appreciative: "No mother couldn't love a child more than
mine did, but her feelings was such that she couldn't bear to see me." He
emphasizes only her generosity to him, and at one point says (as if in
response to a probing, incredulous Mayhew), "Oh, yes; I used to like to
see her very much" (1:331). It is the reader (and presumably Mayhew)
who supplies the heart-wrenching frame for this story, not the seller.

At other times, the man seems on the verge of characterizing himself
as a helpless, afflicted child, as in this passage:

> I feel miserable enough when I see the rain come down of a week
> day, I can tell you. Ah, it *is* very miserable indeed lying in bed all
> day, and in a lonely room, without perhaps a person to come near
> one—helpless as I am—and hear the rain beat against the win-
> dows, and all that without nothing to put in your lips.

This melancholy, lyrical construction of disability, however, is essentially
thrown away by the matter-of-fact assertion that follows it: "I've done *that*
over and over again where I lived before; but where I am now I'm more
comfortable like" (1:330). The image of misery is ephemeral, not something the man expands to define his entire life.

At another melancholy moment, the man uses a Providential frame
to defuse his sense of affliction:

> When I've gone along the streets, too, and been in pain, I've
> thought, as I've seen the people pass straight up, with all the use of
> their limbs, and some of them the biggest blackguards, cussing and
> swearing, I've thought, Why should I be deprived of the use of
> mine? and I've felt angry like, and perhaps at that moment I could-
> n't bring my mind to believe the Almighty was so good and merci-
> ful as I'd heard say; but then in a minute or two afterwards I've
> prayed to Him to make me better and happier in the next world.
> I've always been led to think He's afflicted me as He has for some
> wise purpose or another that I can't see. I think as mine is so hard a
> life in this world, I shall be better off in the next. (1:330–31)

He says he was suicidal when his mother and his guardian died: "I was all alone then, and what could I do—cripple as I was?" The question immediately becomes rhetorical, however, as he details the many things that he *can* do: read and write; build and renovate furniture; and trade in household items (1:331). At one point he had his own shop; after his inability to collect debts caused him to lose it, he hawked kitchen goods. It was illness, not disability, that sent him to the workhouse, and he left it with five shillings (hard-won from the Guardians) to buy stock and try to make his own living. While this venture was not entirely successful, he believes that

> [w]ith a couple of pounds I could . . . manage to shift very well for myself. I'd get a stock, and go into the country with a barrow, and buy old metal, and exchange tin ware for old clothes, and, with that, I'm almost sure I could get a decent living. I'm accounted a very good dealer. (1:332)

The last thing the man says of himself emphasizes his business ability, not his incapacity. It is worth noting, however, that the final image Mayhew gives us—via an interview with one of his friends—is of an "utterly helpless" creature, hurled into the streets by his arms and legs and left shivering against a lamppost for not paying his rent.

Other interviewees collaborate with Mayhew's tendency to characterize them as helpless, suffering children. The blind needle-seller, despite fifteen years of increasing visual impairment, seems not to have adapted at all to his blindness:

> I go along the streets in great fear. If a baby have hold of me, I am firm, but by myself, I reel about like a drunken man. I feel very timid unless I have hold of something—not to support me, but to assure me I shall not fall. . . . if I missed [the banister], I'm sure I should grow so giddy and nervous I should fall from the top to the bottom. (1:343–44)

He further emphasizes his physical and emotional delicacy by asserting that wonderful, colorful dreams "so excite me that I am ill all the next day" (1:343). He summarizes his existence as "a miserable life, sir!—worn out—blind with over work, and scarcely a hole to put one's head in, or a bit to put in one's mouth." (1:341).

"The Crippled Street-Seller of Nutmeg-graters," from *London Labour and the London Poor*, vol. 1 (1861–62). Photo courtesy of Dartmouth Medical School Photography and Illustration.

The needle-seller's lyric lament is at times disrupted by Mayhew's eager questions about blindness, producing passages like this one:

> Oh, yes; if I had all the riches in the world I'd give them every one
> to get my sight back, for it's the greatest pressure to me to be in
> the darkness. God help me! I know I am a sinner, and believe I'm
> so afflicted on account of my sins. No, sir, it's nothing like when
> you shut your eyes. . . . I see a dark mass before me, and never any
> change—everlasting darkness, and no chance of a light or shade
> in this world. But I feel consolated some how, now it is settled;
> although it's a very poor comfort after all. (1:343–44)

In contrast to his verbal prods to the nutmeg-grater seller to bemoan his existence, Mayhew seems here to want to rein in an excessive display of emotion. This characterizes his interview with the crippled street-seller of birds as well. This man looks and feels healthy, is never in pain, and sleeps well. He has a regular place to lodge, with his married sister, and has mostly avoided the workhouse. He maintains himself through a business he enjoys. He discusses, at length, the characteristics and diets of the various birds he sells, accounts himself "a very good judge of birds" and a knowledgeable manager of them, and is confident that "[i]f I had a pound to lay out in a few nice cages and good birds, I think I could do middling" (2:69).

In regard to his disabilities (as well as having no ankle, he has impaired speech), the bird-seller says, "I am quite reconciled to my lameness, quite; and have been for years. O, no, I never fret about that now." At the same time, he repeatedly gives his life a melodramatic frame, in the form of an overriding narrative of affliction that cancels out all conflicting information (2:68). He collapses his beginning and end into the fact of his disability, making himself into a disabled type: "I was born a cripple, sir,' he said, 'and I shall die one." While he says that he likes reading, and jokes, and that "if I had only plenty to live upon there would be nobody happier," he has no interest in the newspaper because "there'll be no change for me in this world" (2:67). Both he and his birds are "prisoners." His Providential narrative, like the needle-seller's, culminates in woe:

> I think of the next world sometimes, and feel quite sure, quite,
> that I shan't be a cripple there. Yes, that's a comfort, for this world

will never be any good to me. I feel that I shall be a poor starving cripple, till I end, perhaps in the workhouse. Other men can get married, but not such as me. . . . I never was in love in my life, never.

Mayhew, who has termed the man "poor fellow" and "poor cripple," and authorized his misery in various ways, seems to run out of patience at this. He comments that "among the vagrants and beggars, I may observe, there are men more terribly deformed than the bird-seller, who are married, or living in concubinage" (2:68).

While pain is not necessarily a component of physical disability, Elaine Scarry's comments on pain are pertinent to the continual project of assessing suffering that *London Labour* enacts in its pages and encourages in its readers (the same project that is a significant component of social agencies' "diagnosis" and classification of applicants for aid).

> When one hears about another person's physical pain, the events happening within the interior of that person's body may seem to have the remote character of some deep subterranean fact, belonging to an invisible geography that, however portentous, has no reality because it has not yet manifested itself on the visible surface of the earth. . . . the pains occurring in other people's bodies flicker before the mind, then disappear. (3–4)

Bodily pain has the ironic status of being both undeniable and unconfirmable, depending on one's perspective; "to have pain is to have *certainty;* to hear about pain is to have *doubt*" (13). Scarry theorizes that bodily pain can be made knowable if "the felt-attributes of pain are . . . lifted into the visible world, *and if the referent for these now objectified attributes is understood to be the human body*," an understanding catalyzed, for example, by "visible body damage or a disease label" (13, 56).

Bodies "visibly damaged" abound in the pages of *London Labour and the London Poor,* yet the body's ability to convey a sense of reality is far from uniform. Mayhew assiduously renders in print his interviewees' bodies, sometimes from three or four different perspectives: seen and described by Mayhew; seen and described by the interviewees themselves; and "seen" and reproduced by daguerreotypes, which are then reproduced as prints. The "sheer material factualness of the human body," however, does not necessarily confer an inalienable sense of the

real (as opposed to the melodramatic) to either these visual representations or the suffering they attempt to convey (Scarry 14).

If the bodies of physically disabled interviewees do convey a sense of
reality, it is a very provisional one. In one case, it may be the reality of
noble suffering; in another, the reality of blind beggars' hypocrisy. Mayhew's assertion that "the faults of the present volume . . . are rather short-
comings than exaggerations" often seems to be undercut by the exces-
siveness of his language, his overprotestations of misery. Autobiographical
statements, likewise, alternately "authenticate" and rebut the emotional
content of disability (1:xv).

Mayhew generally manages to remain the proprietor of most of the
autobiographical narratives, guiding, controlling, and correcting. One
of his most memorable subjects, however, the blind bootlace seller,
places himself within such a complicated set of relationships to disability
and affect that it utterly confounds Mayhew's control. The interviews
with the bootlace seller produce Mayhew's most extensive discourse on
disability, revealing not only his complicated attitudes toward blind people, begging, and work, but also his utter fascination with blindness. This
lively, loquacious informant gives an obviously fascinated Mayhew several pages of material regarding the life and character of the blind in
general and the London street blind in specific. He confirms some
stereotypes (spirituality and love of music) and counters others (blind
women's inability to keep house). He also offers an interesting description of the street blind as a warm and hospitable community, and
glimpses of what could be called blind culture. From his perspective,
"The blind people in the streets mostly know one another; they say they
have all a feeling of brotherly love for each other, owing to their being
similarly afflicted" (1:398).[4]

The bootlace seller's greatest contribution to Mayhew, however, is his
account of his life as a beggar. Most disabled interviewees define themselves against the beggar (of necessity, as this is the identity most likely to
be clapped on them). The bird-seller would rather be twice as lame, than
beg; the nutmeg-grater seller would rather starve. The bootlace seller, in
contrast, details his "fall" into mendicancy with what I can only call
enthusiasm. After fifteen years successfully gathering and selling coal, he
decided to "shake a loose leg" after a conflict with his father. Contacts at
the low lodging-houses persuaded him to use his blindness to make a living; over time he became, as Mayhew puts it, "heart and soul, an
ingrained beggar" (1:407). Now he perambulates the streets of London,

"selling" bootlaces as a cover story for begging. It is a life he calls "dreadful slavery," but one that makes him "a comfortable living—always a little bit in debt" (1:399).

The bootlace seller's acumen as a professional object of charity in many ways confirms him as exactly the kind of person the COS blind registers were designed to thwart. He demonstrates a prodigious memory for the names, addresses, and pensioning habits of upper-class Londoners, and he himself receives several small pensions despite his begging (in theory, a disqualification). His skill at tapping the flows of systematic and casual charity establishes him as much too capable to be an "acceptable" beggar.[5] In terms of his relationship to emotion, however, the bootlace seller confounds the stereotype of a beggar/impostor. In the first place, a really scandalous beggar would seem by Victorian cultural definition a creature devoid of feelings, who cheats pity and alms from others, and eventually hardens their hearts toward even the deserving poor through his abuse of the charitable compact and its emotional dynamic. The worst beggar the middle-class charitable reformer can imagine feels neither affliction nor gratitude, only greed and malicious amusement.

The blind bootlace seller, however, seems to confirm his own description of the blind as "persons of great feeling" (1:401). His accounts of his first travels as a beggar are fervently emotional (albeit toward an unorthodox object). The narrative is suffused with a sense of naive delight, attractive enough to make it an advertisement for begging:

> You see I'd never had no pleasure, and it seemed to me like a new world—to be able to get victuals without doing anything. . . . I didn't think the country was half so big, and you couldn't credit the pleasure I felt in going about it. . . . [at one lodging-house] I found upwards of sixty or seventy, all tramps, and living in different ways, pattering, and thieving, and singing, and all sorts; and that night I got to think it was the finest scene I had ever known. I grew pleaseder, and pleaseder, with the life, and wondered how any one could follow any other. There was no drunkenness, but it was so new and strange, and I'd never known nothing of life before, that I was bewildered, like, with over-joy at it.

In terms of more "appropriate" responses, he weeps while recounting the death of his dog and is "affected, even to speechlessness, at the remembrance of his family troubles." He is similarly moved by Mayhew's stories of other disabled street-sellers (1:406).

Even more provocatively, the bootlace seller's feelings extend beyond what we might call his "personal" life (part of what makes him so fascinating is the lack of separation between his personal and business feelings). His appreciation of the emotional capital of blindness is not only businesslike and distanced, but *also* fervently engaged. His attitude towards his pattering lamentation (one of the tools in the trade of a professional "afflicted child") exemplifies this doubleness. The lament itself, as the man delivers it to Mayhew, is a combination of avowed feeling and professional notes:

You feeling Christians look with pity,
    Unto my grief relate—
Pity my misfortune,
    For my sufferings are great.
I'm bound in dismal darkness—
    A prisoner I am led;
Poor and blind, just in my prime,
    Brought to beg my bread.

When in my pleasant youthful days
    In learning I took delight,
(and when I was in the country I used to say)
And by the small-pox
    I lost my precious sight.
(some says by an inflammation)

I've lost all earthly comforts,
    But since it is God's will,
The more I cannot see the day,
    He'll be my comfort still.
In vain I have sought doctors,
    Their learned skill did try,
But they could not relieve me,
    Nor spare one single eye.

So now in dismal darkness
    For ever more must be,
To spend my days in silent tears
    Till death doth set me free.

But had I all the treasures
    That decks an Indian shore,
Was all in my possession,
    I'd part with that wealthy store,
If I once more could gain my sight,
    And when could gladly view
That glorious light to get my bread,
    And work once more like you.

Return you, tender Christians dear,
    And pity my distress;
Relieve a helpless prisoner,
    That's blind and comfortless.
I hope that Christ, our great Redeemer,
    Your kindness will repay,
And reward you with a blessing
    On the judgment day.

                                                        (1:399)


This is a performance of affliction, presented in exactly the terms that will elicit sympathy without suspicion. As in the document produced by the School for the Indigent Blind, blindness is constructed as a "dark and benighted state, for which no relief can be found on this side of the grave" (*School* n.p.). The *disinterest* in money that seems, ironically, so central to the charitable exchange is displayed as well; the beggar would give untold riches only to see *and work*. At the same time, he has something substantial to transfer to the benevolent donor, his own intimacy with God.

Much of this, of course, contradicts what we have heard of the man's real feelings. He is anything but dismal, devoid of earthly comforts, or desirous of traditional work. At the same time, his comment that the lamentation is "a very feeling thing" is impossible to view with irony alone, when it seems so heartfelt: "Many people stands still and hears it right through, and gives a halfpenny. I'd give one myself any day to hear it well said. I'm sure the first time I heard it the very flesh crept on my bones" (1:399).

Further, as Mayhew's remarks confirm, the bootlace seller's awareness that he is manipulating public emotions for gain has not hardened him to the pleas—or manipulations—of others:

there was, amid the degradation that necessarily comes of habitual mendicancy, a fine expression of sympathy, that the better class of poor always exhibit toward the poor; nor could I help wondering when I heard *him*—the professed mendicant—tell me how he had been moved to tears by the recital of the sufferings of another mendicant—sufferings that might have been as profitable a stock in trade to the one as his blindness was to the other; though it is by no means unusual for objects of charity to have *their* objects of charity, and to be imposed upon by fictitious or exaggerated tales of distress, almost as often as they impose upon others by the very same means. (1:407–8)

Finally unable to categorize the bootlace seller as either an innocent afflicted child or a reviled begging impostor, in spite of his practices, Mayhew presents the man as a sort of demonic child,

a strange compound of cunning and good feeling; at one moment . . . weeping over the afflictions of others . . . the next minute . . . grinning behind his hand, so that his laughter might be concealed from me, in a manner that appeared almost fiendish. (1:407)

The bootlace seller is among the very cheeriest of Mayhew's disabled interviewees. Of all of them, he seems the only one whose relationship with popular stereotypes of blindness has an expansive, not constrictive, effect on his sense of self. Unconcerned with hiding his manipulations of the charity system, he is equally unconcerned with checking the credentials of those who appeal to him. His business is to embody both the beggar and the child, and yet he is neither of these figures; he occupies multiple positions within the emotional economy of disability, weeping freely and making others weep, receiving alms and passing them on. Rather than resisting either emotionally charged figure, he embraces both and puts them to work.

## Middle-Class People with Disabilities

Like *London Labour*'s interviews, life writing by and about middle-class people with physical disabilities alternately authenticates and rebuts the melodramatic stereotypes by which their culture identified them. The

"The Blind Boot-lace Seller," from *London Labour and the London Poor*, vol. 1 (1861–62). Photo courtesy of Dartmouth Medical School Photography and Illustration.

middle-class people I discuss devoted much of their lives to reestablishing disability in material, not emotional terms—advocating for better training and employment, disseminating practical information to other disabled people, and speaking out against "Apostles of Despair" who brought an elegiac mode to discussions of blindness (Holt 69). In contrast to most of Mayhew's interviewees, who were often of necessity "performing affliction" in the eyes of the nondisabled people on whose charitable support they depended, the four middle-class people addressed Victorian constructions of disability directly, in print and in speech.

The middle-class disabled people's responses to the "afflicted child" construction of disability are complex. All four, for the most part, vocally resist the idea that disability produces a physical and moral incapacity to work. One of the notable differences between nondisabled and disabled people's comments on disability is in precisely that realm; Gilbert, for example, specifically constructed disability in social rather than individual terms, and made training and employment the centerpiece of her activism for other blind people. Blind workers, she asserted, bore the burden of "peculiar disadvantages *in obtaining employment*" (Martin 100; emphasis added). The workers her association sponsored affirmed this socioeconomic construction of disability. They wrote that "our Heavenly Father has placed in [Gilbert's] hands the deliverance of the blind from *the worst of their afflictions, namely the Sting of Poverty*" (Martin 103; emphasis added).

Martineau, Kitto, Fawcett, and Gilbert's own working lives attested to the utter inappropriateness of a construction of disability as either incapacity or misery, notwithstanding the fact that all four experienced chronic illnesses as well. While they had far greater financial, educational, and social opportunities than Mayhew's interviewees, all but Gilbert were obliged to work, and all four were in fact tireless workers whose ambitions were directed at contributing meaningful action to the world they inhabited. Further, while they may have had (or, in Kitto's case, made themselves) access to working contexts that were not irretrievably at odds with the place their culture assigned them as disabled people—writing, for example, was a profession in which both gender and disability could be revealed or concealed at the author's discretion—they also all worked in ways that engaged both physical and social discomforts. Fawcett and Gilbert deliberately extended their work into the realms of teaching, politics, and public service, in which gender and class ideologies produced their own messages about the appropriateness of blind gentlemen and ladies "obtruding" themselves into public life. Martineau arguably did this as well, especially in terms of her willingness to write boldly on controversial subjects. Kitto journeyed to the Middle East, including in his writings a history of Palestine and travel books for children. While none was glorified in popular culture in the mode of Milton, the mathematician Saunders, or (in our time) Christopher Reeve, all were public figures to the extent that it is still possible to trace some of the substantial work they achieved.

Despite all these people did to displace disabled stereotypes with material truths, the figure of the afflicted child haunts texts by and about them nearly as much as it does *London Labour and the London Poor*. Biographical texts suggest the dynamics of this haunting, how friends and the larger public, for example, constructed the lives of Henry Fawcett and Elizabeth Gilbert. The various strategies middle-class disabled people used to negotiate the imperative to *be* that emotionally legible figure document the difficulty of producing counternarratives to disabled stereotypes. They underscore how significant it is that disabled Victorians of all classes did produce such narratives, making use of the limited identities available to them and even deriving authority from what would seem the most diminishing of cultural scripts.

## Harriet Martineau

Harriet Martineau (1802–1876) was arguably the nineteenth century's most prominent woman writer of prose nonfiction, especially on the controversial subject of political economy and other social issues. As well as her twenty-five-volume *Illustrations of Political Economy* (1832–34), Martineau published extensively in journals and newspapers, as well as producing travel writing and fiction. Her writing on embodiment includes "Letter to the Deaf" (1834), *Life in the Sickroom* (1844), the novel *Deerbrook* (1839), and her autobiography, written in 1855 and published in 1877.

The causes of Martineau's deafness are unclear. Her mother attributed it to a wet-nurse's insufficient breast milk; Martineau herself says it was "seriously aggravated by nervous excitement, at the age when I lived in revere and vanities of the imagination" but only became noticeable as "a very slight, scarcely-perceptible hardness of hearing" at age twelve. By the time she was sixteen, however, her impairment became "very notice-

**Harriet Martineau. Portrait by Margaret Gillies, reproduced by permission of the Armitt Trust.**

able, very inconvenient, and excessively painful to myself," and at age eighteen, it was "suddenly and severely increased by a sort of accident . . . largely ascribable to disobedience to the laws of nature" (1:55, 441).

In her "Letter to the Deaf," Martineau offers a brief account of her own experiences and a guide to negotiating the hearing world, written for other deaf people. The letter's announced occasion is the desire to help "fellow-sufferers" with the "discipline" of deafness, through which Martineau's own hearing loss "has become, from being an almost intolerable grievance, so much less of one . . . than such a deprivation usually is" (248). One of the guiding principles of this discipline is a resolution to reconstruct deafness in frank and material terms rather than in either delicate silence or emotional speech:

> We must destroy the sacredness of the subject, by speaking of it ourselves; not perpetually and sentimentally, but, when occasion rises, boldly, cheerfully, and as a plain matter of fact. When every body about us gets to treat it as a matter of fact, our daily difficulties are almost gone; and when we have to do with strangers, the simple, cheerful declaration, "I am very deaf," removes almost all trouble. (252)

As she elaborates her program, however, it is laden with discomfort and boredom. After reiterating the familiar idea that deaf people are miserable in society, Martineau seems to advocate that they subject themselves to this misery, for the sake of hearing friends and whatever crumbs of *unsolicited* attention and affection are tossed their way:

> To give the least possible pain to others is the right principle. . . . Social communication must be kept up through all its pain, for the sake of our friends as well as for our own. . . . Society is the very last thing to be given up; but it must be sought . . . under a bondage of self-denial, which annihilates for a time almost all the pleasure. . . . we must bravely go on taking our place in society.
> Taking our place, I say. What is our place? It is difficult to say. Certainly, not that of chief talker, any more than that of chief listener. . . . We must submit to be usually insignificant, and sometimes ridiculous. (251, 253–54)

Martineau advocates this "bondage of self-denial" as a protection against hearing people's sympathy, which is not only inadequate but also a destructive force, one she theorizes as productive of stereotypical "deaf" behavior:

> [T]enderness is hurtful to us in as far as it encourages us to evade our enemy, instead of grappling with it; to forget our infirmity, from hour to hour, if we can; and to get over the present occasion somehow, without thinking of the next. . . . If we see that the partially deaf are often unscrupulous about truth, inquisitive, irrita-

ble, or morose; suspicious, low-spirited, or ill-mannered, it is owing to this. (250)

The danger of sympathy is its disarming tendency, which in Martineau's eyes leaves deaf people without a constant plan for controlling their lives. On the other hand, the role in society that rewards the self-denying deaf person—ridiculousness, or at least insignificance—is uncomfortably close to the cautionary image of an unpleasant deaf "type" that lurks on the borders of Martineau's advice:

> Have we not seen—it sickens me to think of it—restless, inquisitive, deaf people, who will have every insignificant thing repeated to them, to their own incessant disappointment, and the suffering of every body about them, whom they make, by their appeals, almost as ridiculous as themselves. (256)

In contrast to the figure of the deaf person Martineau produces in this document, and the tone of resignation about her situation, she brings energy and delight to her descriptions of her own solitary struggle with the loss of hearing. Becoming a person who asks for nothing is central to Martineau's discipline of deafness, and her greatest source of power is a plan of rigid self-sufficiency through which a deaf person can reassert control over the experience of physiological and emotional loss. All activities that only a hearing person can monitor—musical performance, for example—must be relinquished; if one of the effects of deafness is an "intellectual perversion" brought about by hearing partial sentences, one must "seize or make opportunities for preserving or rectifying . . . associations" (261). Finally, if some experience is about to be lost, Martineau advocates hastening the loss as a way of gaining a sense of mastery:

> How much less pain there is in calmly estimating the enjoyments from which we must separate ourselves, of bravely saying, for once and for ever, "Let them go," than in feeling them waste and dwindle, till their very shadows escape from our grasp! (258)

There is even, Martineau asserts, some pleasure to be derived from being the author of one's inevitable losses:

The thrill of delight which arises during the ready agreement to profit by pain . . . must subside like all other emotion; but it does not depart without leaving the spirit lightened and cheered; and every visitation leaves it in a more genial state than the last. (259)

Good cheer aside, the idea of something delectable in a confrontation with pain puts the dreary martyrdom of the dutiful deaf companion in an entirely new light.

If the critical process is that of becoming triumphantly self-afflicting rather than passively afflicted, it is of paramount importance to construct deafness as an experience of loss. Despite what Martineau says about the effectiveness of her plan, the descriptions of suffering are still the most evocative passages of the "Letter," as the following passage demonstrates:

[W]e find, at the close of each season, that we are finally parting with something; and that the beginning of each, that we have lost something since the last. We miss first the song of the skylark, and then the distant nightingale, and then one bird after another, till the loud thrush itself seems to have vanished; and we go in the way of every twittering under the eaves, because we know that that will soon be silenced too. (258)

Martineau may say that deafness is best managed by removing it of its sacredness. Her most effective strategy, however, seems to have been to retain all the melodramatic value of deafness while authoring the loss so central to that value. In order to continue to derive power from her triumph over the cataclysm of deafness, she must keep alive the (past) reality of deafness as suffering, but detach that suffering from a disempowering interpersonal dynamic of sympathy suggestive of the charitable transaction.

Martineau's two-volume autobiography is explicitly not the story of her disability:

I did once think of writing down the whole dreary story of the loss of a main sense, like hearing; and I would not now shrink from inflicting the pain of it on others, and on myself, if any adequate benefit could be obtained by it. But, really, I do not think that there could. It is true,—the sufferers rarely receive the comfort of adequate, or even intelligent sympathy: but there is no saying that an elaborate account of the woe would create the sympathy, for practical purposes. (*Autobiography* 1:55)

While deafness is only briefly discussed in the *Autobiography*, those and other passages elaborate the complicated significance Martineau gave her loss of hearing, especially as a touchstone for the complex and ambivalent relationship she had with her family, for her passage to adulthood but not to the traditional roles of wife and mother, and for the role of suffering (which she links with deafness) in the rich imaginative life she sustained from an early age and evocatively articulates in her life writing.

While she asserts that "the special duty of the deaf is . . . to spare other people as much fatigue as possible" (1:95), she gives a more convincing picture of the fatigue of the experience of the deafened person, especially in response to the cruel dynamics of a family responding to impairment:

[T]he family of a person who has a growing infirmity are reluctant to face the truth; and they are apt to inflict terrible pain on the sufferer to relieve their own weakness and uneasiness. First, and for long, [my family] insisted that it was all my own fault,—that I was so absent,—that I never cared to attend to anything that was said,—that I ought to listen this way, or that, or the other; and even (while my heart was breaking) they told me that "none are so deaf as those who won't hear." (1:58)

This unknowing mistreatment is much later, and incompletely, compensated by the tenderness her mother shows her because of her deafness, a recurrent plot paradigm in the *Autobiography* in which Martineau's physical or moral pain (earache, for example, or wrongful accusation) is at length recognized by her mother and soothed with exceptional tenderness. These are passages of highly effective melodrama—the realist mode, as Eric Bentley has observed, of childhood itself (217).

While some of the time she seems to discard and efface the notion of her deafness's significance, the autobiography fairly regularly returns to it as a source of deep meanings. In Martineau's self-diagnosis, her deafness has its genesis within the mesh of passions and terrors of her childhood, the subject of some of the most exciting prose of the life story. When a friend of Martineau's childhood loses her leg and is acclaimed for her courage, Martineau is deeply impressed:

> It turned my imagination far too much on bodily suffering, and on the peculiar glory attending fortitude in that direction. I am sure that my nervous system was seriously injured, and especially that my subsequent deafness was partly occasioned by the exciting and vain-glorious dreams that I indulged in for many years after my friend E. lost her leg. All manner of deaths at the stake and on the scaffold, I went through in imagination, in the low sense in which St. Theresa craved martyrdom; and night after night, I lay bathed in cold perspiration till I sank into the sleep of exhaustion. (1:34)

In Dorothy Mermin's persuasive explication of Martineau's view of her deafness, the affliction is in some sense a sacrifice for the gift of imagination, or punishment for imagination's hubris. In this model, the compensation (or self-indulgence) precedes the affliction (or punishment):

> [I]magination is a self-indulgence paid for with the sacrifice of part of the body. . . . Martineau (at least retrospectively) associates imaginative activity with vanity, an insatiable desire for praise and the esteem of others. . . . Martineau's guilt is marked on her body: in deafness, "cold perspiration," exhaustion.

At the same time, Mermin observes, Martineau "was sure that imagination is the highest human faculty and the most beneficial to humanity" (102).

By proposing that she imagined her way into deafness, Martineau empowers the faculty of imagination, the "affliction" of deafness, and herself as an imaginer. As an adult with a disability, Martineau seems to have extracted the most beneficial aspects of this childhood dream of suffering; rather than trying to minimize the pain that she and the world attribute to her situation, she maximizes the power that can be derived from it. In the place of the cold sweats of childhood, she has the thrilling, spirit-lightening experience of authoring her affliction.

And yet, at the point of writing her autobiography in her early fifties,

Martineau has mixed feelings about this construction of deafness. She looks cautiously and critically at this relationship between both aesthetic and Christian narratives of embodiment (the stimulated body; the body transformed by pain and illness) and authorship. Having had many years to examine the relationship, she rejects, as Regenia Gagnier observes, "the romantic myth of inspiration stimulated by either natural or artificial causes" (218). She also rejects the Christian mythology of suffering and power that seems to underwrite much of her work, condemning religious tracts that

> describe the sufferings of illness, and generate vanity and egotism about bodily pain and early death,—rendering these disgraces of our ignorance and barbarism attractive to the foolish and vain, and actually shaming the wholesome, natural desire for "a sound mind in a sound body." . . . every book . . . which sets forth a sickroom as a condition of honour, blessing, and moral safety, helps to sustain a delusion and corruption which have already cost the world too dear. I know too much of all this from my own experience to choose to do anything towards encouragement of the morbid appetite for pathological contemplation,—physical or moral. (*Autobiography* 1:440–41)

While she maintains that her own problematic body was made so largely by her own and others' "disobedience to the laws of nature," Martineau is aware and anxious about her own tendency to transform it from a sign of disobedience to a glorification, especially in print, already the source of public praise about which she is equally ambivalent (1:441). Gagnier has argued that

> women's anxiety concerning self-representation decreases in proportion to [their] participation in other discourse, such as that of religion, family, or human rights, and increases in proportion to women's desire to participate in the male romantic tradition of autonomous genius. (217)

In Martineau's autobiography, what complicates self-representation—especially in terms of representing her disabilities—is her critical awareness of the nuances and consequences of any discourse that enfolds or abuts her writing.[6]

## John Kitto

John Kitto (1804–1854), a stonemason's son and autodidact, was a well-known religious writer and an honorary doctor of divinity, as well as a published poet. Like Martineau, Kitto engages his deafness as a key spur within his coming of age as a writer, and a means of self-authorization. His disability story also emerges, like hers, from an overtly melodramatic and apparently self-effacing narrative.

*The Lost Senses* is a cultural history of deafness *and* blindness, and the latter section is similar in structure and content to Levy's book. The first section, however, is substantially about Kitto's own deafening at age twelve, his management of deafness, and his discovery of his life's work. He justifies this autobiography as something the dearth of biographies of deaf people necessitates (a situation I can confirm). His life story, however, goes completely counter to almost everything he says about the generality of deaf people.

Kitto's representation of deafness, including deaf people's ability to work, is fairly gloomy. From the very start he characterizes himself as a "sufferer" from deafness, "one who has the chief entrance to his inner being closed" and whose eyesight is "the only avenue to the soul. . . . the delicate faculty which alone lies between him and moral death" (19, 46–47). The radical otherness of the deaf person is something to which he emphatically subscribes, even to the point of asserting that deaf people should avoid all but the smallest and most domestic social situations. Like Martineau, he fixes on the dinner party as a scene of especial difficulty for a person who does not hear and asserts that

> it is surely a social duty in the deaf to avoid company, in the assurance that by going into it, or gathering it around him, he is only a stumbling-block to the pleasure of others, and is only laying up for himself a store of mortification and of regret for those terrible disqualifications which, in the solitude of his chamber, or in the presence of his trained domestic circle, he may half forget. (117)

In what seems a cruel stroke, though certainly in line with popular stereotypes, Kitto does not even allot deaf people the compensation of a rich intellectual life; they are not simply devoid of the poetical tendencies of blind people, but intellectually inferior to the blind. For these reasons—and here Kitto goes against the grain of popular belief—he con-

John Kitto, from an engraving reprinted in W. H. K. Wright, *West-Country Poets: Their Lives and Works* (1896). Photo courtesy of University of California–San Diego Medical School Office of Learning Resources.

siders deafness a much worse affliction than blindness, as well as radical disqualification from work:

> In much of that in which lieth the great strength of man, [the deaf person] is impotent; for the great race of life, he is maimed; and his daily walk is beset with petty humiliations, which bear down his

spirit by the consciousness, which he is never allowed to forget, that his is, in one most essential respect,

"Inferior to the vilest now become."

(64)

Speaking in more material terms, he asserts that deafness presents a serious bar to all trades, all professions, and most handicrafts. Handicrafts might in theory present an opportunity for a deaf person, "through the occasional help and ever-ready sympathy . . . workmen are apt to show—at any expense of time or labor—towards an afflicted brother." In practice, however, even if one could pay the necessary premium, "who would readily encumber himself with a deaf apprentice, when he might have a choice of those in full possession of all their senses?" (66).

As Kitto delineates these disqualifications, they are the result of a combination of hearing impairment, socioeconomic status, and public prejudice, but he offers no suggestions for improving any factor in the mix. Instead, having amassed this onerous heap of obstacles to a deaf person's employment, Kitto concludes that

> the utmost usefulness to which one in this position could feasibly aspire, would be that of redeeming himself from entire uselessness by doing *something* towards his own maintenance; and this alone would be so difficult as . . . to become a great and meritorious achievement. (67)

All these remarks are strangely at odds with the evidence of Kitto's own life. Despite his warnings about social life, he describes not only several satisfying relationships with hearing friends (as well as with his wife and family) but also numerous interactions with total strangers in the course of his world travels. He is not simply a success, but famous in a field his book suggests is inhospitable to deaf people, given their supposedly limited intellectualism and lack of "poetical tendencies" (*The Lost Senses* even includes a selection of Kitto's poetry). It is only when we look at the section on deafness as an autobiography of Kitto's disability, and not as the general account it claims to be, that the incongruities seem purposeful rather than absurd.

As Kitto tells it, his story is first and last an account of a father's injury to his son. The father's neglect of his paternal duty originates the chain

of events that lead to the son's fall from a ladder at age twelve and subsequent deafness. He is "a jobbing mason, of precarious employment,"
who deprives Kitto of a solid education through his "inability or *reluctance*
to stand the cost of [his] schooling" and puts him to the work that is the
site of his deafening (11; emphasis added). On the day of Kitto's "down-
fall," as he later calls it, he is preoccupied by thoughts of three things: a
popular book the town crier promised to lend him; a new, adult "smock-
frock" his grandmother is making for him (a garment he likens to a
"toga virilis"); and a young acquaintance's autopsy, taking place in the
very house at which he is working (10). As he carries a load of roof-tiles
to the house, he sees

> a stream of blood . . . flowing through the gutter. . . . The idea that
> this was the blood of the dead youth, whom I had so lately seen
> alive, and that the doctors were then at work cutting him up and
> groping at his inside, made me shudder, and gave what I should
> now call a shock to my nerves. . . . I cannot but think it was owing
> to this that I lost much of the presence of mind and collectedness
> so important to me at that moment; for when I had ascended to
> the top of the ladder, and was in the critical act of stepping from
> it on to the roof, I lost my footing, and fell backward, from a
> height of about thirty-five feet, into the paved court below.

Kitto's only moment of consciousness for the subsequent fortnight is
of his "father, attended by a crowd of people . . . bearing me homeward
in his arms." When he next awakes, he is deaf. The narrative continues,
telling in detail the medical (and social) treatment Kitto received after
his accident (13).

This enigmatic and troubling narrative is marked by the violence of
the scene (both inside and outside Kitto's consciousness), by Kitto's
veiled recriminations of his father (and the father's disappearance from
the story, once he has carried his son home), and by the absence of any
information about the rest of the family. However indirectly and sugges-
tively told, the narrative coheres as one of a father wounding a son on
the verge of manhood. The slow process by which Kitto's father's
deficiencies erode his son's health, education, and prospects is focused
and made concrete in the adjacent image of the autopsy—a violent,
bloody invasion into another young man's corpse.

Significantly, the son's last memory on this day of loss for which "there is no recovery, no adequate compensation" is of his father finally behaving as he should (11). In terms of a melodrama, this is a classic example of justice, or rescue, or love arriving after it is too late to effect anything but a melancholy, "if only—" sort of pleasure. Even worse, the long-term result of deafening seems to be more neglect; Kitto constructs it as the cause of his having to pursue his education without any appreciation or support (77).

The next part of the autobiography, given in fullest form in the chapter "Disqualifications," contains not only the trials of this "poor and deaf boy, in his utter loneliness, devoting himself to objects in which none around him could sympathize, and to pursuits that none could even understand," but also his eventual triumph in literary studies. Kitto subjects himself to a terrible and necessary ordeal, following twelve hours of labor with as much study as he can manage:

> To come home weary and sleepy, and then to have only for mental sustenance the moments which by self-imposed tortures could be torn from needful rest, was a sore trial. . . . thus, without any encouragement of praise or approbation . . . the good most suited to my condition, [was] found. (70)

This time of torment is something Kitto now calls "the turning point of my career." His literary studies not only provided a sense that "the door of exclusion was unlocked," but gave Kitto a perspective he specifically describes in terms of power:

> I had, in fact, learned the secret, that knowledge is power; and if, as is said, all power is sweet; then, surely, that power which knowledge gives, is of all others the sweetest. And not only was it power, but safety. It had already procured for me redress of wrongs which seemed likely to crush my spirit; and thus bestowed upon me the gratifying, I had almost said proud, consciousness, of having secured a means of defence against that state of utter helplessness and dependence upon others, which had seemed to be my lot in life. (71)

The curious thing about this wonderfully melodramatic story of affliction, suffering, and triumph is that the compensation of the found career seems to loom large and satisfying—and to have no effect at all.

Kitto's childhood extends far beyond its proper place in the chronology of his life; beyond establishing the terms on which Kitto came to be deaf, it grounds every later part of his narrative in the stereotype of the afflicted child as well. Thus his general condition is one of suffering, social exclusion, even moral isolation. He has "few joys and many sorrows," despite numerous anecdotes to the contrary. Despite Kitto's claim that he is now "another being, having but slight connection . . . with my former self," his self-representation comprises the child whose suffering still angers him, alongside the triumphant writer who succeeded that child (68).

This strange melodramatic mix of misery and triumph, however, has a clear narrative purpose. Kitto introduces *The Lost Senses* as a pilgrim's report from an unexplored country, even a "record of a condition of which no sufferer has yet rendered an account," an advertisement that is not entirely accurate (9). He feels obliged to tell his story before he dies because of its singularity and extremity: not only has he passed most of his life in "the most intense DEAFNESS to which any living creature can be subjected," but even more importantly, he has risen from that affliction to become a success. As Kitto puts it, "[A] morning of life subject to such crushing calamity has seldom, if ever, been followed by a day of such self-culture . . . and of such active exertion" (9).

In order for his narrative to retain its miraculous quality, it seems to require the ground of utter affliction, even after the triumph has occurred. His success seems to have been achieved, as he insists, without reference to his disability; but his story, like Martineau's (and reminiscent of charitable appeals for schools for the blind or deaf), relies on the extremity of his deafness and misery. The pessimistic remarks on deafness in general, likewise, are in service to the story of Kitto's affliction at the hands of his feckless earthly father and his compensation in a career whereby his "pen became the instrument of redressing that wrong" (71). Kitto's repeated self-construction in terms of *blind* stereotypes rather than deaf ones contributes to the power of this narrative as well, helping to establish him both as someone with "poetical tendencies" and as a poetical subject in himself (deafness is much less often constructed as a "poetical" subject in Victorian culture). It is hardly incidental that Kitto's self-construction is frequently a self-Miltonization.

Kitto's narrative invites psychoanalytic or sociological analysis. Either of these, however, constructs Kitto as primarily an incomplete or damaged person—a conflicted, Oedipally constricted adult or a disabled person at the mercy of the culture. A more productive line of inquiry might be to consider what Kitto gets out of *retaining* (rather than failing to resolve or reject) both suffering and triumph. In a world in which a deaf person's sources of authority or empowerment are extremely limited, the identity of colossal sufferer is hardly one to discount. If one can stretch this "dispensation of Providence" to include a triumphal finish as well (and on Earth, no less), so much the better (Kitto 68). In the emotional economy of disability, Kitto creates a magical version of double-entry bookkeeping in which deafness is an extreme loss, a moral blight, a professional disqualification—*and* a triumphal compensation here on Earth, that which pulled him from the ranks of the artisan class and led him to the work for which God intended him. Both loss and compensation, moreover, are valuable sources of power and authority.

## *Henry Fawcett*

Henry Fawcett (1833–1884) was a Cambridge professor of political economy and a Liberal MP who became the postmaster general of England; his work in the Post Office, as well as that in regard to the preservation of commons, was celebrated in the pages of *Punch* and among working-class groups and the memorials produced at his death included one in Westminster Abbey. Because he wrote no autobiography, Fawcett's representations of his experience of blindness are mediated by other writers' narrative frames: Sir Leslie Stephen's biography of Fawcett, who was his close friend, with references also in Millicent Garrett Fawcett's memoir *What I Remember* (1924) and Winifred Holt's biography of Fawcett, *A Beacon for the Blind* (1915). What emerges from each of these individual texts, and even more clearly from their combined production of the meanings of one man's life, is a continual tension between an individual and a figure. Fawcett, as his biographers all create him, was a man of great practical intelligence, exceptional for his tall stature and ease in his own body, his ebullient energy and love of outdoor sport, his sociability and great charisma, and the ethical tenor of all his ambitions. In the same characterization are threads of anxiety about an equally ambitious and charismatic wife, Millicent Garrett Fawcett, to whom Fawcett was devoted. Almost on a line-by-line basis, however, a blind figure—of speech, but also, inevitably, of an embodied self—enters all three texts to truncate, qualify, and more or less ignore the par-

Henry Fawcett in 1855, from an engraving by Joseph Brown reprinted in Leslie Stephen, *Life of Henry Fawcett*, 5th ed. (1886). Photo courtesy of University of California–San Diego Medical School Office of Learning Resources.

ticulars of the man's life, and summarize all of it within a master frame of blindness.

The fact that the chapter "Blindness" disrupts the orderly chronology of Stephen's *Life of Henry Fawcett* (1886) bespeaks blindness as a condition so radical that it must be considered "outside" the rest of one's life—so powerful that it explodes one's history (one of the curious narrative results is that Fawcett dies twice, the first time in only the second chapter of his biography). In keeping with this structural message, while Stephen's overt stance is that of sophisticated insider—someone qualified to tell the story of Fawcett's resistance to his other friends' naive attempts to make him into an afflicted child—the story to which he seems most drawn is in fact an emotional and melodramatic one.

The fact that his memoir postdates Fawcett's death by only two years is a clear factor in its emotional tenor; the details of Henry Fawcett's accident, furthermore, comprise an emotionally compelling plot both reminiscent of and sharply distinct from Kitto's story, almost like the same plot set in different class contexts. During a hunting outing with his father, who had a cataract beginning in one eye, Fawcett moved out of view; Mr. Fawcett aimed at a bird and shot his son. A pellet of shot passed through each lens of Henry's eyeshades and then through the eyes themselves, lodging permanently behind them. The father's injury to his son was made all the sadder by the fact that this was, according to Stephen, a particularly intimate and healthy relationship, "[a]nd now it seemed that the father's hand had ruined the son's brilliant prospects" (46). To add to the poignancy, the accident took place on a lovely hillside with a vista of the Avon River valley; "Fawcett's first thought, as he told his sister, was that he should never again see the view which he had just been admiring in the light of a lovely autumn afternoon" (43).

This seems to be the last time Fawcett himself publicly acknowledges the sense of loss that plays such a central role in most narratives of disability. He engages this and other conventions of "affliction" with dogged resistance:

> "Nothing," he said [in a speech thirty-three years after the accident] "pained him so much as the letters he received after the accident." The reason, as I gather, was that the letters fell into the ordinary form, and consisted of well-meaning exhortations to resignation, assuming that his life was ruined, though somehow or other, the ruin was to be a blessing! (Stephen 47)

As Stephen represents it, most of Fawcett's friends advocated resignation to a diminished life, advice Stephen critiques on Fawcett's behalf, commenting that "the question remains, what is inevitable? How distinguish between cheerful acceptance of the dictates of fate or Providence and the cowardly abnegation of duty under apparent difficulty?" (47). Fawcett had resolved, in the first ten minutes after his blinding, "to stick to his pursuits as much as possible," a resolution he translated into a successful attempt to become a member of Parliament (44). His daily version of "sticking to his pursuits" seems to have involved massive denial of his blindness, particularly in terms of conversations with other people. He told one friend, for example "he wanted to see the Clarendon Woods, as he understood that the autumn tints were especially fine this year," and commented on how old another was looking, adding, "but when men with hair of that colour turn grey, they do look prematurely old." Stephen explains this "startling" manner of speaking as "part of his system of behaving in his blindness as much as possible as he behaved when he could see" (60). He advised other blind people to follow this same strategy: "Do what you can to act as though you were not blind" (68).

The method produced certain social strains. While Fawcett spoke frequently on behalf of agencies for the blind, "he shrank from such efforts" and always felt extreme nervousness while speaking, in apparent contrast to his experience at the House of Commons. As Stephen explains it,

[H]e no doubt felt the difficulty of citing his own case without appearing in the attitude, most painful to him, of one putting forward a plea for compassion; or in the attitude, only less disagreeable, of one who is making a boast of his own courage. (68)

While Fawcett's avoidance of an identity as a blind person may have enabled him to elide such limitations, Stephen ultimately reinscribes them in this posthumous biography. With one hand he describes Fawcett's resistance to being either patronized or lionized; with the other, he lionizes and patronizes, as in the following passage:

Blind, poor, unknown, he would force his way into the House of Commons. . . . I must ask my readers hereafter to bear in mind what his courageous cheerfulness often tended to make us forget—the fact that everything I have to say of him is said of a blind man. (52–53)

Stephen's final representation of Fawcett emphasizes his identity with the popular stereotype of the gentle, grateful, afflicted child:

[M]isfortune . . . mellowed and sweetened his nature, and strengthened the tenderness which at all times underlay his masculine courage, by making every little service, given or received, a new bond in the great web of kindly attachments . . . Fawcett's friendship always seemed to be blended with gratitude. (72)

Like the Fawcett family, who kept the punctured eyeshades at their home, Stephen retains—fondly, it seems—the sadness of the accident throughout his discussion of the prominence and pleasure Henry Fawcett achieved.

While Millicent Garrett Fawcett's memoir says almost nothing about Henry Fawcett's blindness, the fact of his happy marriage to one of the most important women of the century has a particular and persuasive narrative pull worth mentioning. For modern scholars of the Victorian period, or indeed, for anyone whose cultural education in the meanings of gender relations and blindness has included Charlotte Brontë's 1847 novel *Jane Eyre,* the happy seventeen-year marriage between two people passionate for politics and temperamentally compatible in all life activities but fishing evokes one of the best-loved feminist texts of disability and gender equality.

As the thesis goes, the temporary blinding of the novel's arrogant hero Rochester is what facilitates his happy marriage to Jane by making their relationship more democratic (Gilbert and Gubar 368–69). Henry Fawcett was already blind—as well as a Cambridge professor and an MP—when he met Millicent Garrett (1847–1929), who would become a well-known suffragist, political economist, and writer. While it is engaging to theorize that his experience of social disenfranchisement may have encouraged Henry Fawcett's feminism and support of his wife's work, assuming blindness was the key influence on his gender politics is risky, and one unsubstantiated by his wife. Their meeting, at a party in 1865 hosted by a radical MP, was occasioned by Millicent's reaction to the death of Abraham Lincoln, which the eighteen-year-old characterized as a greater single loss to the world than "the loss of any of the crowned heads of Europe" (54). Henry Fawcett immediately asked his hostess to introduce them. They were married in 1867 and spent their lives between London and Cambridge, enjoying a busy social life with the other political and intellectual figures of their time. Henry advocated equal rights for women before ever meeting Millicent; he supported her activism and urged her to write and publish.

While Millicent Fawcett has much to say about her husband, she has little to say about his blindness, specifically leaving that aspect of his life to Winifred Holt's earlier biography. While that volume is probably the fullest description available of Henry Fawcett's life, incorporating much of Stephen's biography but also including more personal anecdotes from people who knew him, it is a fully mediated life text, given that Holt herself did not know Fawcett. It is also clearly a work of imaginative prose, in which Holt creates from her sources passages like this, whose construction of Fawcett mixes popular beliefs about blind people's sensual connection to nature and details from an individual life:

> He loved the smells of spring, and seemed to feel the pushing and striving in the dank earth and to divine the fragrance about to burst forth. Like a giant lizard he revelled and basked in the heat of the summer sun, and rejoiced in the contrast of the cool shadow beneath the heavy-laden trees, the smell of the hot grass and of fully opened fragrant flowers, and the sedate "brum" of the bourgeois bumble-bee. (126)

Even were each strand of the mix not inescapably implicated in the other, it would be impossible to establish the source of this odd and engaging reptilian moment, nor assess its "accuracy," and the same is true of much of the book.

As well as stock passages building Fawcett into a saintly "beacon" and speculating about whether "either Miss Keller or Fawcett, without their spur from blindness, without that need of iron determination and unflinching pluck to win their race in the dark, would, as seeing people, have attained their respective distinction and have been such great servants of humanity," Holt's biography offers substantial detail about Fawcett's public and private life, narrated in an easy and enjoyable style (65). It also presents a chronological map of Fawcett's gradual inroads against various cultural barriers that affected blind people, from the belief that they could not or should not engage in sport (Fawcett was an avid and, according to Holt, sometimes reckless sportsman who loved ice-skating, riding, and fishing) to the belief that they could not be effective statesmen, all told in the form of lively, richly suggestive anecdotes. When his friends proposed him for membership in the Reform Club, for example, the committee

> was loath to admit a blind man. It was felt that he would be helpless and in the way. . . . He received the news with entire good

humour and calmness. . . . But the attitude of Thackeray, who was a member of the club, was quite different; he felt the ruling was outrageous, and said so, exclaiming "It is ridiculous—if Mr. Fawcett is only brought into the dining-room or the library every one of us there will forget that he is blind, and he will find his way about without any difficulty." (Holt 127)

This story, like many others in the book, informs us both about the content of resistance—fear of people being "helpless and in the way"—and about the terms of acceptance: "every one of us there will forget that he is blind." The shape of this plot characterizes other moments in Holt's biography as well as moments in many other stories about disability. It completely elides, for example, the possibility of accepting Fawcett *as* blind, engaging that fact with an unpredictable mix of remembering and forgetting, and framing blindness as, whatever else it might be, a combination of the human universals of dependence and independence.

This engaging life narrative can leave us completely in thrall to Holt's Henry Fawcett, but even less sure of where to locate, much less pursue, the question of how he "really" felt about his blindness. One intertextual moment illustrates how problematic it is to represent any life, particularly those lives in which the personal is especially marked as "always already" the cultural. The only area in which Henry Fawcett seems have faltered in his support of Millicent was in the case of her desire to climb the Swiss Alp Monte Rosa. Millicent writes that Henry, usually "completely cheerful," was out of spirits in "a place where hardly anything but external beauty and grandeur were spoken of" and experienced "a fever of anxiety" while she climbed with one of their friends (103–4). Placed side by side with what Stephen says about Henry Fawcett's concerted engagement of sighted, externalist rhetorics, Millicent Fawcett's remarks suggest that while his personality may indeed have "carried him for the most part light-heartedly over the inevitable privations of blindness" (57), some of the light-heartedness may have been a performance dictated by gender and ableism, carried out at a personal emotional cost these same dictates forced him to keep private.

This anecdote is even more interesting, however, read next to Holt's biography, which asserts that Fawcett "loved great heights and mountains" and was an enthusiastic climber himself, asking his fellow climbers to describe the views. Further, Holt's biography tells of an earlier incident in which Millicent fell from a horse and lost consciousness, and

Fawcett "could not be convinced that her stupor was not death, and that his friends were not deceiving him. The grief and uncontrollable weeping of the big man were infinitely touching" (133). This context suggests a very different frame for Fawcett's anxiety in the Alps: that of a husband passionately devoted to his wife, logically concerned about her safety during an Alpine climb and pressured beyond logic by an unforgettable prior trauma.

Ultimately, the question of who can supply the authoritative view of Henry Fawcett cannot be resolved. While my own bias is to read Millicent Garrett Fawcett's words as the closest to Henry's own experience, this is obviously a dangerous assumption. What is hardest to "read" about Henry Fawcett is the kind of effort his performance of "normalcy" required.

The most interesting facet of the textual life of Henry Fawcett, generalizable to the larger question of how culture narrates disability, is precisely this failed fit of narrative pieces and the ability of nineteenth-century and modern British culture to absorb Fawcett's material life, achievements, and physical presence without altering its idea of blindness at all. It should have been impossible to affirm affliction and dependence as the master narrative of blindness, given the apparent facts about a particularly lovable, energetic, and capable person. While his strengths combined made him exceptional, each one of those strengths seems to have fallen within the "normal" range of human experience; in other words, he was a particularly good example of what a person can do if he has reasonable access and accommodation. Yet the figure of a blind man as afflicted child, burdened by personal tragedy or overcoming it to achieve an unthinkable personal triumph, inhabits the biographies without being dislodged by the life they chronicle.

### Elizabeth Gilbert

Elizabeth Gilbert (1826–1884), founder of the Association for Promoting of the General Welfare of the Blind, is one of the few nineteenth-century disabled activists whose work is acknowledged by twentieth-century histories; unlike Fawcett, she did not attempt to bracket this aspect of her life in relation to its other parts, but rather used her work to define her life. In fitting contrast to Leslie Stephen's compartmentalization of Fawcett's blindness within his biography, the entirety of Frances Martin's

Elizabeth Gilbert, from an engraving by Sir William Boxall reprinted in Frances Martin, *Elizabeth Gilbert and Her Work for the Blind* (1886). Photo courtesy of University of California—San Diego Medical School Office of Learning Resources.

*Elizabeth Gilbert and Her Work for the Blind* is about blindness. Gilbert was only three when she was blinded by scarlet fever, and spent all her adult life in work for blind people, a story Martin, her longtime friend, tells in loving detail from Gilbert's first interest in poor blind people in the 1850s to her immobilization with ill health in 1875 and death in 1884. Martin, like Stephen, presents a mixed stance toward her subject's disability.[7] She is both a sophisticated critic of emotional representations of blindness and an adherent to exactly this construction of her dear and recently dead friend.

She places Gilbert's life, for example, in the context of an era in which "kindly and intelligent men and women could gravely implore 'the Almighty' to 'take away' a child merely because it was blind . . . [and] argue that to teach the blind to read, or . . . work, was to fly in the face of Providence." One of the major functions of the biography is to publicize Gilbert's substantial efforts to dismantle such received beliefs, to "overcome prejudice and superstition [and] to show that blindness, though a great privation, is not a disqualification" (viii).

Martin also displays a rueful understanding of the painful effect of popular stereotypes on her friend's own life. Gilbert, whose father was principal of Brasenose College, Oxford, and later the bishop of Chichester, was part of a large, lively, and close-knit family. Both parents were devoted to the idea of giving her as normal a life as possible:

> [S]he should be trained, educated and treated like the other children . . . she should share their pleasures and their experience, and should not be kept apart from the mistaken notion of shielding her from injury. . . . There was no invention, no educational help for the blind which they did not inquire into and procure; but these were only used in the same way that one child might have one kind of pencil and another child another pencil. (4)

Gilbert's childhood was physically and intellectually stimulating, filled with rambunctious games and distinguished and interesting adult visitors. Her personality, like her daily life, was completely at odds with the idea of affliction, as Martin documents with a series of anecdotes about Gilbert's strong will and passionate temper:

> One incident remembered against her was that at seven or eight years old she seized one of the high schoolroom chairs and hurled it, or intended to do so, at a governess who had offended her. . . . when she was somewhat younger, at the close of their daily walk, she and a little sister hurried on to enjoy the luxury of ringing the front door bell. It was just out of reach, and the little girls on tiptoe were straining to get at it. An undergraduate, passing by, thought to do them a kindness and pulled the bell. Bessie

stamped with anger, and turned upon him a little blind passionate face: "Why did you do it? You knew I wanted to ring."

"A most affectionate nature, unselfish, generous, but passionate and obstinate; so obstinate no one could turn her from the thing she had resolved on," says one of the sisters. (6)

Though Martin seems to succumb to the obvious temptations of making these stories emblems of Gilbert's passionate blind life, they also are interesting indicators that if Gilbert's early life was constrained in any way, those constraints were anchored to childhood itself, not disability.

Outside her immediate family, however, loving relations were eager to make her into a pathetic and poetic object. Her maternal grandfather renamed her "Little Blossom" after she became blind, because "she was never to develop into flower or fruit . . . on account of her great affliction, and the limitations that it must entail" (Martin 26). A family friend's sonnet for the ten-year-old Gilbert expresses the same desire to submerge a lively child in a kind of relished gloominess:

> Forgive the thought, but I have learnt to love
> What others deem privation; I have seen
> How more than recompensed thy loss has been,
> Dear gentle child! by Him who from above
> Guides thy dark steps; and I have yearned to prove
> The store of heavenly peace, that thou dost glean
> From angels' steps, unseen, who round thee move.
> Yes, I have owed thee much; thou are a thing
> For sharpest grief to gather round, and grow
> To mellowness; where sorrow loves to cling,
> And tune to gospel strains the tears that flow
> In harshest discord, sullen murmuring,
> That will not learn the blessedness of woe.
>
> (Martin 34–35)

Despite her awareness of how damaging these views were to Gilbert, Martin herself devotes ample energy to summarizing Gilbert's substantial life's work in terms of just such melodramatic commonplaces, a contradiction that substantially undercuts her support of Gilbert's cause. She repeatedly portrays Gilbert as a being isolated by personal nobility from both her sighted peers and the poor blind people whose cause she promoted:

Free from any taint of selfishness or self-seeking, all her thought [was] for the helpless, the poor, the friendless. Her pity was boundless. There was nothing she could not forgive the blind, no error, no ignorance, no crime. She knew the desolation of their lives, their friendless condition, and understood how they might sink down and down in the darkness because no friendly hand was held out to them. (ix)

As an alternative to this impossibly good figure, Martin repeatedly (and approvingly, it seems) presents recollections of Gilbert that shrink her into a physically weak, emotionally truncated girl in white muslin, an object at the center of a melodramatic tableau:

She was standing apart on the grass; standing peaceful, motionless, with a sweet still face, and all the sad suggestion of the large darkened glasses that encased her eyes. The little boy picked daisies and took them to her and showed her the gold in the center. She smiled as she took them, and her slender fingers fluttered about them. And the children, the flowers, the sunlight, and those beautiful gardens in the early summer, made a picture in which this friend always loved to enshrine her memory of "Little Blossom." (37–38)

Martin typically begins chapters with poetic epigraphs and closes them with such tableaux. In one, Gilbert's poetic essence is authenticated by William Wordsworth himself, a visitor to Gilbert's childhood home:

One day she was in the drawing-room alone, and Wordsworth entered. For a moment he stood silent before the blind child. The little sensitive face, with its wondering, inquiring look, turned towards him. Then he gravely said, "Madam, I hope I do not disturb you." She never forgot that "Madam," grave, solemn, almost reverential. (13)

In correspondence with her construction of Gilbert as saintly, frail, and poetic, Martin depicts many of the working-class blind people with whom Gilbert spent most of her time as inveterate beggars, "often even more degraded and vicious than poor," who "meant *alms* when they said *wages,* and drew back in disgust from the offer to teach them a trade and make them self-supporting" (116). Gilbert was also "open to the influence of the fanatics," those blind activists Martin characterizes as radical discontents. At times, the biography seems much more concerned with these people's depredations of Gilbert's energy than with representing Gilbert's own beliefs about them. This protective and patronizing attitude extends to Gilbert's support of many "radical" ideas, which Martin explains in terms of her naïveté about the real world:

> There can be no doubt that she was influenced throughout life by her own early training, which had made it impossible for her to believe in the numerous so-called "disabilities" of the blind. Some of her friends thought that she had not an adequate notion of what these really were. Perhaps those who are born blind, or who have lost sight at so early an age that no memory of it remains, do not adequately realise their privation. Sight is to them a "fourth dimension," a something that it is absolutely impossible to realise. They can talk about it, but it is impossible for them to understand it. (26)

The physical and emotional agonies of Gilbert's last years clearly encourage Martin's focus on her frailty. A degenerative spinal condition left her immobile, deaf, and in constant pain; not only did both parents and a sister die, but worst of all, it seems, so did her associate W. Hanks Levy, "the faithful servant and friend of her whole life" (267). She did not sit up, or leave her bed, for nine years.

At the same time, as we have seen in Mayhew, the narrative frame of a life story, not necessarily its details or their chronology, directs its tone. With a variety of emphases possible, Martin chooses to adopt a reverent melancholy as the governing tone that encompasses this energetic life. The introduction announces that there is

> a sacred privacy in the life of a blind person. . . . [who is] led apart from much of the ordinary work of the world, and is unaffected by many external incidents which help to make up the important events of other lives. It is passed in the shade and not in the open sunlight of eager activity. (ix)

The book's close echoes the same tone, peculiar for a biography of a social activist, as Martin encapsulates Gilbert's life in a few disconcerting paragraphs:

No murmur escaped her lips from early youth to age. She stood
trembling with awestruck face when, after she had said, "Oh how I
should like to see the sun!" her companion solemnly assured her,
"And so you shall see," and turned the sightless face towards the
glowing sky. All was dark, the young girl could only answer, "I see
nothing," as she turned and went slowly homewards. She accepted
her blindness. It was the will of God. . . . Again there came a time
when a great cause had been entrusted to her, when she felt that
it was prospering in her hands, when she hoped to raise the whole
condition of the blind, to lift them up out of poverty and dependence, and place them on a level with all industrious and intelligent citizens. But a hand was laid upon her in the darkness. "I can
do nothing," she said; and once again she turned and went slowly
without a murmur, without repining, down the dark pathway to
the grave and gate of death. (306–7)

Martin's tone threatens to submerge Gilbert's wide range of working
abilities, the physically and mentally exhausting schedule she followed,
and the decidedly unromantic view she had of herself (this was a person
who, when confined to bed, compared herself to a train left on a siding).
Despite Martin's extensive description of Gilbert's work, the predominant plot of the biography is a passionate child's transformation into a
subdued, saintly blind woman. As Martin phrases it,

In after life we find a temper under perfect control, and a will
developed and trained to sweet firmness and unwavering
endurance; but these showed themselves in the fitful irregularity
of a somewhat wilful childhood. (6–7)

The transformation is something Martin perceives as complete
enough to permit her to narrate Gilbert's life without much reference to
that "irregularity." "There are but few incidents in her peaceful life," she
writes. "It was torn by no doubt, distracted by no apprehensions, it
reached none of the heights of human happiness, and sounded none of
the depths of despair" (x). This hardly seems a likely life portrait of a person who once brandished a chair at her governess.

Martin explains Gilbert's emotional development with a narrative
that serves as the thematic core of the biography and that has particular
relevance to the fiction addressed in chapter 2. At age twenty, as Martin
describes it, Gilbert experienced a crisis in the form of a realization that

she would never marry. Her attainment of marriageable age and failure to enter the world of courtship set off a series of changes in her position both inside and outside family life:

> In childhood and youth the blind daughter was the centre of all activity and pleasure; but the blind woman inevitably receded more and more. She no longer leads; she can with difficulty follow; and at a distance which increases as the years go on. . . . Without any fault of her own, she discovered that blindness would be a permanent bar to activity. Sisters began to marry and be sought in marriage. A home of her very own, a beautiful life, independent of the family life, and yet united to it; fresh interests and added joy to all; the hope of this, which was her ideal of marriage, she had to renounce. (73–74)

Martin never elaborates Gilbert's inability to marry, simply stating that "matrimony was seen to be not possible or even desirable for some women, such, for example, as Bessie Gilbert" (79). When we learn in the course of the biography that Gilbert herself believed blind people should marry if so inclined, and supported marriages in which both partners were blind, her own situation becomes even more enigmatic. The COS Special Committee on the Blind, of which Gilbert was a member, prepared the following resolution:

> [I]n consideration of the well-known suffering and misery which result from marriages between two blind persons, the Committee strongly recommends that such marriages be discouraged and prevented by all reasonable means, especially by the proper authorities providing entirely separate accommodation for the two sexes, in schools, workshops and at all gatherings of blind persons under their control; and by making it a rule that in case any blind person receiving the benefits of their institution or charity do, after having been duly warned, marry another blind person, both such persons shall forfeit the benefits of such institution, or charity, unless it be otherwise decided by the Committee of an institution in exceptional cases. (*COR*, 18 March 1880, 71)

According to Martin, however,

Bessie warmly approved of marriage for the blind, and was sometimes charged with promoting it injudiciously. . . . She used to say
that blindness was the strongest possible bond of sympathy
between husband and wife; and as she did not for herself witness
the untidiness and discomfort in the homes where man and wife
are both blind, and the almost unavoidable neglect of young children, she could not share the objection of many members of the
Committee to marriage between the workpeople. (282)

Martin herself was something of a "new woman" who shared a lodging with another unmarried writer, Dinah Maria Mulock [later, Craik],
and she elaborates Gilbert's crisis beyond the immediate issue of marriage (much as Craik does for the character Olive Rothesay, and Yonge
does for Ermine Williams; Gilbert clearly knew both writers, as both
wrote in the 1860s of visiting her workshop). The arrival of the season of
courtship, as Martin presents it, heralded a series of new exclusions in
Gilbert's life. Initially, the change is not even tied to disability; as Martin
expresses it, "the five or ten years that elapse after she is twenty, form the
turning point in the life of a woman, whether married or unmarried"
(73). For Gilbert, however, this turning point becomes instead a point of
immobility, figurative and literal. No future life has been articulated for
her, nor is there even a set of potential futures toward which to dream:

Up to a certain point she has gone hand in hand with sisters and
brothers; if not indeed in advance of them. She reaches that point
full of ardour and enthusiasm, eager to learn, to live, to work, and
suddenly the way is barred. Blindness stands there as with a drawn
sword, and she can go no farther.
    The limitations of her condition touched her first on the side of
pleasure. She could join in a quadrille at Chichester, could dine at
the palace when there was a party, and "what she was to take" had
been arranged in the morning. But in London there were no balls
for her, no dining out except with a few very old friends, no possibility of including her in the rapid whirl of London life. She had
many disappointments, and tried hard to conceal them. (Martin 72)

Martin's vagueness on the exact circumstances through which
Gilbert knew she could not marry extends to other social prohibitions as

well. Was it simply the size and commotion of London that made her parents preclude her involvement in balls, or was this prohibition simply a way of phasing her out of a courtship pattern in which she had no clear role? Gilbert not only became depressed, but also rebelled. According to one of her sisters, she began at this time "to want to do impossible things, to go out alone in London, to go alone in a cab, and if she might not go alone . . . to give her own orders to the cabman" (72). It was a vain rebellion.

In the narrative's resolution, as Martin tells it, the experience of loss became something Gilbert not only articulated in terms of blindness but also remedied through her identification with other blind people.

> She asked about the blind around her, those who had to earn their bread; and the same answer came from all. She saw them led up to the verge of manhood and womanhood, and then, as it were, abandoned. They were set apart by their calamity, even as she was. Their sufferings were not less, but greater than her own. Poverty was added to them, and the enforced indignity of a beggar's life. (74)

Shortly after, she learned to write with a Foucault frame and began her correspondence with Levy, a teacher of the blind and blind himself. The first workshop was opened in 1854, and the Association for Promoting the General Welfare of the Blind was formed some two years later.

For Martin, the role of impairment per se in this narrative of crisis seems secondary; the real cataclysmic loss is that of a position in one's culture. Suddenly Gilbert feels that "work in the world, even a place in the world, there seemed to be none for her," and it is only after this primary loss that she perceives her blindness as a limitation. The compensations are similarly mixed. It is ultimately because she is denied a domestic role that Gilbert finds her profession. On the other hand, the crisis seems to drain the child Bessie's emotional range and volatility and leave her with a limited register of feelings—no highs and lows. As Martin writes the story of loss and compensation, the consolation of work hardly balances the loss of both her earlier selves, the sighted baby with "flashing black eyes" and the passionate, bright young woman on the verge of adulthood (1).

Gilbert's own stance, as we can piece it together from her actions, her published writings, and Martin's excerpts from her commonplace book, vacillates between resistance and acquiescence to popular ideologies of blindness. Regardless of whether or not her devotion to her work was a strategy to compensate for a lost domestic life, it is certain that the daily tasks that comprised it were material strategies for dismantling stereotypes. Her daily work for the association ranged from learning basket-making so she could teach it to other women, advising workers about such things as bleach and disinfecting fluids, visiting them at their homes, and writing fund-raising letters to a host of Victorian luminaries that included Queen Victoria and John Ruskin (the former became a patron; the latter declined to contribute). The activities she most often records in her commonplace book (at least, in the excerpts Martin gives us) are the workaday ones, for example, the sale of products. As Martin puts it, Gilbert would always "gladly throw aside anything else in order to 'sell two brushes'" on behalf of blind workers (181). Prime Minister William Gladstone's endorsement of her work, particularly in terms of its integrity in relation to political economy, highlights Gilbert's dogged efforts to ground discussions of the blind poor in material facts rather than popular beliefs about beggars and afflicted innocents.

Gilbert's work not only changed public opinion about the capabilities of blind workers, but offered an example of the work a middle-class blind woman could do. Further, in becoming a social worker (as opposed to the object of poetry her friends tried to make her, or the object of charity she would have been in another class), Gilbert attempted to change her position within the received narrative of how nondisabled and disabled people related to one another. Her remarks on blind education indicate how much she was aware of this paradigm and its limitations:

> I am sure that the necessity of [blind people] being the objects of affection is often too exclusively dwelt upon, and that sufficient opportunity for showing their gratitude towards their fellow-creatures is not afforded them. I believe this to be the cause of much apathy or irritability . . . among them. (Qtd. in Martin 143)

At the same time, she was diplomatically if uncomfortably silent in the face of close relations' refusal to see her life beyond that of an afflicted blind child.

Even more curiously, while the Association for Promoting the General Welfare of the Blind was one of the greatest nineteenth-century forces against the stereotype of blindness as childlike incapacity, Gilbert's own letter to the COS Special Committee closes with a passage that recalls Stephen's last fond picture of Fawcett. In addition to numerous practical goals, such as "to endeavor to lessen, as far as possible, the difference in speed between the work of the Blind and that of the sighted, while making it the first object to secure good and efficient work," she suggests that the committee

> do everything to reduce the dependence of the Blind as far as possible, while endeavouring, by Christian instruction, to enable them to accept the unavoidable dependence of their condition in a spirit of humility and thankfulness which will soften and sweeten it to them, and will turn this dependence into one of their greatest blessings, as it will be the means of uniting them more closely to their fellow-creatures. (*COR*, 11 November 1874, 321)

Elsewhere, her beliefs and behavior form a similar patchwork of bold resistance and delicate withdrawal. She was often at adds with her notable blind colleagues at the COS; for example, while most of them proclaimed music as the way to blind self-sufficiency, Gilbert remarked drily, "Many adult persons lose their sight, but the loss does not entail a love of music" (Martin 273). While they issued a special resolution against marriages between blind people, she asserted that "blindness was the strongest possible bond of sympathy between husband and wife" (Martin 281). In her own life, however, she accepted the idea that it was impossible for her to marry.

Gilbert's experience with solitary travel exemplifies her complicated stance. By her early thirties, Gilbert had gained authority over every aspect of her life but this one, which her parents forbade (not surprisingly, given her social class). "She submitted, but often wished to ascertain for herself, and by experience, if the prohibition was necessary," and sent her maid into another train car on one trip to London. A gentleman rushed in as the train pulled away, and then, when it failed to stop at the next stop, realized he had boarded an express train and "swore—an *oath*" (Martin 130).

> She referred to this as one of the most painful adventures of her life, and said she passed through an agony of apprehension and

suspense until the train arrived at the terminus. This journey took from her all desire to travel alone, and she made no further experiment in that direction. (Martin 131)

The retreat from her bold adventure on the train indicates just how difficult the work Gilbert pursued must have been for her, despite the fact that it saved her from the placelessness of life as a blind adult. As an activist for the blind with influence on both sides of the Atlantic, she rarely withdrew from other challenging public spaces.

⁂    ⁂    ⁂

The intertwined threads of class, religion, and gender are especially note-worthy features of these life stories. Many of the people who "speak" in *London Labour* construct the loss of work as part of a larger loss that is "affliction." The compensations they construct for their loss are generally passive or deferred: the comforts of spirituality and music; a more reflective life; and above all, happiness in the afterlife. Many of the street folk with disabilities, forced continually to seek subsistence, are ironically precluded from deriving life-changing satisfactions from work, a situation which reproduces their cultural identities as unhappy nonworkers.

Mayhew's interviewees had financial reasons to portray themselves as afflicted children. The blind street-seller of needles clearly thinks that Mayhew's published interviews will have the function of promoting his cause; his narrative ends with a plea for someone to recommend him to "Mr. Day's Charity for the Blind" (4:344).[8] Despite Mayhew's respect for the blind needle-seller and distress about the blind bootlace seller, the former's plea for a recommendation to Day and Martin's charity is not all that different from the beggar's request for direct alms, and a lament is at the core of both the "deserving" man's plea and the beggar's "canting" performance. This self-promotion was reinforced by the activities of schools, charitable agencies, and medical professionals, all of whom had a vested interest in displaying their objects' affliction. In this context, the self-promotion of the blind needle-seller has something of an entrepreneurial aspect to it, if nothing like that of the bootlace seller.

In large part because the middle-class people with disabilities had greater access to meaningful work, they often transform the Providential frame of Divine affliction and compensation into a complex and nuanced narrative that articulates work as something triumphant, even an earthly version of the compensation poor people anticipate in Heaven. Martineau constructs deafness as a discipline that yields power through triumph over suffering, and links it with the imagination and intellectual ability that were central to her writing. Kitto specifically writes "affliction" and his literary antecedents into a double source of power, identifying himself both as an afflicted child and as a triumphant, Divinely compensated writer. Even Fawcett and Gilbert, who refuse in various ways to consider disability a cataclysmic *loss,* clearly regard work with the reverence appropriate to a cataclysmic *gift.* Fawcett's determination to stick to his vocational pursuits becomes his means of denying and thus surviving the impact of his blindness; Gilbert calls her activities "working to live," and records family weddings and other entertainments in her diary with the terse phrase, "Unavoidably, nothing done" (164).

Concern with presenting oneself in a manner befitting one's religious connections may also have shaped disabled people's representations of their lives. In the case of highly religious people like Gilbert and Kitto, it seems possible that affirming one's affliction is in a sense submitting, humbly, to the will of God rather than fighting it. Kitto refers directly to this issue in his defense of his writerly ambitions:

> [S]ome will be disposed to ask whether self-advancement is a legitimate object of exertion; and whether it was not rather my duty to have been content in the station to which it had pleased God to call me. Now, by "self-advancement" I mean amelioration of the evils of my condition; and no one can object to that without affirming that it was my duty to lie still, to be content and happy, under the unmitigated calamities of the condition to which I had been reduced. I believe that *this* was not required of me. (74)

Even if a person does not necessarily believe that this "affliction" is a form of chastening by the Deity for a previous hubris, it may still be impolitic for Christians *not* to affect a humility appropriate to such chastening. Obviously, when there was a fund-raising aspect to one's life, like Gilbert's, it would be professionally important not to blatantly refuse this role, regardless of one's personal feelings.

This "hands of heaven" thread of Providentiality particularly marks Victorian life writing in comparison to its modern counterparts. While disability narratives in our own time are often called "melodramatic" because their emotionality is focused on the self, a parallel situation in nineteenth-century auto/biography is complicated by the fact that the self, as theorized by the devout, does not exist as such; within an Evangelical Christian melodrama, the engine that drives emotion is not a notion of the self but a notion of God's plan. In both autobiography and biography, Christian melodrama can have the effect of effacing both the subjectivity of the disabled person and the material and historical realities that shape his or her existence, in favor of a larger plan that would seem to negate any possibility of resistance to the roles for disabled people dictated by society. It seems a mode of self-representation inherently at odds with disability activism, as well as alien to a more generalized twenty-first-century ableist notion of autonomy and individualism.

As convenient as it is to dismiss Elizabeth Gilbert's assertion that dependency is a blessing as a sign of cultural brainwashing, or to patronize Mayhew's fluttery, emotionally fragile needle-seller as someone who needs to join an activist group, these dismissals obscure the complexity of reading texts across cultural and historical gaps. The melodramatic paradigm is a useful thinking point here. With performance theory part of the latest critical wave, many of us in the academy have added the concept of performativity to our habitual modes of talking about embodiment. The more general use of the concept usually references Judith Butler's work, particularly her essay on the performance of gender, but Victorian theater and cultural studies scholars have explored the performance of the self in more local ways, and not always with reference to Butler. Elaine Hadley suggests, notably, that the self was not only interpersonally but also dramatically constructed in eighteenth-century culture, and that nineteenth-century melodrama continued to suggest this mode of identity formation. Against an earlier critical paradigm in which interiority was a precondition for subjectivity, and in which the nineteenth-century novel's movement from the humoral or dramatic characters of Dickens to the psychologically complex ones of Eliot set the stage for modernism and the widespread acceptance of Freudian psychology, Hadley quite brilliantly posits a dynamic and interpersonal process through which selves found their meaning (15–16). James Eli Adams, developing the work of Juliet John, made a similar argument about the early Dickens articulating sexuality as "an affect cut adrift from structures of deep psychology" and constructed as public and interpersonal rather than internalized and "deep," which in the early Dickens, Adams argues, is always a pejorative term.

The performance of disability in Victorian culture forms an even richer and more complex exemplar of this paradigm of identity-formation. For a disabled Victorian person, especially within the working classes, life and identity were materially constituted by a series of performative and relational bodily events. People who lived by alms must deliver a good enough show of bodily pain and abjection—or a moving enough version of that painful story, in a verse lament—to generate alms and stay alive outside of the workhouse. Those who went into the workhouse must pass the harsh tests for malingerers, or they would be kept at hard labor in order to earn their government support. Those who tried to work, rather than beg, outside the "House" must somehow "pass" as a worker in a culture that disavowed productive labor by disabled people as impossible. In middle-class social life, as Harriet Martineau details it, the deaf person at the dinner table must perform an expression of pleasant comprehension regardless of whether or not s/he is following the conversation, and must never ask to have a comment repeated. Henry Fawcett saw fit to pass linguistically as sighted—not by using conventional expressions like "I see what you mean," or "It's good to see you," but by pointedly commenting on the appearance of the sunset and his friends' hair. For a Victorian with a disability, the "stylized repetition of acts"—which Judith Butler (270) theorizes as constitutive of gender identity—to confirm social membership on whatever terms it was offered was a daily necessity, and these terms included the verbal positioning of disability with reference to Providence.

The disabled person's social body was a palimpsest, if not a construction, of discussions of how blind people felt about charity, the ways that disability might be faked, or the low spirits that might attend deafness, in the pages of social reform periodicals, medical journals, and newspapers, to say nothing of novels and plays.

It is crucial, then, as well as intellectually liberatory, to read every statement a person with a disability makes as potentially embedded in the requirements of this performative context, and to assess the range of strategies people adopted to maintain consistency of self as rhetorical and performative stances with the potential to create, protect, and promote a self within a limited set of cultural scripts for "afflicted" selfhood. This is not to discount the genuine religious belief that may indeed have informed the pervasive Providential frameworks, or to make them palatable by suggesting an ironic gap between performance and some hidden reality (quite the contrary). It is to suggest, however, that referencing a Providential framework was integral to the larger, multifaceted, constant performance that was disabled identity in Victorian Britain.

The necessarily relational dynamic of performance is also an area in which Victorian disability narratives offer complex sites of study for modern theories of the construction of subjectivity. Regenia Gagnier's comments on class and gender differences and their impact on self-representation and implied concepts of the self as discrete or relational are particularly transferable to life writing on disability. Gagnier points out, for example, that women did not use discourses of autonomy (that of the artist or genius, for example) to underwrite their self-representations "in part because women were not autonomous but were culturally and biologically at least as other-regarding as self-regarding" (217). Created within an industrialized culture that values an unreasonably high degree of physical autonomy (while retaining a strong suspicion of its intellectual equivalent), disability is automatically (and then institutionally and structurally) constructed as a condition that produces "dependence" on others, and a lack of the prized autonomy (i.e., a tendency to be "other-regarding"). Despite and even because of the habitual shaming of this experience (and of writing and scholarship about it), however, disability produces an important reminder of the reality that almost all lives *are* based on interdependence and mutuality, and that sorting people into "disabled" or "able" in no way effects a parallel sorting into the dependent and the independent. Gagnier's phrase "other-regarding" suggests a wonderful reframing of the devalued "dependence" as an ethical stance of attentiveness to the perspectives of others, an indicator of the riches a revaluation of these categories can yield.[9]

Gender issues clearly permeate all these life narratives. The questions raised by the interaction of gender, class, and disability, all of which are simultaneously and situationally constructed, and whose meanings are often forged in terms of each other, are too complex to answer with any simple theory, like the feminizing effects of disability. What makes it possible for Kitto to embrace affect? What forces guide Henry Fawcett's emphatic use of sighted rhetoric? What would Gilbert have done were she male, or a woman of the working classes? Her professional development can hardly be considered apart from the constraints of gender and class, not only those of cultural constructions of blindness. Her groundbreaking achievements for blind workers could never have taken place without growing acceptance of social work as a role for middle-class women and a changing definition of what it meant to be a gentlewoman.[10] Similarly, the question of work is for both Gilbert and Martineau constructed in relation to the other vocational and social roles they did not or could not play, those of wife and mother.

These issues are particularly interesting in comparison to literary works. We might expect to see life writing by and about disabled middle-class women focusing on the marriage plot that is featured by literary works and problematized by medical and social work texts, and we might expect that for women of the working class and men across classes, work would be the predominant concern. Gilbert's biography and Martineau's autobiography do emphasize the significance of the period in a woman's life in which she is eligible to marry. While Martin makes much of Gilbert's loss of the fantasy of domestic life, the specific reasons that she cannot marry are never spelled out. In Martineau's text, the marriage plot is fraught with narrative tension, misunderstandings, and even the death of a fiancé, but deafness plays only a minor role. Martineau writes regretfully of the fiancé's suffering but is equally fervent about her good fortune in not becoming a wife and mother, a role for which she "was, or believed myself unfit" (I:100–101). If her reflections are in some ways reminiscent of the discourse in *Olive* on the benefits of being a "different" woman, they are striking for their use of the language of Victorian neo-eugenics *without* reference to deafness or the body. Concerns about hereditary transmission of disability, then, are more pronounced both in most nonfiction and fiction of the period than they are in these works of life writing. Further, both women's lives are narrated with at least as much concern with meaningful (and in Martineau's case, remunerative) work as are the lives of middle-class men and working-class people of both genders.

Gender difference and gender definitions permeate disabled people's specific work as activists as well. While Elizabeth Gilbert concerned herself with providing blind women a range of industrial work opportunities, Levy's writing advocates training blind women to keep house, and firmly reinscribes the stereotypes of dependent affliction he resists when they are applied to blind men.

> Woman without the aid of man is naturally weak, and how incomparably so must they be who are not only debarred from having man's aid, but are also deprived of the inestimable blessing of sight! Weak in body, fearful in mind, utterly without friends and pecuniary resources, and their condition almost rendered hope-

less by that greatest of all afflictions, blindness, the position of the greater number of our poor sightless sisters is indeed exceedingly wretched. (373)

Finally, Henry Mayhew's changing response to disabled men offers a final example of the complexity of gender's role in Victorian treatments of disabled life stories. The harshness Henry Mayhew is ready to show the blind bootlace seller is partly a function of his being a cheerful non-working male, as well as exhibiting the tears that mark the "afflicted child" blind needle-seller's distance from masculinity; Mayhew seems happy with other disabled men who weep and do not work.

The afflicted child, the begging impostor, and the unmarriageable woman were reproduced over and over again in Victorian culture because they were eminently functional representations, useful for mediating the anxieties and desires of a host of different segments of the nondisabled public. These desires and anxieties often complemented each other, for example, when the desire to enjoy sympathy for afflicted children cooperated with the fear of addressing the problem of disabled, unemployed adults, or when the suspense of marriage plots about disabled women shunted away fear about dysgenic birth and degeneration. While disabled people were virtually born into the context of these representations at the moment of their impairment, they also were virtually required to participate in their existence. To some extent, then, the life narratives of this chapter exemplify the process of making a virtue of necessity (after Milton, that most eminent salvager of the rhetoric of affliction). At the same time, the degree to which nineteenth-century people created lives that were not only satisfactory but even highly rewarding—without widespread awareness of the minority status of "afflicted" people, and often without communities of other people with disabilities to support them in this awareness—makes them important artifacts of the historical strength of people with physical impairments. It is both easy and appropriate to recast the villain in this story of disability as discrimination, not fate; at the same time, as these nineteenth-century texts document, it is inaccurate and dangerous to continue to cast people with impairments as helpless victims.

Even working-class people, rather than simply submitting to emotional stereotypes (a scenario that reinscribes them as weak, afflicted children), may have been making use of one of the few sources of identity and importance the culture could yield them. Both Scripture and melodrama place disability within a context that not only promises special compensation in the afterlife, but also confers special significance in the here and now. If being an afflicted child meant being under God's special protection—even if daily life gave no evidence of such Divine preference—that concept could be empowering, as could seeing oneself as a poetical subject, or as the literary descendant of Milton or Homer. The limitations of a melodramatic identity notwithstanding, it might still confer a much-needed sense of cultural place. Even Gilbert, after all, growing up in a comfortable, loving, and progressive family, experienced a sudden conviction that "work in the world, even a place in the world, there seemed to be none for her" (Martin 74). Using melodrama, disabled Victorians could write themselves that place.

# Conclusion

𝒯homas Elsaesser has observed that the popularity of melodrama and other "romantic" dramas "coincides with periods of intense social and ideological crisis" (45). The particular nineteenth-century crises most critics identify as pertinent to melodrama are those of women and the poor, for whom it functions as both a social control and a potential source of power. Disabled people, while they were not perceived as central to any widespread social or ideological crisis, were decidedly constituted as a social problem in need of a program of management.[1]

Both literary and nonfictional texts constituted part of this program, even when the placement and management of physically disabled people within Victorian culture was not the solitary or even primary goal of such cultural work. In making a significant aesthetic place for disabled characters, melodramatic literature fashioned potential identities for disabled people in Victorian culture. These identities were probably mostly constructed to fulfill the wishes and allay the fears of nondisabled people; however, some women characters may be read to convey agency and confer rewards to disabled people. Melodrama, like detective fiction and other popular genres, is habitually constructed as either a conservative or subversive cultural force, but as Elsaesser points out, these very categories are "relative to the given historical and social context," and melodrama not only has the potential to be subversive *or* conservative, but also the potential to do both at once, as the culture requires it (47).

The wide range of nonfictional texts that addressed disabled people as a newly visible group within Victorian culture simultaneously activated and attempted to manage the idea that disabled people's place might be within the marriage bed and the productive economy, in the mainstream of culture, rather than at its afflicted and isolated margins. Melodrama and fiction, rather than hermetically sealed sanctuaries for essential truths about disability, worked with nonfiction to process these and other emotionally charged concerns—and in the process, change the landscape in which disability had meaning.

The question of how to feel about disability, and why, is far from settled. It is a question that many of us actively face or refuse to face on a daily basis, regardless of where in culture we locate ourselves or our bodies. If we are seen as "different" by the culture in which we live, we may choose to avoid or embrace, disown or engage, this status; we may find it impossible, however, to ignore others' assumptions about the radically different identities we inhabit as a result of our different bodies. If, on the other hand, our culture sees us as "same" or unmarked, the problem of how culture assigns meaning to bodily difference will be easy to push out of our consciousness.

This unawareness—or forgetting—might go on forever, but for the fact that while most people will never experience a change of gender or racial identity, we will all experience impairment some day, given the fact of life's unpredictability or simply the fact of having lived a long life. As the baby boom ages, it will become statistically normal in the United States to be physically impaired in some way.

There is no telling what this experience will be like. The cultural category "disability" houses a widely heterogeneous group of conditions, its contents shifting based on different cultural contexts. The physical experience of impairment may be minor or severe, a constant or intermittent life focus, the subject of one or many medical interventions. We may have to live with a greater degree of dependence on other people or agencies than we had before; or we may not. The changes in our bodies may or may not require a realignment of perspective, a change in life priorities, or a reevaluation of ourselves, our work, and our relationships with others.

If our impairment and the accommodations for it are visible and noticeable—if others see us and we see ourselves as disabled, rather than able-bodied—we may have major, potentially traumatic, adjustments to make for which our culture has prepared us mostly in negative and destructive ways. If we become disabled after living identified as able-bodied, the big adjustment may not be to accommodate our changed bodies, but rather to accommodate attitudes (including our own) toward physical impairment, corporeal difference, and perhaps toward the interdependency that characterizes all of our lives. Our worst daily struggle, for example, may be to manage mobility, but the feelings of nondisabled culture will be at the heart of the things that obstruct our motion.

It is personal experience that moves most of us to change and act. The personal reality that a generation of temporarily able-bodied baby boomers will have to face is as follows: how will we cope when we move from the satisfying cultural position of able-bodied person to the new and not always satisfying one of disabled person? How will we handle the disadvantages we have learned and reinforced from our earliest years? In short, how will we live disabled in the ableist culture we have helped to maintain?

I began the book as a youngish person and am ending it as a bona fide middle-aged one. While my experience of embodiment in my forties has been overall very fortunate, an experience of pleasure rather than pain, both my own and my family's experiences with chronic and acute illness have continually forced me to realize the urgency of thinking differently about physical impairment and about the issues of dependence and independence that can accompany it. As I leave this book, I feel more and more urgently the need to find a way to make disability, illness, and aging experiences that our culture constructs in livable ways, changing those factors that can be changed and rethinking those that cannot. Recent articles on aging all too often sell the experience to baby boomers by minimizing its impact: with modern technological developments, they reassure us, aging will not necessarily mean physical impairment; nothing much will be lost. This strikes me as one more way of not addressing our cultural problem with disability. If we improve our health care and change the stairways, we can indeed minimize both the incidence and severity of impairment and the disabling impact of our social environment. But we still will not know how to feel about impairment as need or impairment as strength.

We need to reexamine, in particular, the question of interdependence and its cultural value, to interrogate the impetus to see need as something shameful and disfiguring. Above all, we need to see what is almost always ignored in constructions of disability, its capacity to catalyze the development of mental, emotional, and physical capabilities in order to accommodate the experience of living in a body for which your culture is not designed. These are not solely features of "Supercrip" narratives, or of those people who write (or are written into) their own narratives of overcoming; these real strengths exist, often unrecognized, in anyone who has learned to get to work in a wheelchair, raise a child while chronically ill, or answer, repeatedly, the question, "What happened to you?" In short, we need to rethink our feelings about physical impairment, for all of us who will live the realities those feelings create.

Melodrama still dominates how we imagine disability, as two recent news stories in a regional daily paper illustrate. In one, a Marine "who lost his right hand in the fight" with Iraq had come home to recover; in the other, "a man with cerebral palsy" was "accused of soliciting sex acts from boys at neighborhood parks."[2] In the first story, impairment and the melodramatic intensity of life itself resonate with a national melodrama of war and survival. In the second, the relevance of cerebral palsy is much less clear, but it isn't much farther from these news reports to horror movies with disabled villains or weepies about lost body parts and gained insights. Disability is still emotional shorthand, a word where sorrow, suspicion, and a host of other emotions love to cling.

The desire to keep disability individual, sentimentalized, or vilified as a failure of volition or a mark of improvidence, well apart from the realms in which we talk about sexuality and reproduction or meaningful work—in short, to keep it "Victorian," not even exploring the question of affliction with the energy the Victorians themselves devoted to it—seems powerful and deep. More exploration is necessary: not only of what makes examining disability as a cultural construct so traumatic, but also of what is so satisfying about *not* examining disability's cultural and political history, its interpersonal, social dynamics, its embeddedness in our lives.

This book does not posit a new right way to feel about disability, the one way that will set right all the errors of the past, any more than it calls for an end to Tiny Tim or other affect-laden representations of physical impairment. It does not ask that we stop enjoying melodrama, as I reminded myself while I wept happily through at least five showings of *Terms of Endearment* on television as I worked on this book. It insists, however, that we need to keep examining the question of how and where and why we learn how to feel about disability. What cultural texts take the impaired body for their rightful territory, and how are these bodies placed in narrative? What feelings do plots about disability encourage most energetically, and why? How wide is the range of possible ways to feel, if we look at the affective paradigms supplied by our novels and films, magazine advertisements and radio journalism, medical textbooks and insurance prospectuses, social work periodicals and cereal boxes, church bulletins and graffiti and elementary school readers? To what degree are we encouraged to be flexible to unprescribed emotions about impairment, and how much and by what means are we bound to such affective dyads as "pity and fear"? How devoted are we to the idea that feelings are the core of our individuality, and not collective and public products as well as private ones?

From a purely utilitarian standpoint, it will be an unusual person who does not have an experience of disability in his or her life, either personally or contiguously, as a family member, friend, or loved one of a person with disabilities. For the greatest good of the greatest number, or simply for the greater good of even one more person, we need to be willing to attend to what choices have been made and what alternatives occulted. If we are teachers, doctors, parents, scientists, lawyers, or others who will adjudicate questions of disability and identity in part on the basis of our feelings, and will shape others' minds and direct their feelings, we particularly need to include disability in our taxonomies of "difference" and our concomitant training of students as critical, questioning readers of literature and culture. These are not intellectual games but essential learning for anyone who has a body.

# Appendix

## *Physically Disabled Characters in*
## *Nineteenth-Century British Literature*

This is a far from exhaustive list and includes a few works on the cusp between the late Victorian and modern periods.

| Author | Character | Title | Date |
|---|---|---|---|
| | **BLIND CHARACTERS** | | |
| Sir Walter Scott | Bessie McClure | *Old Mortality* | 1816 |
| | Blind Alice | *The Bride of Lammermoor* | 1819 |
| | Wandering Willie | *Redgauntlet* | 1824 |
| Sir Edward Bulwer-Lytton | Nydia | *The Last Days of Pompeii* | 1834 |
| Charles Dickens | Stagg | *Barnaby Rudge* | 1841 |
| | Bertha Plummer | *The Cricket on the Hearth* | 1846 |
| Charlotte Brontë | Rochester | *Jane Eyre* | 1847 |
| Frederick Marryat | Edward Jackson | *The Little Savage* | 1848 |
| Elizabeth Gaskell | Margaret Jennings | *Mary Barton* | 1848 |
| Charles Kingsley | Amyas Leigh | *Westward Ho* | 1855 |
| Dinah Craik | Muriel Halifax | *John Halifax, Gentleman* | 1856 |

| Author | Character | Title | Date |
|---|---|---|---|
| Elizabeth Barrett Browning | Romney Leigh | *Aurora Leigh* | 1857 |
| Wilkie Collins | Leonard Frankland | *The Dead Secret* | 1857 |
| | Lucilla Finch | *Poor Miss Finch* | 1872 |
| George Eliot | Bardo | *Romola* | 1862–63 |
| Mary Elizabeth Braddon | William Crawford | *The Lady's Mile* | 1865–66 |
| Thomas Hardy | Clym Yeobright | *The Return of the Native* | 1878 |
| Robert Louis Stevenson | Pew | *Treasure Island* | 1883 |
| | Duncan Mackiegh | *Kidnapped* | 1886 |
| Walter Besant | Mrs. Monument | *The Children of Gibeon* | 1886 |
| Rudyard Kipling | Dick Heldar | *The Light That Failed* | 1891 |
| | Miss Florence | "They" | 1904 |
| J. M. Barrie | Blinder | *Sentimental Tommy* | 1896 |
| George du Maurier | Barty Josselin | The *Martian* | 1897 |
| Joseph Conrad | Capt. Whalley | *The End of the Tether* | 1903 |
| H.G. Wells | Pedro et al. | "The Country of the Blind" | 1904 |
| Arthur Conan Doyle | Andreas | *Sir Nigel* | 1906 |

### DEAF CHARACTERS

| Author | Character | Title | Date |
|---|---|---|---|
| Charles Dickens | The Deaf Gentleman | *Master Humphrey's Clock* | 1841 |
| | Baby Turveydrop | *Bleak House* | 1851 |
| | Sophy Marigold | "Doctor Marigold" | 1865 |
| Mary Elizabeth Braddon | Peters | *The Trail of the Serpent* | 1861 |
| Wilkie Collins | Madonna Blyth | *Hide and Seek* | 1854 |
| | "The Cur" | *The Guilty River* | 1886 |

### "CRIPPLED" CHARACTERS

| Author | Character | Title | Date |
|---|---|---|---|
| Jane Austen | Mrs. Smith | *Persuasion* | 1818 |
| Harriet Martineau | Maria Young | *Deerbrook* | 1839 |
| Charles Dickens | Tiny Tim | *A Christmas Carol* | 1843 |
| | Mrs. Clennam | *Little Dorrit* | 1857 |
| | Silas Wegg, Jenny Wren | *Our Mutual Friend* | 1864–65 |
| | Phoebe | "Mugby Junction" | 1866 |
| Elizabeth Gaskell | Franky | "The Three Eras of Libbie Marsh" | 1847 |
| | Nest Gwynn | "The Well at Pen-Morfa" | 1850 |
| | Thurstan Benson | *Ruth* | 1853 |
| Dinah Craik | Olive Rothesay | *Olive* | 1850 |
| | Earl of Cairnforth | *A Noble Life* | 1861 |
| Charlotte Yonge | Charles Edmonstone | *The Heir of Redclyffe* | 1853 |
| | Margaret May | *The Daisy Chain* | 1856 |
| | Ermine Williams, Alick Keith | *The Clever Woman of the Family* | 1865 |
| | Geraldine Underwood | *The Pillars of the House* | 1873 |

| Author | Character | Title | Date |
|---|---|---|---|
| Wilkie Collins | Lavinia Blyth | *Hide and Seek* | 1854 |
| | Mrs. Milroy | *Armadale* | 1866 |
| | Rosanna Spearman | *The Moonstone* | 1868 |
| | Limping Lucy | "" | |
| | Sir Patrick Lundie | *Man and Wife* | 1870 |
| Anthony Trollope | Madeline Neroni | *Barchester Towers* | 1857 |
| | Mary Belton | *The Belton Estate* | 1866 |
| George Eliot | Philip Wakem | *The Mill on the Floss* | 1860 |
| R. L. Stevenson | Long John Silver | *Treasure Island* | 1883 |
| Mary Elizabeth Braddon | Lord Lashmar | *One Thing Needful* | 1886 |
| Mary Augusta Ward | Jim Hurd | *Marcella* | 1894 |
| Lucas Malet | Sir Richard Calmady | | |
| | (elder and younger) | *Sir Richard Calmady* | 1901 |

### PEOPLE OF SMALL AND LARGE STATURE

| Author | Character | Title | Date |
|---|---|---|---|
| Sir Walter Scott | Jeffrey Hudson | *Peveril of the Peak* | 1823 |
| Charles Dickens | Quilp | *The Old Curiosity Shop* | 1840–41 |
| | The Marchioness | "" | |
| | circus folk | "" | |
| | Miss Mowcher | *David Copperfield* | 1849–50 |
| | Tpschoffski | "Going into Society" | 1858 |
| | Pickleson | "Doctor Marigold" | 1865 |
| Wilkie Collins | Reburrus | *Antonina* | 1850 |

### PEOPLE WITH FACIAL "DISFIGUREMENTS"

| Author | Character | Title | Date |
|---|---|---|---|
| Charles Dickens | Rosa Dartle | *David Copperfield* | 1850 |
| Wilkie Collins | Mannion | *Basil* | 1852 |
| Ellen Price Wood | Isabel Vane | *East Lynne* | 1861 |
| George Gissing | Clara Hewett | *The Nether World* | 1889 |

### MULTIPLE DISABILITIES

| Author | Character | Title | Date |
|---|---|---|---|
| Wilkie Collins | Miserrimus Dexter | *The Law and the Lady* | 1875 |
| Hall Caine | Naomi | *The Scapegoat* | 1881 |

### CHRONIC ILLNESS OR UNSPECIFIED DISABILITIES

| Author | Character | Title | Date |
|---|---|---|---|
| Charles Dickens | Smike | *Nicholas Nickleby* | 1838–39 |
| Charlotte Brontë | Mme. Walravens | *Villette* | 1853 |
| Dinah Craik | Phineas Fletcher | *John Halifax, Gentleman* | 1856 |
| Wilkie Collins | Frederick Fairlie | *The Woman in White* | 1858 |
| | Matilda Wragge | *No Name* | 1862 |
| | Oscar Dubourg | *Poor Miss Finch* | 1872 |
| Charlotte Yonge | Margaret May | *The Trial* | 1864 |
| George Meredith | Emma Dunstane | *Diana of the Crossways* | 1885 |
| R.L. Stevenson | Edward Hyde | *The Strange Case of Dr. Jekyll and Mr. Hyde* | 1886 |

# Notes

### PREFACE

1. Robert Lee Hotz, "Mapping Emotions," *LA Times,* reprinted in *Valley News,* 18 December 2000, C1.

2. See Bérubé; Cassuto; Roof and Wiegman; and Mayberry.

### INTRODUCTION

1. For example, any ethical debate involving the concept of "quality of life" or "a life worth living" has trouble excluding a cultural history of narratives that teach us that certain kinds of lives are tragic. See Jordanova for an argument about the social construction of medical knowledge that can be extrapolated to any presumably "objective" realm in which decisions are made about the differential social and ontological value of bodies, and Biklen's discussion of representations of disability and their impact on public policy.

2. See Auerbach, Hadley, and Vlock on the pervasiveness of melodrama and the "theatrical" in Victorian life and culture; Brooks's discussion extends to the twentieth century.

3. The essays in Freedman and Holmes, *The Teacher's Body,* explore such issues.

4. Linton distinguishes between having a disability or disabilities and positively identifying as a disabled person, claiming disability as inseparable from one's valued identity. It is related but not rhetorically identical to the kinds of claiming asserted in concepts like crip culture or queer theory. While the people

I write about did not necessarily see disability as a valued identity, they mostly did claim it as integral to themselves. In listening to students become more open about "having" disabilities, but reluctant to be "disabled people," I am inclined to think that disability is actually more stigmatized in our own time in the sense that it is much less a speakable identity.

5. See Maudsley's "Galstonian Lecture II on the Relations Between Body and Mind" for an example of what is asserted directly and indirectly by most Victorian medical texts.

6. See Garland-Thomson, *Freakery,* and "Narratives of Deviance and Delight." See also Rachel Adams's *Sideshow USA,* Erin O'Connor's *Raw Material,* and Peter W. Graham and Fritz H. Oehlschlager's *Articulating the Elephant Man.* William Holladay and Stephen Watt's "Viewing the Elephant Man" considers melodramatic framings of Merrick.

7. See Garland-Thomson, "Seeing the Disabled," for a useful historico-cultural schema of modes of looking at disabled bodies.

CHAPTER ONE

1. See Booth; Disher; Gledhill, "The Melodramatic Field"; Rahill; and J. L. Smith. Elsaesser is useful in considering melodrama as permitting both conservatism and subversion; Hays and Nikolopolou's introduction reminds us that these assessments must be grounded in the changing contexts, including class contexts, for melodramatic theater in the nineteenth century.

2. See Eigner, for example, on the significant differences among melodrama, pantomime, and harlequinade, and the way the different subgenres can inform separate rhetorical threads within one work by Dickens. The relationship between the melodramatic, the sentimental, and the sensational has yet to be defined in a useful way. For explorations of the sentimental on both sides of the Atlantic, see Samuels and Kaplan.

3. I do not address comedy, whose connections to disability are rich and multiple but exceed the scope of this book. See Bratton for a discussion of the comic subplots of melodrama and a commentary on critical neglect of this recurrent feature of the genre.

4. For the visuality of melodrama, see Meisel, "Scattered Chiaroscuro," and Eisenstein; for visuality and melodrama with particular reference to gender, see Doane and Williams; for the visuality of Victorian culture in general, see Meisel, *Realizations,* and Flint.

5. Like Mitchell and Snyder in *Narrative Prosthesis* (8), I want to encompass the ways in which the failure of some functions of melodrama contributes to the overall impact of the genre.

6. Warhol, "As You Stand," explores both this experience and the historical dynamism of what "being made to cry" means; see Shattuc for an important discussion of the feminist problem of response to melodramatic film.

7. See, for example, "Overcoming Obstacles" (http://www.mindspring .com /~deloggio /homepage/faq/diversty/obstacle.htm); and "The Drama of Being on Stage" (http://psychological.com /2001d_case_management.htm).

8. Specific examples of "excess as too-real" and "excess as too-fake" follow in chapters 2 and 4.

9. This is less true of theater studies in general as more disability studies scholarship is coming into print. See Lewis; Sandahl; Albright; Kuppers; and Auslander and Sandahl.

CHAPTER TWO

1. In terms of relationships between disabled and nondisabled people, consider for example offhand comments like Frederic Golden's, that Albert Einstein's first wife, "afflicted with a limp, and three years his senior," was "nonetheless a soul mate" (62). In terms of relationships between disabled people, consider the responses that have met Deaf partners' desire to have Deaf children.

2. See Pykett 164–65; Poovey's introduction; Helsinger, Sheets, and Veeder; Russett; and Auerbach. For a complex discussion of the gendered "politics of affect" in nineteenth- and twentieth-century culture, see Cvetkovich. See also Crosby and Warhol, "As You Stand." For an important discussion of the representation of women's bodies in Victorian culture, see Michie, *The Flesh Made Word*.

3. See Klages, especially the introduction and chapter 1, "The Semiotics of Disability."

4. See McGann for a rich discussion of the progression from sensibility to sentimentality, including its shift in emphasis, within concepts of mind-body relations, from the mind to the body. For a study of Victorian sentimentality, see Kaplan.

5. Most recently, the play loosely informed Jean Rollins's 1995 film *Les Deux Orphelines Vampires*. See Norden for an excellent discussion of the film and its history from a disability studies perspective. Brooks ("Melodrama Body, Revolution") discusses the play as an example of the body's conveying a hysterical meaning, but he does not, surprisingly, address Louise's blindness specifically. For discussions of *The Sisters Gerard*, the Russian production of the play, see Law and Gerould. I draw here on more than one English version, including Jackson, Oxenford, and Gideon, while retaining the original "Henriette" and "Louise" as the sisters' names even when quoting from Gideon, who anglicizes them into "Margaret" and "Lilian."

6. See, for example, Tonna 64, and Poovey 214 n. 53.

7. Twersky writes that Nydia is, like Bertha Plummer, "pure and sweet, if less sickeningly" (30). Victorian critics seem equally to have ignored Nydia's sexuality and potential for evil.

8. For a delightful discussion of "falling" scenes in Dickensian melodrama, see Saunders.

9. For a compelling and fascinating argument for Dickens's engagement with a "literary tradition of blindness and ocular cure" in a text "dotted with eyes" and references to other stories about blindness, see Gitter, "The Blind Daughter."

10. For a clear and thorough discussion of definitions of disability based on care versus rights, see Silvers, Wasserman, and Mahowald.

11. This kind of scene continues to be reenacted in our own time, arguably with more serious consequences given the assumption that in a culture of technological and medical expertise, all babies will be "perfect." See Block and Landsman.

12. I am indebted to Cindy LaCom for introducing me to this novel and for her insightful reading of Ermine, which was germinal to my own. See her discussion in "It Is More Than Lame."

13. I am grateful to Leila Granahan for the idea that Jenny's "golden bower" of hair is a literal bower, a generative space like, or metonym of, her verbal creativity.

14. See Gitter, "The Blind Daughter" 679, for a brilliant analysis of the visually oriented sadism of *The Cricket on the Hearth.*

15. See Michie, *Sororphobia,* for an important discussion of the representation of differences among women and their cultural functions.

16. See Hamlin for a useful discussion of the complex rhetorics and social dynamics of contagionist-anticontagionist debates. See Ackerknecht, "Anticontagionism," for the germinal essay on this subject. See Lomax, "Hereditary or Acquired Disease?" for an excellent discussion of the mysterious scrofula. See Spongberg for an extensive discussion of Victorian theories of disease and heredity with reference to venereal disease.

17. See *Medical and Surgical Reporter,* 3 October 1868, 287; 10 October 1868, 307; 31 October 1868, 359; and 2 January 1869, 16. See Rosenberg for a fascinating discussion of how both feminists and antifeminists mobilized the mother's centrality in the development of the child. For more on impressions, see Huet.

18. As medical science in our own time reconnects not only the mind and the body, but also the parents' behaviors and habits (particularly, alcohol consumption) with the health and capabilities of the unborn child, it becomes harder and harder to simply scoff at Victorian hereditarian thought. "The Bitter Fruit," Rosenberg's indispensable essay on nineteenth-century hereditarian thought, was published prior to widespread public discussions of fetal alcohol syndrome.

19. Hurley, Pick, and Greenslade are particularly helpful and readable regarding degeneration theory.

20. As well as Spongberg, see Gilman for the permutation of the "Other" over time and the relationships among the various categories of people represented as dangerously different. See Poovey, Showalter, and Shuttleworth for important critiques of the ambiguity of Victorian medical discourse's representations of women.

21. While Jenny and Lizzie present a possible example, I have more in mind Limping Lucy and Rosanna Spearman of Collins's *The Moonstone.* See Robert McRuer's provocative investigation of a related dynamic in contemporary film, an analysis less subject to the dangers of eliding historical change in conventional behaviors of same-sex relationships (see Smith-Rosenberg).

22. It also seems, speaking very generally, that women characters whose dis-

abilities are characterized as located in the body rather than in the mind are treated differently by many fictions, as long as they are seen as mentally ill rather than intellectually "deficient." Madwomen are both sexualized and fairly readily classed as villainesses; women with intellectual disabilities, on the other hand, are either pathetic or comic figures, but generally not sexualized. Gilman and Showalter are essential reading on the representation of madness and sexuality in terms of each other.

CHAPTER THREE

1. See Kleege for an excellent discussion of these patterns.

2. This story of adoption as passionate "rescue" invokes a recurrent strand in both Victorian literature and other Victorian writing about disability. Dickens produced not only some of the more familiar literary examples, from Oliver Twist to Johnny Harmon of *Our Mutual Friend* to Sophy Marigold of "Doctor Marigold," but also a famous journalistic narrative in his account of the deaf-blind American girl Laura Bridgman. After visiting Bridgman at the Perkins Institution for the Blind in Boston, Dickens wrote: "There she was, before me; built up, as it were in a marble cell, impervious to any ray of light, or particle of sound; with her poor white hand peeping through a chink in the wall, beckoning to some good man for help" (*American Notes* 32).

Foreshadowing Madonna, even down to the outstretched hand, Bridgman as envisioned by Dickens is seeking neither to be more powerful in herself, nor to find a community that will make her feel at home, but one good man to help her. *Hide and Seek,* similarly, presents Valentine Blyth as the only savior for Madonna and promotes this connection by presenting adoption as imperative and by constructing the adoptee's situation as one of both physical, and probably sexual, abuse (the threat of moral danger is what finally sways Mrs. Peckover to cede Madonna to Valentine).

3. James Kincaid's *Child-Loving* is an important counteractive to the quick outrage this scene can provoke.

4. The multiple contexts in which this scene resonates include debates over Sign versus oralism, which would culminate in the 1880s with a resolution against Sign, and Victorian gender ideologies. See Gitter, "Deaf-Mutes and Heroines," for positioning of *Hide and Seek* with reference to these issues. See Nayder for a discussion of Collins's use of Madonna's deafness and Lavinia's spinal infirmity to critique and challenge repressive ideals of femininity; especially interesting is her development of Collins's concurrent normalization of deafness and pathologization of the female norm. See Baynton, *Forbidden Signs,* for a more developed history of oralism, focused on the United States but very pertinent to Victorian Britain as well.

5. This passage echoes a similar one in Gavin Douglas's description of Philip Davis, "the celebrated blind traveler of Plymouth," in the 1830s: "Animal sensibility was his chief dependence; and so exquisite was his sense of touch, of hearing, and of smell, that his whole body might be said to receive impressions from the external world" (10–11). It also connects more humorously with Holt's

description of Henry Fawcett basking in the sun like a giant lizard; see chap. 5, p. 169.

6. For more on nineteenth-century discussions of deafness and heredity, see Groce 94–95.

7. See Kleege and Linda Williams for more discussion.

8. For art used as a framing device in nineteenth-century literature, and the dangers to heroines who step outside the frame, see Michie, *The Flesh Made Word* 79–123.

9. For a discussion of disabled women's complex relationship to stereotypical feminine roles, see Fine and Asch, introduction. For an important early essay on literary representations of disabled women and their relationship to traditional plots for women, see Kent.

CHAPTER FOUR

1. See Garland-Thomson, "Seeing the Disabled," for a discussion of the sentimental mode in which Tim and later figures of disabled children participate. See also Longmore, "Conspicuous Contribution and American Cultural Dilemmas."

2. Curiously, given Dickens's personal interest and public endorsement of both contexts for disabled children, as well as his recurrent representations of schoolboys, there are no disabled schoolchildren in his fiction with the exception of Sophy Marigold, whose education in a school for the deaf is not described in the Christmas story *Doctor Marigold*.

3. In 1870, concurrent with the Elementary Education Act, the Poor Law Guardians were empowered to provide for "the maintenance, education, and training of all the indigent afflicted classes, both children and adults . . . by sending them to either public or charitable institutions, and paying their full cost therein."

These "afflicted and neglected" classes were comprised of "(1) the blind; (2) deaf; (3) dumb; (4) lame children; (5) deformed children; (6) idiotic; (7) imbecile . . . [and] (8) insane" (*COR*, 5 January 1876, 1). State support of eligible children was not considered parochial relief and thus neither disenfranchised their fathers nor stigmatized the entire family as paupers. These provisions seem to have had questionable, possibly negative, practical effects. One writer asserts in 1878 that

> no single case is known in which the Guardians have sent to, and paid the full cost of a blind or deaf and dumb child at any of the voluntary charities, and the mere existence of the legislative powers, although entirely unused, appears to have acted as a preventive against proper institutions being provided by the Government. (*COR*, 28 February 1878, 43)

In 1893–94, the Elementary Education (Blind and Deaf) Act passed control of statutory provisions from the Guardians to the boards of education and made it compulsory for blind and deaf children to be in school from ages seven to sixteen. Other provisions limited class size in schools for disabled children. In theory, at least, statutory provisions for disabled children were more comprehensive than those for nondisabled ones.

4. According to Groce, this was a commonplace in the nineteenth century; it was assumed that "those deaf who were not fortunate enough to be educated at a school or institution lived, as the educator Camp described it, in a 'degraded condition, but little superior to that of the brute creation'" (102). The character of the uneducated deaf child clearly presents something of a contrast to that of the blind one. While a state of isolation from social and economic life is central to descriptions of both, the superior spirituality and morality attributed to even uneducated blind people becomes spiritual and even moral "lowness" in deaf people.

5. As E. F. Lonsdale's lecture on surgical manipulation demonstrates, texts from multiple disciplines advertised the benefits of treatments for disability and by portraying disabled people before treatment as abject sufferers. See chap. 1, p. 28.

6. See Brooks, *The Melodramatic Imagination* 63–64, for remarks on melodramatic theater sets as "iconic texts."

7. Raymond Williams completely discounts the nostalgic picture of the Elizabethan poor laws that recurs in nineteenth- and twentieth-century social work texts (86).

8. The category of "undeserving" was replaced in 1886 by "not likely to benefit"; in 1888 it became simply "not assisted" versus "assisted" (Owen 19).

9. For an interesting historical view on these possibilities, see J. Davis.

10. See Liachowitz for a fuller discussion with reference to American society.

11. From another perspective, charity profanes business. The superintendent of the Edinburgh Blind Asylum writes,

> Trade and charity . . . must be kept thoroughly distinct both as regards the Blind and as regards the sale of manufacture. I mean a blind man must get no credit from charity for his work, and the public must get no occasion to say they give charity when purchasing from the blind institutions. Again, the Committee must have distinctly in view the maintenance of the God-made family tie, and also that, to send a blind tradesman home to work at his trade is *injurious* to family relations. He must get a workshop, like any other man. He must have his work sold for him; as when he presents himself at a door to sell an article, let it be never so cheap, it is so absolutely connected with charity that the party buying makes a beggar of him. (*COR*, 11 November 1878, 321)

12. Among other things, the alert evinces a public misunderstanding of the various forms of visual impairment usually classified as "blindness," some of which do not preclude reading the newspaper. See Kleege for a richer context for this article and its continued pertinence to modern understandings of disability.

13. For an excellent discussion of Mayhew, see Humpherys.

14. See Gallagher for an exemplary discussion of Mayhew in the context of Victorian attempts to classify bodies as "productive" or "nonproductive." While

she does not mention the disabled interviewees, her discussion of vigorous street arabs and enfeebled workers has useful connections to the oppositions I discuss.

### CHAPTER FIVE

1. For more on the uses of autobiography as a self-preserving counternarrative, see Couser, *Recovering Bodies;* see also Couser's "Conflicting Paradigms" for a discussion of some of the specific generic models on which disabled autobiographies draw. For a useful overview of Victorian life writing, see Peltason.

2. See Auerbach, *Private Theatricals,* for a discussion of the Victorians' anxiety about theatricality as directly opposed to authenticity.

3. For a provocative discussion of begging, imposture, and performances of identity, see Jaffe. Crosby's chapter on Mayhew and melodrama is a valuable reference point as well.

4. The narrative of the blind woman who sells small wares offers an interesting contrast to this account. She says, "I don't associate with blind people. I wasn't brought up, like, to such a thing, but am in it by accident" (1:395). Her implication is that blindness is a learned social role, and that blind culture is produced and shared by people blind from an early age; later, she says that if "you lose your sight as I did, sir, when you're not young, it's a long time before you learns to be blind'" (1:394). For a twentieth-century perspective, see Scott's *The Making of Blind Men.*

5. I am indebted to Kelly Hurley for observing that the vilification of "professional" alms-seekers like the bootlace seller occurs during an age of increasing professionalism in traditional work.

6. Lee Chambers-Schiller alerted me to one of the signs of deafness's uncertain valence in the *Autobiography,* a passage in which Martineau laughs about the "three griefs" of her adolescence: "my bad hand-writing, my deafness, and the state of my hair" (1:69). As Chambers-Schiller observed, classing deafness with bad hair days indicates that we should not accept wholesale the notion that Martineau posits deafness as the tool of her own martyrdom and glorification.

7. If I have drawn Martin and Stephen as unduly acquiescent to the cultural pull of disabled stereotypes, tending to inflate their subjects into heroes and saints while simultaneously shrinking them to pathetic, grateful objects of charity, I should also acknowledge the private and public contexts that shaped their books. Not only were both biographers mourning friends recently dead; they were also writing books that would be read by many of their subjects' intimates, including the very people who pained Fawcett and Gilbert with their well-meaning, patronizing remarks. In choosing to write and commemorate these lives, they entered into the cultural production of disability with at least some self-awareness, bearing the attendant responsibilities and risks. Engaged in a similar project, I can see both the conflicts in their work and the degree to which conflict and disjuncture were unavoidable, given the complexity of the cultural formation into which their words ventured, and am ultimately grateful that they chose to write at all.

8. In the 1830s, Charles Day, of the City firm Day and Martin, left to blind charity a legacy of one hundred thousand pounds, which Chancery elected to deploy in small pensions (Owen 173).

9. For a more nuanced discussion of dependence/ independence/interdependence, see Wendell; see also Silvers, Wasserman, and Mahowald.

10. See, for example, Vicinus, *Independent Women* 22–23. The fact of Gilbert's envisioning her work in terms of living with her disability—transforming her own struggle into activism for others—also seems to be gender-linked.

## CONCLUSION

1. See Arney and Bergen for a provocative account of nineteenth-century management of people with anomalous bodies in terms of a "socio-moral discourse [that] deploys a *programme of compassion* whose principal purpose is to find for a person a proper place in society" (8). This sociomoral discourse was both linked to and separate from a medical discourse that treated diseases rather than patients.

2. See Walsh and City [of San Diego] News Service.

# Works Cited

*An Account of the School for the Indigent Blind, in St. George's Fields, Surrey.* London: Philanthropic Society, 1830.

Ackerknecht, Erwin H., M.D. "Anticontagionism between 1821 and 1867." *Bulletin of the History of Medicine* 22 (1948): 569–93.

———. *A Short History of Medicine.* Baltimore and London: Johns Hopkins University Press, 1982.

Adams, James Eli. " 'Always Suspect Everyone': Producing Transgression in Early Dickens." Paper presented to the Annual Meeting of the Modern Language Association, New Orleans, 2001.

Adams, Rachel. *Sideshow USA: Freaks and the American Cultural Imagination.* Chicago: University of Chicago Press, 2001.

Albright, Ann Cooper. *Choreographing Difference: The Body and Identity in Contemporary Dance.* Hanover, N.H.: University Press of New England for Wesleyan University Press, 1997.

Anderson, Thomas. *Observations on the Employment, Education and Habits of the Blind.* London: Simpkin, Marshall, and Co., 1837.

Arney, William Ray, and Bernard J. Bergen. "The Anomaly, the Chronic Patient, and the Play of Medical Power." *Sociology of Health and Illness* 5 (1983): 1–24.

Ashley, Robert P. *Wilkie Collins.* London: Barker, 1952.

Auerbach, Nina. *Private Theatricals: The Lives of the Victorians.* Cambridge: Harvard University Press, 1990.

———. *Woman and the Demon: The Life of a Victorian Myth.* Cambridge: Harvard University Press, 1982.

Auslander, Philip, and Carrie Sandahl, eds. *Bodies in Commotion: Disability and Performance.* Ann Arbor: University of Michigan Press, forthcoming.

Baynton, Douglas C. "Disability and the Justification of Inequality in American History." In *The New Disability History: American Perspectives,* ed. Paul K. Longmore and Lauri Umansky, 33–57. New York and London: New York University Press, 2001.

———. *Forbidden Signs: American Culture and the Campaign against Sign Language.* Chicago: University of Chicago Press, 1996.

Bedell, Jeanne F. "Wilkie Collins." In *Twelve Englishmen of Mystery,* ed. Earl F. Bargainnier, 8–32. Bowling Green, Ohio: Bowling Green University Popular Press, 1984.

Bentley, Eric. *The Life of the Drama.* New York: Applause, 1964.

Bérubé, Michael. "On the Cultural Representation of People with Disabilities." *Chronicle of Higher Education,* 30 May 1997, B4–B5.

Biklen, Douglas. "The Culture of Policy: Disability Images and Their Analogues in Public Policy." *Policy Studies Journal* 15 (1987): 515–35.

Block, Laurie. *Beyond Affliction: The Disability History Project.* 4 audiocassettes. Part 4, "Tomorrow's Children." Conway, Mass.: Straight Ahead Pictures,1998.

Booth, Michael R. *English Melodrama.* London: Herbert Jenkins, 1965.

Bratton, Jacky. "The Contending Discourses of Melodrama." In *Melodrama: Stage Picture Screen,* ed. Jacky Bratton, Jim Cook, and Christine Gledhill, 38–49. London: British Film Institute, 1994.

Bratton, Jacky, Jim Cook, and Christine Gledhill, eds. *Melodrama: Stage Picture Screen.* London: British Film Institute, 1994.

Brooks, Peter. "Melodrama, Body, Revolution." In *Melodrama: Stage Picture Screen,* ed. Jacky Bratton, Jim Cook, and Christine Gledhill, 11–24. London: British Film Institute, 1994.

———. *The Melodramatic Imagination.* New Haven: Yale University Press, 1976.

Bulwer-Lytton, Edward. *The Last Days of Pompeii.* 1839. *Novels of Sir Edward Bulwer Lytton.* Vol. 3. Boston: Little, Brown, 1896.

Butler, Josephine. *Josephine Butler, an Autobiographical Memoir.* Ed. George W. Johnson and Lucy A. Johnson. Bristol: Arrowsmith; London: Simpkin, Marshall, Hamilton, Dent & Co., 1909.

Cassuto, Leonard. "Whose Field Is It Anyway? Disability Studies in the Academy." *Chronicle of Higher Education,* 19 March 1999, A60.

Chalmers, Thomas. *On Political Economy in Connexion with the Moral State and Moral Prospects of Society.* 1832. New York: Augustus M. Kelley, Reprints of Economic Classics, 1968.

———. *Problems of Poverty: Selections from the Economic and Social Writings of Thomas Chalmers D.D.,* ed. Henry Hunter. London and New York: T. Nelson, 1912.

*Charity Organisation Reporter* [*COR*]. 1872–1900.

City [of San Diego] News Service. "Charges Added in Poway Sex Solicitation Case." *North County Times,* 10 April 2003, B3.

Collins, Wilkie. *Basil.* 1852. New York: Dover, 1980.

———. *Hide and Seek.* 1861. New York: Dover, 1981.

———. *The Moonstone.* 1868. Oxford: Oxford University Press, 1982.

————. *Poor Miss Finch*. In *The Works of Wilkie Collins*. Vol. 15. New York: Peter Fenelon Collier, [1900].

Colquhoun, Patrick. *A Treatise on Indigence*. London: J. Hatchard, 1806.

Coote, Holmes. "On the Nature and Treatment of Deformities." *London Lancet* 1, no. 5 (1860): 399–401.

Cott, Nancy. "Passionlessness: An Interpretation of Victorian Sexual Ideology, 1790–1850." In *Women and Health in America*, ed. Judith Walzer Leavitt, 57–69. Madison: University of Wisconsin Press, 1984.

Couser, G. Thomas. "Conflicting Paradigms: The Rhetorics of Disability Memoir." In *Embodied Rhetorics: Disability in Language and Culture,*ed. James C. Wilson and Cynthia Lewiecki-Wilson, 78–91. Carbondale: Southern Illinois University Press, 2001.

————. *Recovering Bodies: Illness, Disability, and Life Writing*. Madison: University of Wisconsin Press, 1997.

Craik, Dinah Maria Mulock. *Olive*. 1850. Oxford: Oxford University Press, 1996.

Crosby, Christina. *The Ends of History: Victorian Writers and the "Woman Question."* New York: Routledge, 1991.

Cvetkovich, Ann. *Mixed Feelings: Feminism, Mass Culture, and Victorian Sensationalism*. New Brunswick: Rutgers University Press, 1992.

Davidson, Luke. "'Identities Ascertained': British Ophthalmology in the First Half of the Nineteenth Century." *Social History of Medicine* 9 (1996): 313–33.

Davies, Robertson. "Playwrights and Plays." In *The Revels History of Drama in English*, ed. Michael R. Booth et al., 6:145–263. London: Methuen, 1975.

Davis, Jim. "The Gospel of Rags: Melodrama at the Britannia, 1863–74." *New Theatre Quarterly* 7 (1991): 369–89.

Davis, Lennard J., ed. *The Disability Studies Reader*. New York: Routledge, 1997.

de la Mare, Walter. "The Early Novels of Wilkie Collins." In *The Eighteen-Sixties: Essays by Fellows of the Royal Society of Literature*, ed. John Drinkwater, 51–101. Cambridge: Cambridge University Press, 1932.

D'Ennery, Adolphe Philippe, and Eugène Cormon. *The Two Orphans, or In the Hands of Heaven*. Trans. N. Hart Jackson. 1870. In *Melodrama Classics,* ed. Dorothy Mackin, 121–74. New York: Sterling, 1982.

Deutsch, Helen, and Felicity Nussbaum, eds. *"Defects": Engendering the Modern Body*. Ann Arbor: University of Michigan Press, 2000.

Dickens, Charles. *American Notes*. 1846. Oxford: Oxford University Press, 1957.

————. *A Christmas Carol*. In *Christmas Books*. 1852. Oxford: Oxford University Press, 1954.

————. *The Cricket on the Hearth*. In *Christmas Books*. 1852. Oxford: Oxford University Press, 1954.

————. *The Letters of Charles Dickens*. Ed. Kathleen Tillotson. Vol. 4. Oxford: Clarendon Press, 1977.

————. *Nicholas Nickleby*. 1838–39. Oxford: Oxford University Press, 1950.

————. *Our Mutual Friend*. 1864–65. Harmondsworth: Penguin, 1987.

"Diseases of the Eye Produced by Impure Air." *Lancet*, 25 March 1848, 343.

Disher, Maurice. *Blood and Thunder: Mid-Victorian Melodrama and Its Origins*. New York: Haskell House, 1974.

Doane, Mary Ann. "The Clinical Eye: Medical Discourses in the 'Woman's Film' of the 1940s." In *The Female Body in Western Culture*, ed. Susan Rubin Suleiman, 152–74. Cambridge: Harvard University Press, 1985.

Douglas, Gavin. *Authentic Anecdotes and Biographical Sketches of Remarkable Blind Persons*. London, 183[?].

Easson, Angus. "Emotion and Gesture in *Nicholas Nickleby*." *Dickens Quarterly* 5, no. 3 (Sept. 1988): 136–51.

Eigner, Edwin M. *The Dickens Pantomime*. Berkeley and Los Angeles: University of California Press, 1989.

Eisenstein, Sergei M. "Dickens, Griffith and the Film Today." In *Selected Works*, 3:193–228. London: British Film Institute; Bloomington, Indiana University Press, 1988–96.

Ellis, Sarah Stickney. *The Women of England, Their Social Duties, and Domestic Habits*. London: Fisher, Son & Co. [1839].

Ellison, Julie. *Cato's Tears and the Making of Anglo-American Emotion*. Chicago: University of Chicago Press, 1999.

Elsaesser, Thomas. "Tales of Sound and Fury: Observations on the Family Melodrama." In *Home Is Where the Heart Is: Studies in Melodrama and the Woman's Film*, ed. Christine Gledhill, 43–69. London: British Film Institute, 1987.

Farrell, Gabriel. *The Story of Blindness*. Cambridge: Harvard University Press, 1956.

Fawcett, Millicent Garrett. *What I Remember*. London: Unwin, 1924.

Fiedler, Leslie. *Pity and Fear: Images of the Disabled in Literature and the Popular Arts*. New York: International Center for the Disabled, 1981.

Fine, Michelle, and Adrienne Asch, eds. *Women with Disabilities: Essays in Psychology, Culture, and Politics*. Philadelphia: Temple University Press, 1988.

Flint, Kate. *The Victorians and the Visual Imagination*. Cambridge: Cambridge University Press, 2001.

Frawley, Maria. "'A Prisoner to the Couch': Harriet Martineau, Invalidism, and Self-Representation." In *The Body and Physical Difference*, ed. David T. Mitchell and Sharon L. Snyder, 174–88. Ann Arbor: University of Michigan Press, 1997.

Freedman, Diane P., and Martha Stoddard Holmes, eds. *The Teacher's Body: Embodiment, Identity, and Authority in the Academy*. Albany: State University of New York Press, 2003.

Freud, Sigmund. "The Uncanny." In *The Standard Edition of the Complete Psychological Works of Sigmund Freud*, ed. and trans. James Strachey, 17:219–52. London: Hogarth, 1953.

Gagnier, Regenia. *Subjectivities: A History of Self-Representation in Britain, 1832–1910*. New York: Oxford University Press, 1991.

Gallagher, Catherine. "The Body versus the Social Body in the Works of Thomas Malthus and Henry Mayhew." In *The Making of the Modern Body*, ed. Catherine Gallagher and Thomas Laqueur, 83–106. Berkeley and Los Angeles: University of California Press, 1987.

Garland-Thomson, Rosemarie. "The Beauty and the Freak." In *Points of Contact:*

*Disability and Culture,* ed. Susan Crutchfield and Marcy Epstein, 181–96. Ann Arbor: University of Michigan Press, 2000.

———. *Extraordinary Bodies: Figuring Physical Disability in American Culture and Literature.* New York: Columbia University Press, 1997.

———. "Narratives of Deviance and Delight: Staring at Julia Pastrana, the 'Extraordinary Lady.'" In *Beyond the Binary: Reconstructing Cultural Identity in a Multicultural Context,* ed. Timothy B. Powell, 39–60. New Brunswick: Rutgers University Press, 1999.

———. "Seeing the Disabled: Visual Rhetorics of Disability in Popular Photography." In *The New Disability History,* ed. Paul K. Longmore and Lauri Umansky, 335–74. New York: New York University Press, 2001.

———, ed. *Freakery: Cultural Spectacles of the Human Body.* New York: New York University Press, 1996.

Gerould, Daniel. "Melodrama and Revolution." In *Melodrama: Stage Picture Screen,* ed. Jacky Bratton, Jim Cook, and Christine Gledhill, 185–98. London: British Film Institute, 1994.

Gideon, Emanuel. *Blind Among Enemies.* [1885?] Frank Pettingell Collection of Plays, ms. B04. University of Kent Library, Canterbury.

Gilbert, Sandra M., and Susan Gubar. *The Madwoman in the Attic: The Woman Writer and the Nineteenth-Century Literary Imagination.* New Haven: Yale University Press, 1979.

Gilman, Sander. *Difference and Pathology: Stereotypes of Sexuality, Race, and Madness.* Ithaca, N.Y.: Cornell University Press, 1985.

Gitter, Elisabeth G. "The Blind Daughter in Charles Dickens's *Cricket on the Hearth.*" *Studies in English Literature* 39 (autumn 1999): 675–89.

———. "Deaf-Mutes and Heroines in the Victorian Era." *Victorian Literature and Culture* 20 (1992): 179–96.

Gledhill, Christine. "The Melodramatic Field: An Investigation." In *Home Is Where the Heart Is: Studies in Melodrama and the Woman's Film,* ed. Christine Gledhill, 5–39. London: British Film Institute, 1987.

Golden, Frederic. "Albert Einstein: Person of the Century." *Time,* 31 December 1999, 62–81.

Graham, Peter W., and Fritz H. Oehlschlager. *Articulating the Elephant Man.* Baltimore: Parallax, 1992.

Greenslade, William M. *Degeneration, Culture, and the Novel, 1880–1940.* Cambridge: Cambridge University Press, 1994.

Groce, Nora Ellen. *Everyone Here Spoke Sign Language: Hereditary Deafness on Martha's Vineyard.* Cambridge: Harvard University Press, 1985.

Greg, W. R. "The False Morality of Lady Novelists." *National Review* 8 (1859): 144–67.

Hadley, Elaine. *Melodramatic Tactics: Theatricalized Dissent in England's Marketplace, 1800–1885.* Stanford: Stanford University Press, 1995.

Hahn, Harlan. "Can Disability Be Beautiful?" *Social Policy* 18, no. 3 (winter 1988): 26–32.

Hamlin, Christopher. "Predisposing Causes and Public Health in Early Nineteenth-Century Medical Thought." *Social History of Medicine* 5 (April 1992): 43–70.

Hays, Michael, and Anastasia Nikolopolou. *Melodrama: The Cultural Emergence of a Genre.* New York: St. Martin's Press, 1996.

Helsinger, Elizabeth K., Robin L. Sheets, and William Veeder. *The Woman Question: Society and Literature in Britain and America, 1837–1883.* 3 vols. Chicago: University of Chicago Press, 1983.

Herndl, Diane Price. *Invalid Women: Figuring Feminine Illness in American Fiction and Culture, 1840–1940.* Chapel Hill: University of North Carolina Press, 1993.

*An Historical Sketch of the Asylum for Indigent Deaf and Dumb Children, Surrey.* London: Edward Brewster, 1841.

Holladay, William E., and Stephen Watt. "Viewing the Elephant Man." *PMLA* 104 (October 1989): 868–81.

Holt, Winifred. *A Beacon for the Blind: Being a Life of Henry Fawcett the Blind Postmaster-General.* London: Constable, 1915.

Houghton, Walter E. *The Victorian Frame of Mind, 1830–1870.* New Haven: Yale University Press, 1957.

Huet, Marie-Hélène. *Monstrous Imagination.* Cambridge: Harvard University Press, 1993.

Humpherys, Anne. *Travels into the Poor Man's Country: The Work of Henry Mayhew.* Athens: University of Georgia Press, 1977.

Hurley, Kelly K. *The Gothic Body: Sexuality, Materialism, and Degeneration at the Fin de Siècle.* Cambridge: Cambridge University Press, 1996.

"Intermarriage and Its Results." *London Lancet* 1 (1864): 69–70.

Jacobus, Mary, Evelyn Fox Keller, and Sally Shuttleworth, eds. *Body/Politics: Women and the Discourses of Science.* New York: Routledge, 1990.

Jaffe, Audrey. *Scenes of Sympathy: Identity and Representation in Victorian Fiction.* Ithaca, N.Y.: Cornell University Press, 2000.

James, Louis. "The Rational Amusement: 'Minor' Fiction and Victorian Studies." *Victorian Studies* 14 (1970): 193–99.

Jewsbury, Geraldine. Unsigned review of *Hide and Seek. Athenaeum,* 24 June 1854, 775.

John, Juliet. *Dickens's Villains: Melodrama, Character, Popular Culture.* Oxford: Oxford University Press, 2001.

Johnson, Edgar. *Charles Dickens: His Tragedy and Triumph.* 2 vols. New York: Simon and Schuster, 1952.

Jordanova, Ludmilla J. "The Social Construction of Medical Knowledge." *Social History of Medicine* 8 (1998): 361–82.

Kaplan, Fred. *Sacred Tears: Sentimentality in Victorian Literature.* Princeton: Princeton University Press, 1987.

Kent, Deborah. "In Search of a Heroine: Images of Women with Disabilities in Fiction and Drama." In *Women with Disabilities: Essays in Psychology, Culture, and Politics,* ed. Michelle Fine and Adrienne Asch, 90–110. Philadelphia: Temple University Press, 1988.

Kincaid, James R. *Child-Loving: The Erotic Child and Victorian Culture.* New York: Routledge, 1992.

———. *Dickens and the Rhetoric of Laughter.* Oxford: Clarendon Press, 1971.

Kitto, John. *The Lost Senses.* 1845. New York: Robert Carter and Brothers, 1852.

Klages, Mary. *Woeful Afflictions: Disability and Sentimentality in Victorian America.* Philadelphia: University of Pennsylvania Press, 1999.

Kleege, Georgina. *Sight Unseen.* New Haven: Yale University Press, 1999.

Kuppers, Petra, ed. Special issue "Disability and Performance." *Contemporary Theatre Review* 11 (2001).

LaCom, Cindy. "'It Is More Than Lame': Infirmity and Maternity in Victorian Fiction." In *The Body and Physical Difference,* ed. David T. Mitchell and Sharon L. Snyder, 189–201. Ann Arbor: University of Michigan Press, 1997.

Landsman, Gail H. "Reconstructing Motherhood in the Age of 'Perfect' Babies: Mothers of Infants and Toddlers with Disabilities." *Signs* 24 (1998): 69–99.

Lang, Andrew. "Mr Wilkie Collins's Novels." *Contemporary Review* 57 (January 1890): 20–28.

Law, Alma. "The Two Orphans in Revolutionary Disguise." In *Melodrama,* ed. Daniel Gerould, 7:106. New York: New York Literary Forum, 1980.

Lawrence, William. "Lectures on the Anatomy, Physiology, and Diseases of the Eye." I. *Lancet,* 22 October 1825, 144–51.

———. "Lectures on the Anatomy, Physiology, and Diseases of the Eye." XI. *Lancet,* 4 February 1826, 628–30.

———. "Lectures on the Anatomy, Physiology, and Diseases of the Eye." XIII. *Lancet,* 25 March 1826, 849–55.

———. "Lectures on the Anatomy, Physiology, and Diseases of the Eye." XIV. *Lancet,* 1 April 1826, 1–7.

Levy, W. Hanks. *Blindness and the Blind: or, A Treatise on the Science of Typhology.* London: Chapman and Hall, 1872.

Lewes, George Henry. "The Lady Novelists." *Westminster Review* 58 (1852): 129–41.

Lewis, Victoria Ann. "The Dramaturgy of Disability." *Michigan Quarterly Review* 37 (1998): 525–40.

Liachowitz, Claire H. *Disability as a Social Construct.* Philadelphia: University of Pennsylvania Press, 1988.

Linton, Simi. *Claiming Disability: Knowledge and Identity.* New York: New York University Press, 1998.

Lomax, Elizabeth. "Hereditary or Acquired Disease? Early Nineteenth Century Debates on the Cause of Infantile Scrofula and Tuberculosis." *Journal of the History of Medicine* 32 (1977): 356–74.

———."Infantile Syphilis as an Example of Nineteenth Century Belief in the Inheritance of Acquired Characteristics." *Journal of the History of Medicine* 34 (1979): 23–39.

Lonoff, Sue. *Wilkie Collins and His Victorian Readers.* New York: AMS Press, 1982.

Longmore, Paul K. "Conspicuous Contribution and American Cultural Dilemmas: Telethon Rituals of Cleansing and Renewal." In *The Body and Physical*

*Difference,* ed. David T. Mitchell and Sharon L. Snyder, 134–58. Ann Arbor: University of Michigan Press, 1997.

Longmore, Paul K., and Lauri Umansky, eds. *The New Disability History.* New York: New York University Press, 2001.

Lonsdale, E. F. "A Course of Lectures on Surgical Manipulation." *London Lancet* 1 (January 1851): 3–12.

Lonsdale, Susan. *Women and Disability.* New York: St. Martin's Press, 1990.

Marshall, David. *The Surprising Effects of Sympathy: Marivaux, Diderot, Rousseau, and Mary Shelley.* Chicago: University of Chicago Press, 1988.

Martin, Frances. *Elizabeth Gilbert and Her Work for the Blind.* London: Macmillan, 1884.

Martineau, Harriet. *Harriet Martineau's Autobiography.* Ed. Maria Weston Chapman. 2 vols. Boston: Osgood, 1877.

———. "Letter to the Deaf." In *Miscellanies.* Boston: Hilliard, Gray and Company, 1836. Reprint, New York: AMS Press, 1975.

Maudsley, Henry. "Galstonian Lecture II on the Relations Between Body and Mind." *Lancet,* 30 April 187, 609–12.

Mayberry, Katherine J., ed. *Teaching What You're Not: Identity Politics in Higher Education.* New York: New York University Press, 1996.

Mayhew, Henry. *London Labour and the London Poor.* 4 vols. 1861–62. New York: Dover, 1968.

McGann, Jerome J. *The Poetics of Sensibility: A Revolution in Literary Style.* Oxford: Oxford University Press, 1996.

McRuer, Robert. "Compulsory Able-Bodiedness and Queer/Disabled Existence." In *Disability Studies: Enabling the Humanities,* ed. Sharon L. Snyder, Brenda J. Brueggemann, and Rosemarie Garland-Thomson, 88–99. New York: Modern Language Association, 2002.

Meisel, Martin. *Realizations.* Princeton: Princeton University Press, 1983.

———. "Scattered Chiaroscuro: Melodrama as a Way of Seeing." In *Melodrama: Stage Picture Screen,* ed. Jacky Bratton, Jim Cook, and Christine Gledhill, 65–81. London: British Film Institute, 1994.

Mermin, Dorothy. *Godiva's Ride: Women of Letters in England, 1830–1880.* Bloomington: Indiana University Press, 1993.

Michie, Helena. *The Flesh Made Word.* Oxford: Oxford University Press, 1987.

———. *Sororphobia: Differences among Women in Literature and Culture.* Oxford: Oxford University Press, 1992.

———. "'Who Is This in Pain?': Scarring, Disfigurement, and Female Identity in *Bleak House* and *Our Mutual Friend.*" *Novel* 22 (1989): 199–212.

Miller, J. Hillis. *Charles Dickens: The World of His Novels.* 1958. Cambridge, Mass.: Harvard University Press, 1965.

Mitchell, David T., and Sharon L. Snyder. *Narrative Prosthesis.* Ann Arbor: University of Michigan Press, 2000.

———, eds. *The Body and Physical Difference.* Ann Arbor: University of Michigan Press, 1997.

Mitchell, Sally. *Dinah Mulock Craik.* Boston: Twayne, 1983.

———. "Sentiment and Suffering: Women's Recreational Reading in the 1860s." *Victorian Studies* 21, no. 1 (autumn 1977): 29–45.

Modleski, Tania. "Time and Desire in the Woman's Film." In *Home Is Where the Heart Is: Studies in Melodrama and the Woman's Film*, ed. Christine Gledhill, 326–38. London: British Film Institute, 1987.

Morgenthaler, Goldie. *Dickens and Heredity: When Like Begets Like*. New York: St. Martin's Press, 2000.

Mulvey, Laura. *Visual and Other Pleasures*. Bloomington: Indiana University Press, 1989.

Nayder, Lillian. *Wilkie Collins*. New York: Twayne/Simon Schuster, 1997.

Norden, Martin. *The Cinema of Isolation: A History of Physical Disability in the Movies*. New Brunswick: Rutgers University Press, 1994.

O'Connor, Erin. *Raw Material: Producing Pathology in Victorian Culture*. Durham: Duke University Press, 2000.

Owen, David. *English Philanthropy, 1660–1960*. Cambridge: Belknap Press of Harvard University Press, 1964.

Oxenford, John. *The Two Orphans*. London, 1874.

Page, Norman, ed. *Wilkie Collins: The Critical Heritage*. London: Routledge and Kegan Paul, 1974.

Paulson, William R. *Enlightenment, Romanticism, and the Blind in France*. Princeton: Princeton University Press, 1987.

Peltason, Timothy. "Life Writing." In *A Companion to Victorian Literature and Culture*, ed. Herbert F. Tucker, 356–72. Malden, Mass. and Oxford: Blackwell, 1999.

Peters, Catherine. *The King of Inventors: A Life of Wilkie Collins*. Princeton: Princeton University Press, 1991.

Phillips, Walter C. *Dickens, Reade, and Collins: Sensation Novelists*. New York: Columbia University Press, 1919.

Pick, Daniel. *Faces of Degeneration: A European Disorder, c.1848–c.1918*. Cambridge: Cambridge University Press, 1989.

Pinch, Adela. *Strange Fits of Passion: Epistemologies of Emotion, Hume to Austen*. Stanford: Stanford University Press, 1996.

Poovey, Mary. *Uneven Developments: The Ideological Work of Gender in Mid-Victorian England*. Chicago: University of Chicago Press, 1988.

"Popular Literature—Tracts." *Blackwood's Edinburgh Magazine* 85, no. 523 (May 1859): 515–32.

Pykett, Lyn. *The "Improper" Feminine: The Women's Sensation Novel and the New Woman Writing*. London: Routledge, 1992.

Rahill, Frank. *The World of Melodrama*. University Park: Pennsylvania State University Press, 1967.

Roof, Judith, and Robyn Wiegman, eds. *Who Can Speak? Authority and Critical Identity*. Urbana: University of Illinois Press, 1995.

Rooff, Madeline. *Voluntary Societies and Social Policy*. London: Routledge and Kegan Paul, 1957.

Rosenberg, Charles. "The Bitter Fruit: Heredity, Disease, and Social Thought in Nineteenth-Century America." *Perspectives in American History* 8 (1974): 189–235.

Ruskin, John. "Fiction Fair and Foul—I." *The Complete Works of John Ruskin*, 34: 265–302. London: George Allen, 1908.

Royal Commission on the Blind, the Deaf and Dumb, &c., of the United Kingdom. *Report*. London: HMSO, 1889.

Russett, Cynthia Eagle. *Sexual Science: The Victorian Construction of Womanhood.* Cambridge: Harvard University Press, 1989.

Samuels, Shirley, ed. *The Culture of Sentiment: Race, Gender, and Sentimentality in Nineteenth-Century America.* Oxford: Oxford University Press, 1992.

Sánchez-Eppler, Karen. *Touching Liberty: Abolition, Feminism, and the Politics of the Body.* Berkeley and Los Angeles: University of California Press, 1993.

Sandahl, Carrie. "Ahhhh Freak Out! Metaphors of Disability and Femaleness in Performance." *Theatre Topics* 9 (1999): 11–30.

Saunders, Mary. "Lady Dedlock Prostrate: Drama, Melodrama, and Expressionism in Dickens's Floor Scenes." In *Dramatic Dickens,* ed. Carol Hanbery MacKay, 68–80. New York: St. Martin's Press, 1989.

Scarry, Elaine. *The Body in Pain: The Making and Unmaking of the World.* Oxford: Oxford University Press, 1985.

Schor, Hilary M. *Dickens and the Daughter of the House.* Cambridge and New York: Cambridge University Press, 1999.

Scott, Robert A. *The Making of Blind Men.* New York: Russell Sage Foundation, 1969.

*School for the Blind.* School for the Indigent Blind, Liverpool, 1818.

Shattuc, Jane. "Having a Good Cry over *The Color Purple.*" In *Melodrama: Stage Picture Screen,* ed. Jacky Bratton, Jim Cook, and Christine Gledhill, 147–56. London: British Film Institute, 1994.

Showalter, Elaine. *The Female Malady: Women, Madness, and English Culture, 1830–1980.* New York: Pantheon, 1985.

Shuttleworth, Sally. *Charlotte Brontë and Victorian Psychology.* Cambridge: Cambridge University Press, 1996.

Silvers, Anita, David Wasserman, and Mary B. Mahowald. *Disability, Difference, Discrimination.* Lanham, Md.: Rowman and Littlefield, 1998.

Smith, Adam. *The Theory of Moral Sentiments.* 1759. London: George Bell and Sons, 1907.

Smith, James L. *Melodrama.* London: Methuen, 1973.

Smith-Rosenberg, Carroll. "The Female World of Love and Ritual." In *Disorderly Conduct: Visions of Gender in Victorian America.* Oxford: Oxford University Press, 1985.

Snyder, Sharon L., Brenda J. Brueggemann, and Rosemarie Garland-Thomson, eds. *Disability Studies: Enabling the Humanities.* New York: Modern Language Association, 2002.

Snyder, Sharon L., and David T. Mitchell. "Re-engaging the Body: Disability Studies and the Resistance to Embodiment." *Public Culture* 13, no. 3 (2001): 367–89.

Spongberg, Mary. *Feminizing Venereal Disease: The Body of the Prostitute in Nineteenth-Century Medical Discourse.* New York: New York University Press, 1997.

Stephen, Leslie. *Life of Henry Fawcett.* London: Smith, Elder, 1886.

Stern, Julia. *The Plight of Feeling: Sympathy and Dissent in the Early American Novel.* Chicago: Chicago University Press, 1997.

Stewart, Garrett. *Dickens and the Trials of Imagination.* Cambridge, Mass.: Harvard University Press, 1974.

Stone, Deborah. *The Disabled State.* Philadelphia: Temple University Press, 1984.

Swinburne, Algernon C. "Wilkie Collins." *Fortnightly Review* (1889): 589–99.

Symons, Julian. Introduction. *The Woman in White* by Wilkie Collins. Harmondsworth: Penguin, 1974.

Tonna, Charlotte Elizabeth. *Personal Recollections*. New York: John S. Taylor, 1845.

Twersky, Jacob. *Blindness in Literature*. New York: American Foundation for the Blind, 1955.

Vicinus, Martha. "'Helpless and Unfriended': Nineteenth-Century Domestic Melodrama." *New Literary History* 13 (1981): 127–43.

———. *Independent Women: Work and Community for Single Women, 1850–1920*. Chicago: University of Chicago Press, 1985.

Vlock, Deborah. *Dickens, Novel Reading, and the Victorian Popular Theatre*. Cambridge: Cambridge University Press, 1998.

Vrettos, Athena. *Somatic Fictions: Imagining Illness in Victorian Culture*. Stanford: Stanford University Press, 1995.

Walker, Alexander. *Intermarriage, or The Mode in Which, and the Causes Why, Beauty, Health, and Intellect Result from Certain Unions, and Deformity, Disease, and Insanity from Others*. 1838. New York: Langley, 1844.

Walker, John. "Stimulant Treatment of Purulent Ophthalmia." *Lancet*, 8 March 1834, 884–85.

Walsh, Erin. "Marine Recovering in O'side." *North County Times*, 10 April 2003, B1.

Warhol, Robyn. "As You Stand, So You Feel and Are: The Crying Body and the Nineteenth-Century Text." In *Tattoo, Torture, Mutilation, and Adornment: The Denaturalization of the Body in Culture and Text*, ed. Frances E. Mascia-Lees and Patricia Sharpe, 100–125. Albany: State University of New York Press, 1992.

———. *Having a Good Cry: Effeminate Feelings and Pop-Culture Forms*. Columbus: Ohio State University Press, 2003.

Wendell, Susan. *The Rejected Body: Feminist Philosophical Reflections on Disability*. London: Routledge, 1996.

Wilkins, John. *The Blind Wife*. Frank Pettingell Collection of Plays, ms. Bm53. [1850?] University of Kent Library, Canterbury.

Williams, Linda. "When the Woman Looks." In *Re-vision: Essays in Feminist Film Criticism*, ed. Mary Ann Doane, Pat Mellencamp, and Linda Williams, 83–99. Frederick, Md.: University Publications of America and the American Film Institute, 1984.

Williams, Raymond. *The Country and the City*. New York: Oxford University Press, 1973.

Wood, Jane. *Passion and Pathology in Victorian Fiction*. Oxford: Oxford University Press, 2001.

Wright, W. "On the Causes and Treatment of Deafness, No. II." *Lancet*, 9 July 1831, 464–66.

Yonge, Charlotte M. *The Clever Woman of the Family*. 1865. New York: Penguin, 1986.

Young, A. F., and E. T. Ashton. *British Social Work in the Nineteenth Century*. London: Routledge and Kegan Paul, 1956.

# Index

Adams, James Eli, 185
*Affair to Remember, An* (film), 3
"afflicted child," 95–96, 100–102,
    107–8, 123, 126, 128, 131, 135,
    138, 145, 147, 149–50, 163, 166,
    167, 171, 182–84, 189–90
Anderson, Thomas, 105–7, 115
Anzaldúa, Gloria, viii
Aristotle, 37
Armitage, Thomas Rhodes, 116
Ashton, E. T., 109, 113
Association for Promoting the Gen-
    eral Welfare of the Blind, 107, 116,
    121
Asylum for Indigent Deaf and Dumb
    Children (Surrey), 103–4
autobiography. *See* life writing

*Barnaby Rudge* (Dickens), 92, 95, 99
*Basil* (Collins), 83
Baynton, Douglas, 12
*Beacon for the Blind, A* (Holt), 164,
    169–71

beggars and "begging impostors,"
    8–9, 18, 30, 32, 38, 65, 94, 95–96,
    100–102, 107, 117, 120–31, 133,
    135, 142–47, 175, 180, 183, 189
*Belinda the Blind; or, the Stepmother's
    Vengeance* (Pitt), 23
Bentley, Eric, 18–19, 21–22, 155
biography. *See* life writing
*Bleak House* (Dickens), 10, 59, 92
*Blind among Enemies* (Gideon), 38
*Blind Boy, The* (Kenney), 19, 23
blindness: causes of, 26–27, 63–66,
    68, 70, 88, 141, 145, 166, 172;
    childhood, 64–66, 88; and educa-
    tion, 101–7, 116, 173, 181; in
    fiction, 40–48, 57, 74–76, 84–93;
    and life writing, 164–83; and mar-
    riage, 7, 15, 35, 39, 44–47, 57, 68,
    72–73, 75–76, 84–89, 91, 93, 164,
    168, 177–80, 182, 188; and medi-
    cine, 26–27, 63–70, 88–89, 91; and
    sensuality, 169; and sexuality, 7, 35,
    38–48, 64–65, 70, 72–73, 76,

blindness (*continued*)
84–90, 178; in stage melodrama,
23, 35, 38–39; stereotypes of, 84,
105–7, 127, 143, 147, 163, 167,
169, 173–78, 182, 188–89; and
work, 102–3, 107, 116–17, 119–22,
125–31, 139, 143–50, 164, 168,
171–77, 179–84, 188–90
*Blindness and the Blind* (Levy), 65–66,
107, 119, 121–22, 158, 188–89
*Blind Wife, The* (Wilkins), 17–18, 23,
35
Booth, Michael, 23, 25, 36
British and Foreign Blind Association,
116
Brontë, Charlotte, 22, 57, 168
Brooks, Peter, 23–25, 31
Bulwer-Lytton, Edward, 6, 7, 34–35,
39–43, 48–49, 55–56, 61, 70, 72,
89, 91
Butler, Josephine, 111
Butler, Judith, 20, 185–86

Campbell, Francis, 116
Chadwick, Edwin, 109, 115
Chalmers, Thomas, 112–13, 121, 136
charity: and Christianity, 51, 97, 112,
114, 133, 145–46; and disability, 8,
26, 30, 48, 58, 70, 95, 104–5,
113–22, 124, 126, 128–29, 131,
144, 147, 181, 183; and performance, 113, 136
*Charity Organisation Reporter* (*COR*),
30, 102, 116–20, 122, 133, 178,
182
Charity Organisation Society (COS),
26, 110–12, 114, 116–20, 122, 131,
144, 178, 182
Christianity, 2, 51, 69, 97, 104–5,
114, 134, 145–46, 157, 164, 166,
173, 182–86
*Christmas Carol, A* (Dickens), 1–2, 5,
11, 18, 43, 48, 72, 95–99, 103, 131
*Clever Woman of the Family, The*
(Yonge), 6, 7, 17, 35, 48, 51–56,
58, 70, 72, 98, 179

Collins, Wilkie, 7, 17, 23, 73–93, 95;
compared to Dickens, 90, 93; criticism of disabled characters, 23,
73–74, 90–93; as disabled authorial
body, 73–74, 91–93
Colquhoun, Patrick, 112
Cormon, Eugène, 5–6, 23, 32, 35,
38–40, 44, 47, 70, 73, 82, 85
courtship plots, 5–7, 10, 15, 30,
34–95, 98, 188–89
Craik, Dinah Maria Mulock, 6–7, 35,
47–52, 54–56, 60, 70, 72, 89, 179,
188
*Cricket on the Hearth, The* (Dickens), 6,
15, 17–18, 35, 39, 43–48, 55–56,
61, 70, 72, 75, 85, 93, 133
"cripples": causes of, 65–66, 70–71;
and marriage, 6, 15, 48–59, 72, 83,
89, 93; and work, 15, 52, 130,
139–41, 158
Crosby, Christina, 24

*David Copperfield* (Dickens), 59, 92
Davies, Robertson, 24
Day and Martin's Charity for the
Blind, 183
deafness: causes of, 65, 68, 70,
77, 79, 83, 88, 150–51, 156,
160–61; and education, 29,
102–4, 116, 162; in fiction, 74–83;
and life writing, 150–64; and marriage, 68, 75, 98, 188; and sensuality, 79–80, 82; and sexuality, 76–83;
in stage melodrama, 23; stereotypes
of, 136, 158–60; and work, 102,
130–31, 149, 158–60, 164, 184,
188
*Deerbrook* (Martineau), 150
deformity, 10, 28, 37, 48–50, 68, 70,
73, 92
degeneration theory, 66, 189
de la Mare, Walter, 90
D'Ennery, Adolphe Phillipe, 5–6, 23,
32, 35, 38–40, 44, 47, 70, 73, 82,
85
dependence, 52, 96, 101, 107,

120–21, 162, 170, 182, 187, 192–93

Descartes, René, 37

Deutsch, Helen, 12

*Deux orphelines, Les,* 5, 6, 23, 32, 35, 38–40, 44, 47, 70, 73, 82, 85

Dibdin, Thomas, 20

Dickens, Charles, 1–2, 5–8, 10–11, 15, 17–20, 30, 35, 39, 43–49, 55–61, 70, 72–74, 76, 85, 88–90, 92–93, 95–99, 103, 131, 133, 185

disability: and Christianity, 2, 51, 69, 97, 104–5, 114, 134, 145–46, 157, 164, 166, 173, 182–86; and compensation, 31, 50–51, 156–58, 162–64, 174, 181, 183–84, 190; and courtship plots, 5–7, 10, 15, 30, 34–95, 98, 188–89; and dependence; 52, 96, 101, 107, 120–21, 162, 170, 182, 187, 192–93; and education, 4–5, 26, 29–30, 79, 95, 101–8, 116, 125, 131, 135, 162, 173, 181; and gender, viii, 5, 7, 35, 38–39, 43, 48, 51, 59, 61–62, 70, 72, 76, 83, 90, 94, 132, 134–35, 149, 168, 170, 183, 185–89, 192; and heredity, 4–5, 7, 31–33, 60, 62–63, 66–69, 88, 188; and homosociality, 52, 55, 58, 98–99; and indigence, 5, 8, 64, 111–14; and interdependence, 52, 187, 193; and life writing, 9, 133–90; and literary scholarship, ix, 9–14, 23, 59–62, 73–74, 90–93; as loss, 86, 153–55, 161–62, 164, 166, 174, 183–84, 188; and marriage, viii, 4, 5–7, 15, 26, 30, 31, 34–73, 75–76, 83, 84–89, 91, 93, 94, 98, 168, 177–80, 182, 188–89, 192; and medicine, 7, 12–13, 26–27, 30, 62–71, 79, 88–89, 91, 161, 184, 186, 188, 192, 195; and performance, 9, 56, 72, 77, 113, 137, 146, 170–71, 183, 185–87; and sensuality, 58, 70, 79–80, 82, 169; and sexuality, viii, 3, 7, 10, 32, 35, 37–48, 50, 56, 58–59, 64–65, 69–70, 72–73, 76–90, 96, 132, 178, 194; and social class, 63, 119–20, 134, 147, 149, 181, 182–84, 186, 188; in stage melodramas, 4–5, 16–25, 35–36, 38–39, 75; and sympathy, 29–30, 46, 70, 95–100, 111, 115, 125, 128, 130, 146–47, 152–55, 160, 179, 182, 189; and visibility/visuality, 10–12, 14, 17, 22, 24, 30, 35, 38, 40, 70, 86, 97, 113–15, 119, 142–43, 192–93; and work, 4, 8, 15, 26, 30–31, 48, 52, 94, 96, 99, 101–3, 107–8, 114, 116–32, 139–41, 143–50, 158–60, 164, 168, 171–77, 179–84, 186, 188–90, 192, 194. *See also* blindness; "cripples"; deafness

disability studies, ix–x, 12, 59; and cultural studies classes, vii–ix

disease, 5, 26, 62–66, 68–70, 88, 92, 124, 142; anticontagionist (miasmist) theory of, 63, 88; as cause of impairments, 62–65, 68–70, contagionist theory of, 63–64

"Doctor Marigold" (Dickens), 88

*Dumb Man of Manchester, The* (Rayner), 23

Easson, Angus, 98

education, 4–5, 26, 29–30, 79, 95, 101–8, 116, 125, 131, 135, 162, 173, 181

Eliot, George, 15, 185

*Elizabeth Gilbert and Her Work for the Blind* (Martin), 171–83, 188, 190

Ellis, Sarah Stickney, 36

Ellison, Julie, x, 13

Elsaesser, Thomas, 191

emotion: and the academy, ix–xi; and science, xi

emotional excess, 3–8, 16–22, 30–31, 35, 38–39, 42, 47–48, 55, 57, 60, 62, 72, 75–76, 84–85, 95, 99, 100, 111–13, 135. *See also* melodrama

eugenics, 7, 31, 188

Farrell, Gabriel, 64, 120
Fawcett, Henry, 9, 116, 134, 149–50, 164–71, 182, 184, 186–87
Fawcett, Millicent Garrett, 164, 168, 170–71
Fiedler, Leslie, 72, 94
Frawley, Maria, 14
freaks, 14–15
Freud, Sigmund, 15, 20, 185

Gagnier, Regenia, 157, 187
Garland-Thomson, Rosemarie, 12–13, 22, 61–62
gender, viii, 3, 5, 7, 11, 14, 17, 20, 35–39, 43, 48, 51, 57, 59, 61–62, 70, 72, 76, 79–80, 83, 90, 94, 132, 134–35, 149, 168, 170, 183, 185–89, 192
Gideon, Emanuel, 38
Gilbert, Elizabeth, 9, 102, 116, 120, 134, 149, 150, 171–85, 187–88, 190
Gilbert, Sandra, 168
Gladstone, William, 181
Greg, W. R., 36
Griffith, D. W., 38
Gubar, Susan, 168
Guild of the Brave Poor Things, 26

Hadley, Elaine, 25, 185
Hahn, Harlan, 70
Halliday, Andrew, 65, 123, 129, 136
*Harriet Martineau's Autobiography*, 134, 150–51, 154–57, 188
heredity, 4, 5, 7, 31–33, 60, 62–63, 65–69, 88, 188
Herndl, Diane Price, 14
*Hide and Seek* (Collins), 7, 74–83, 85, 88, 93
Holcroft, Thomas, 23
Holt, Winifred, 149, 164, 169–70
homosociality, 52, 55, 58, 98–99
Houghton, Walter, 111
Hume, David, 37
Hunt, Evelyn, 69

illness, 2, 7, 9–10, 14, 52, 63, 66, 74, 77, 92–93, 98, 139, 149, 157, 193
impressions, maternal, 65–66
incest, 75, 83
indigence, 5, 8, 64, 111–14
*Indigence* (Colquhoun), 112
interdependence, 52, 187, 193

Jackson, N. Hart, 38
Jaffe, Audrey, 10–11, 13
*Jane Eyre* (Brontë), 22, 57, 168
Jerry's Kids, 2, 103
Jewsbury, Geraldine, 83
John, Juliet, 20, 186
Johnson, Edgar, 56, 95

Kenney, James, 19, 23
Kimmins, "Sister Grace," 26
Kitto, John, 9, 79–80, 82, 134, 149–50, 158–64, 166, 184, 187
Klages, Mary, 13, 37

*Last Days of Pompeii, The* (Bulwer-Lytton), 6, 7, 34–35, 39, 40–43, 48–49, 55–56, 61, 70, 72, 75, 85, 89, 91
Lawrence, William, 26–28, 31, 63–64
"Letter to the Deaf" (Martineau), 134, 150–54
Levy, W. Hanks, 65–66, 107, 116, 119, 121–22, 158, 176, 180, 188–89
*Life in the Sickroom* (Martineau), 150
*Life of Henry Fawcett* (Stephen), 164–72, 182
life writing, 9, 133–90; and blindness, 164–83; and deafness, 150–64
Linton, Simi, vii, 13
Locke, John, 37
London Association for the Prevention of Pauperism and Crime, 110
*London Labour and the London Poor* (Mayhew), 9, 15, 65, 96, 101, 108, 110, 123–32, 135–48, 150, 183
London Society for Organising Charitable Relief and Repressing Men-

dicity. *See* Charity Organisation
Society
Longmore, Paul, 12
Lonoff, Sue, 93
Lonsdale, E. F., 28
Lonsdale, Susan, 114–15
*Lost Senses, The* (Kitto), 79–80, 134,
158–64, 166, 184

*Man and Wife* (Collins), 95
March of Dimes, 103
marriage, viii, 4, 5–7, 15, 26, 30, 31,
34–73, 75–76, 83–89, 91, 93–94,
98, 168, 177–80, 182, 188–89, 192.
*See also* courtship plots
Martin, Frances, 171–83, 188, 190
Martineau, Harriet, 9, 134, 149–58,
163, 184, 186, 187–88
*Master Humphry's Clock* (Dickens), 95
Maudsley, Andrew, 66, 68
Mayhew, Henry, 9, 15, 65, 96, 101,
108, 110, 123–32, 135–48, 150,
183
McRuer, Robert, 24
medicine, 7, 12, 26–27, 30, 63–70,
88–89, 91, 161, 184, 186, 188, 192
melodrama: acting styles, 16, 20, 25,
136–37; and antimelodrama, 4, 74,
138; definitions of, 4–5, 16–22; in
educational writing, 103–7; in life
writing, 133–90; in *London Labour
and the London Poor*, 101, 125,
135–38, 141; in medical writing,
26–28; and the melodramatic stage,
4–5, 16–25, 35–40, 43, 75, 136–37;
and realism, 19–22; and social class,
23–24; and social problems, 191; in
social reform writing, 111, 122; and
subversion, 191–92; and visuality,
17–18; and women, 36–38, 79. *See
also* emotional excess
*Melodrame Mad!* (Dibdin), 20
Mendicity Society, 110, 129–30
Mermin, Dorothy, 156
Merrick, Joseph, 14
Michie, Helena, 10–11, 59, 61,

Miller, J. Hillis, 57
*Mill on the Floss, The* (Eliot), 15
Milton, John, 26, 31, 150, 163,
189–90
Mitchell, David, x, 11–13, 24
Mitchell, Sally, 52, 60
Modleski, Tania, 36
Moon, William, 116
Morgenthaler, Goldie, 7, 59
Mulvey, Laura, 24, 60

National League for the Blind, 120
*Nicholas Nickleby* (Dickens), 19, 92,
97–99, 103
Nussbaum, Felicity, 12

*Observations on the Employment, Educa-
tion, and Habits of the Blind* (Ander-
son), 105–7, 115
*Old Curiosity Shop, The* (Dickens), 15,
59, 92, 95, 99
*Olive* (Craik), 6–7, 35, 47–52, 54–56,
70, 72, 89, 179, 188
*On Political Economy* (Chalmers), 121
*One True Thing* (film), 18
*Orphans of the Storm* (film), 38
*Our Mutual Friend* (Dickens), 6–7, 10,
35, 56–60, 70, 72, 93, 96, 98–99,
131
Owen, David, 109–10
Oxenford, John, 34, 38

performance theory, 185
Peters, Catherine, 93
Pinch, Adela, 13
Pitt, George Dibdin, 23
Poor Law, New, 30, 33, 109–11,
114–17, 119, 121
poor laws, Elizabethan, 100, 108–9
*Poor Miss Finch* (Collins), 7, 73–75,
84–89, 91–92
*Problems of Poverty* (Chalmers), 112

Rayner, B. F., 23
realism, 19, 59, 74, 75, 90, 155
Reeve, Christopher, 21, 150

Reid, Thomas, 37
religion. *See* Christianity
Rooff, Madeline, 111, 116
Royal Commission on the Blind, Deaf
    and Dumb, etc., 116, 121
Ruskin, John, 92, 181

Samuels, Shirley, 13
Sánchez-Eppler, Karen, 13
Saunders, William, 150
Scarry, Elaine, 142–43
*Scent of a Woman* (film), 2
School for the Indigent Blind (Liver-
    pool), 100, 104–5, 146
School for the Indigent Blind (Sur-
    rey), 103
sexuality, viii, 3, 7, 10, 32, 35, 37–48,
    50, 56, 58–59, 64–65, 69–70,
    72–73, 76–90, 96, 132, 178, 194
Showalter, Elaine, 14
Shuttleworth, Sally, 14
*Sleepless in Seattle* (film), 3
Smith, Adam, 11, 37, 96
Snyder, Sharon, x, 11–13, 24
social class, 115, 120; and disability,
    119–20, 134, 147, 149, 181–84,
    186, 188; and melodrama, 23–24
social reform, nineteenth-century, 8,
    101, 108–22, 131, 136, 186
Society for the Relief of Distress, 110
Spongberg, Mary, 69
Stephen, Sir Leslie, 164–72, 182
Stern, Julia, 13
Stevenson, Robert Louis, 95, 99
Stone, Deborah, 8, 100
*Strange Case of Dr. Jekyll and Mr. Hyde,
    The* (Stevenson), 95
Swinburne, Algernon, 91
Symons, Julian, 90

sympathy, 10–11, 29–30, 46, 70,
    95–100, 111, 115, 125, 128, 130,
    146–47, 152–55, 160, 179, 182,
    189

*Tale of Mystery, A* (Holcroft), 23
*Terms of Endearment* (film), 18, 194
Thackeray, William Makepeace, 170
*Theory of Moral Sentiments, The*
    (Smith), 11, 37, 96
*Treasure Island* (Stevenson), 95, 99
"twin structure," 38–39, 45, 50, 58, 61
*Two Orphans, The* (Jackson), 38
*Two Orphans, The* (Oxenford), 34, 38

Umansky, Lori, 12

Victoria, Queen, 181
Vrettos, Athena, 14

Warhol, Robyn, 13, 20
*Waterdance, The* (film), vii
*What I Remember* (Fawcett, M.), 164,
    168, 170
Wilkins, John, 17, 23, 35
Wilkinson, W. M., 119
Wood, Jane, 14
Wordsworth, William, 175
work, 4, 8, 15, 26, 30–31, 48, 52, 94,
    96, 99, 101–3, 107–9, 114, 116–32,
    139–41, 143–50, 158–60, 164, 168,
    171–77, 179–84, 186, 188–90, 192,
    194
workhouses, 107–9, 114–15, 118–19,
    121, 127–30, 139–42, 186

Yonge, Charlotte Mary, 7, 17, 35, 48,
    51–56, 58, 70, 72, 98, 179
Young, A. F., 109, 113

Martha Stoddard Holmes is Associate Professor of Literature
and Writing Studies at California State University, San Marcos.